Bloom's Modern Critical Views

African-American
  Poets: Volume 1
African-American
  Poets: Volume 2
Aldous Huxley
Alfred, Lord Tennyson
Alice Munro
Alice Walker
American Women
  Poets: 1650–1950
Amy Tan
Anton Chekhov
Arthur Miller
Asian-American
  Writers
August Wilson
The Bible
The Brontës
Carson McCullers
Charles Dickens
Christopher Marlowe
Contemporary Poets
Cormac McCarthy
C.S. Lewis
Dante Aligheri
David Mamet
Derek Walcott
Don DeLillo
Doris Lessing
Edgar Allan Poe
Émile Zola
Emily Dickinson
Ernest Hemingway
Eudora Welty
Eugene O'Neill
F. Scott Fitzgerald
Flannery O'Connor
Franz Kafka
Gabriel García
  Márquez
Geoffrey Chaucer
George Orwell
G.K. Chesterton

Gwendolyn Brooks
Hans Christian
  Andersen
Henry David
  Thoreau
Herman Melville
Hermann Hesse
H.G. Wells
Hispanic-American
  Writers
Homer
Honoré de Balzac
Jamaica Kincaid
James Joyce
Jane Austen
Jay Wright
J.D. Salinger
Jean-Paul Sartre
John Donne and the
  Metaphysical Poets
John Irving
John Keats
John Milton
John Steinbeck
José Saramago
Joseph Conrad
J.R.R. Tolkien
Julio Cortázar
Kate Chopin
Kurt Vonnegut
Langston Hughes
Leo Tolstoy
Marcel Proust
Margaret Atwood
Mark Twain
Mary Wollstonecraft
  Shelley
Maya Angelou
Miguel de Cervantes
Milan Kundera
Nathaniel Hawthorne
Native American
  Writers

Norman Mailer
Octavio Paz
Paul Auster
Philip Roth
Ralph Ellison
Ralph Waldo
  Emerson
Ray Bradbury
Richard Wright
Robert Browning
Robert Frost
Robert Hayden
Robert Louis
  Stevenson
The Romantic Poets
Salman Rushdie
Samuel Taylor
  Coleridge
Stephen Crane
Stephen King
Sylvia Plath
Tennessee Williams
Thomas Hardy
Thomas Pynchon
Tom Wolfe
Toni Morrison
Tony Kushner
Truman Capote
Walt Whitman
W.E.B. Du Bois
William Blake
William Faulkner
William Gaddis
William Shakespeare:
  Comedies
William Shakespeare:
  Histories
William Shakespeare:
  Romances
William Shakespeare:
  Tragedies
William Wordsworth
Zora Neale Hurston

Bloom's Modern Critical Views

FRANZ KAFKA
New Edition

Edited and with an introduction by
Harold Bloom
Sterling Professor of the Humanities
Yale University

BLOOM'S
LITERARY CRITICISM
An imprint of Infobase Publishing

Bloom's Modern Critical Views: Franz Kafka—New Edition
Copyright © 2010 by Infobase Publishing
Introduction © 2010 by Harold Bloom

All rights reserved. No part of this publication may be reproduced or utilized in any form or by any means, electronic or mechanical, including photocopying, recording, or by any information storage or retrieval systems, without permission in writing from the publisher. For more information contact:

Bloom's Literary Criticism
An imprint of Infobase Publishing
132 West 31st Street
New York NY 10001

Library of Congress Cataloging-in-Publication Data
Franz Kafka / edited and with an introduction by Harold Bloom. — New ed.
    p. cm. — (Bloom's modern critical views)
  Includes bibliographical references and index.
  ISBN 978-1-60413-806-1
  1. Kafka, Franz, 1883–924—Criticism and interpretation.   I. Bloom, Harold.
  PT2621.A26Z7166 2010
  833'.912—dc22

                                 2009032385

Bloom's Literary Criticism books are available at special discounts when purchased in bulk quantities for businesses, associations, institutions, or sales promotions. Please call our Special Sales Department in New York at (212) 967-8800 or (800) 322-8755.

You can find Bloom's Literary Crticism on the World Wide Web at
http://www.chelseahouse.com.

Contributing editor: Pamela Loos
Cover design by Alicia Post
Composition by IBT Global, Troy NY
Cover printed by IBT Global, Troy NY
Book printed and bound by IBT Global, Troy NY
Date printed: January, 2010
Printed in the United States of America

10 9 8 7 6 5 4 3 2 1

This book is printed on acid-free paper.

All links and Web addresses were checked and verified to be correct at the time of publication. Because of the dynamic nature of the Web, some addresses and links may have changed since publication and may no longer be valid.

Contents

Editor's Note

My introduction is a speculative overview of the Jewish negative in the only modern rival of Sigmund Freud as a dark guide to the spiritual future of any secular Jewish culture.

Anthony Thorlby, with a sensitive rigor, catches the Kafkan endless parabasis of verbal transmemberment, while Walter H. Sokel shrewdly argues for the autonomy of Kafka's art.

"A Country Doctor," which is a sublimely outrageous brief masterpiece, erupts in two outbursts of song by the peasants, sinuously noted by Henry Sussman.

Steven D. Dowden rightly finds Kafka's wisest counsel is for spiritual patience, after which Robert Alter studies the Kafkan fluid, almost dissolving sense of the Hebrew Bible.

"In the Penal Colony" seems to Stanley Corngold part of Kafka's despair of narrative art, while Russell A. Berman reads "The Judgment" as another parable of the betrayal of canonical tradition.

Clayton Koelb gives a hopeful view of Kafka's final rhetorical art, since as his readers we can absolve this superb writer from his curious guilt as to his indubitable vocation.

Martin Puchner sees in Kafka an agon with theatrical representation, after which Patrick Reilly risks a Dantean reading of Kafka, while acutely noting that: "Disagreeing with Kafka seems almost like quarreling with nature."

This volume concludes with Simon Ryan's persuasive interpretation of *The Metamorphosis* as a more than ironic vision of the absurdities of Jewish assimilation into a hostile pseudoculture.

HAROLD BLOOM

Introduction

In her obituary for her lover, Franz Kafka, Milena Jesenská sketched a modern Gnostic, a writer whose vision was of the *kenoma*, the cosmic emptiness into which we have been thrown:

> He was a hermit, a man of insight who was frightened by life.... He saw the world as being full of invisible demons which assail and destroy defenseless man.... All his works describe the terror of mysterious misconceptions and guiltless guilt in human beings.

Milena—brilliant, fearless, and loving—may have subtly distorted Kafka's beautifully evasive slidings between normative Jewish and Jewish Gnostic stances. Max Brod, responding to Kafka's now-famous remark—"We are nihilistic thoughts that came into God's head"—explained to his friend the Gnostic notion that the Demiurge had made this world both sinful and evil. "No," Kafka replied, "I believe we are not such a radical relapse of God's, only one of His bad moods. He had a bad day." Playing straight man, the faithful Brod asked if this meant there was hope outside our cosmos. Kafka smiled, and charmingly said: "Plenty of hope—for God—no end of hope—only not for us."

Kafka, despite Gershom Scholem's authoritative attempts to claim him for Jewish Gnosticism, is both more and less than a Gnostic, as we might expect. Yahweh can be saved, and the divine degradation that is fundamental to Gnosticism is not an element in Kafka's world. But we were fashioned out of the clay during one of Yahweh's bad moods; perhaps there was divine dyspepsia or sultry weather in the garden that Yahweh had planted in the East. Yahweh is hope, and we are hopeless. We are the jackdaws or crows, the *kafkas* (since that is what the name means, in Czech) whose impossibility is what the heavens signify: "The crows maintain that a single crow could destroy the heavens. Doubtless that is so, but it proves nothing against the heavens, for the heavens signify simply: the impossibility of crows."

In Gnosticism, there is an alien, wholly transcendent God, and the adept, after considerable difficulties, can find the way back to presence and fullness. Gnosticism therefore is a religion of salvation, though the most negative of all such saving visions. Kafkan spirituality offers no hope of salvation and so is not Gnostic. But Milena Jesenská certainly was right to emphasize the Kafkan terror that is akin to Gnosticism's dread of the *kenoma*, which is the world governed by the Archons. Kafka takes the impossible step beyond Gnosticism by denying that there is hope for us anywhere at all.

In the aphorisms that Brod rather misleadingly titled "Reflections on Sin, Pain, Hope and the True Way," Kafka wrote: "What is laid upon us is to accomplish the negative; the positive is already given." How much Kabbalah Kafka knew is not clear. Since he wrote a new Kabbalah, the question of Jewish Gnostic sources can be set aside. Indeed, by what seems a charming oddity (but I would call it yet another instance of Blake's insistence that forms of worship are chosen from poetic tales), our understanding of Kabbalah is Kafkan anyway, since Kafka profoundly influenced Gershom Scholem, and no one will be able to get beyond Scholem's creative or strong misreading of Kabbalah for decades to come. I repeat this point to emphasize its shock value: We read Kabbalah, via Scholem, from a Kafkan perspective, even as we read human personality and its mimetic possibilities by way of Shakespeare's perspectives, since essentially Freud mediates Shakespeare for us, yet relies on him nevertheless. A Kafkan facticity or contingency now governs our awareness of whatever in Jewish cultural tradition is other than normative.

In his diaries for 1922, Kafka meditated, on January 16, on "something very like a breakdown," in which it was "impossible to sleep, impossible to stay awake, impossible to endure life, or, more exactly, the course of life." The vessels were breaking for him as his demoniac, writerly inner world and the outer life "split apart, and they do split apart, or at least clash in a fearful manner." Late in the evening, K. arrives at the village, which is deep in snow. The Castle is in front of him, but even the hill on which it stands is veiled in mist and darkness, and there is not a single light visible to show that the Castle was there. K. stands a long time on a wooden bridge that leads from the main road to the village, while gazing, not at the village, but "into the illusory emptiness above him," where the Castle should be. He does not know what he will always refuse to learn, which is that the emptiness is "illusory" in every possible sense, since he does gaze at the *kenoma*, which resulted initially from the breaking of the vessels, the splitting apart of every world, inner and outer.

Writing the vision of K., Kafka counts the costs of his confirmation, in a passage prophetic of Scholem, but with a difference that Scholem sought to negate by combining Zionism and Kabbalah for himself. Kafka knew better, perhaps only for himself, but perhaps for others as well:

> Second: This pursuit, originating in the midst of men, carries one in a direction away from them. The solitude that for the most part has been forced on me, in part voluntarily sought by me—but what was this if not compulsion too?—is now losing all its ambiguity and approaches its denouement. Where is it leading? The strongest likelihood is that it may lead to madness; there is nothing more to say, the pursuit goes right through me and rends me asunder. Or I can—can I?—manage to keep my feet somewhat and be carried along in the wild pursuit. Where, then, shall I be brought? "Pursuit," indeed, is only a metaphor. I can also say, "assault on the last earthly frontier," an assault, moreover, launched from below, from mankind, and since this too is a metaphor, I can replace it by the metaphor of an assault from above, aimed at me from above.
>
> All such writing is an assault on the frontiers; if Zionism had not intervened, it might easily have developed into a new secret doctrine, a Kabbalah. There are intimations of this. Though of course it would require genius of an unimaginable kind to strike root again in the old centuries, or create the old centuries anew and not spend itself withal, but only then begin to flower forth.

Consider Kafka's three metaphors, which he so knowingly substitutes for one another. The pursuit is of ideas, in that mode of introspection that is Kafka's writing. Yet this metaphor of pursuit is also a piercing "right through me" and a breaking apart of the self. For "pursuit," Kafka then substitutes humankind's assault, from below, on the last earthly frontier. What is that frontier? It must lie between us and the heavens. Kafka, the crow or jackdaw, by writing, transgresses the frontier and implicitly maintains that he could destroy the heavens. By another substitution, the metaphor changes to "an assault from above, aimed at me from above," the aim simply being the signifying function of the heavens, which is to mean the impossibility of Kafkas or crows. The heavens assault Kafka through his writing; "all such writing is an assault on the frontiers," and these must now be Kafka's own frontiers. One thinks of Freud's most complex "frontier concept," more complex even than the drive: the bodily ego. The heavens assault Kafka's bodily ego, *but only through his own writing*. Certainly such an assault is not un-Jewish and has as much to do with normative as with esoteric Jewish tradition.

Yet, according to Kafka, his own writing, were it not for the intervention of Zionism, might easily have developed into a new Kabbalah. How are we to understand that curious statement about Zionism as the blocking agent that prevents Franz Kafka from becoming another Isaac Luria? Kafka darkly and immodestly writes: "There are intimations of this." Our teacher Gershom Scholem governs our interpretation here, of necessity. Those intimations belong to Kafka alone or perhaps to a select few in his immediate circle. They cannot be conveyed to Jewry, even to its elite, because Zionism has taken the place of messianic Kabbalah, including presumably the heretical Kabbalah of Nathan of Gaza, prophet of Sabbatai Zvi and of all his followers down to the blasphemous Jacob Frank. Kafka's influence on Scholem is decisive here, for Kafka already has arrived at Scholem's central thesis of the link between the Kabbalah of Isaac Luria, the messianism of the Sabbatarians and Frankists, and the political Zionism that gave rebirth to Israel.

Kafka goes on, most remarkably, to disown the idea that he possesses "genius of an unimaginable kind," one that either would strike root again in archaic Judaism, presumably of the esoteric sort, or more astonishingly "create the old centuries anew," which Scholem insisted Kafka had done. But can we speak, as Scholem tried to speak, of the Kabbalah of Franz Kafka? Is there a new secret doctrine in the superb stories and the extraordinary parables and paradoxes, or did not Kafka spend his genius in the act of new creation of the old Jewish centuries? Kafka certainly would have judged himself harshly as one spent withal, rather than as a writer who "only then began to flower forth." Kafka died only two and a half years after this meditative moment, died, alas, just before his forty-first birthday. Yet as the propounder of a new Kabbalah, he had gone very probably as far as he (or anyone else) could go. No Kabbalah, be it that of Moses de Leon, Isaac Luria, Moses Cordovero, Nathan of Gaza, or Gershom Scholem, is exactly easy to interpret, but Kafka's secret doctrine, if it exists at all, is designedly uninterpretable. My working principle in reading Kafka is to observe that he did everything possible to evade interpretation, which only means that what most needs and demands interpretation in Kafka's writing is its perversely deliberate evasion of interpretation. Erich Heller's formula for getting at this evasion is: "Ambiguity has never been considered an elemental force; it is precisely this in the stories of Franz Kafka." Perhaps, but evasiveness is not the same literary quality as ambiguity.

Evasiveness is purposive; it writes between the lines, to borrow a fine trope from Leo Strauss. What does it mean when a quester for a new negative, or perhaps rather a revisionist of an old negative, resorts to the evasion of every possible interpretation as his central topic or theme? Kafka does not doubt guilt but wishes to make it "possible for men to enjoy sin without guilt, almost without guilt," by reading Kafka. To enjoy sin almost without guilt is to evade interpretation, in exactly the dominant Jewish sense of interpretation. Jewish tradition, whether normative or esoteric, never teaches you to ask Nietzsche's question: "Who is the interpreter, and what power does he seek to gain over the text?" Instead, Jewish tradition asks: "Is the interpreter in the line of those who seek to build a hedge about the Torah in every age?" Kafka's power of evasiveness is not a power over his own text, and it does build a hedge about the Torah in our age. Yet no one before Kafka built up that hedge wholly out of evasiveness, not even Maimonides or Judah Halevi or even Spinoza. Subtlest and most evasive of all writers, Kafka remains the severest and most harassing of the belated sages of what will yet become the Jewish cultural tradition of the future.

* * *

The jackdaw or crow or Kafka is also the weird figure of the great hunter Gracchus (whose Latin name also means a crow), who is not alive but dead, yet who floats, like one living, on his death-bark forever. When the fussy Burgomaster of Riva knits his brow, asking: "And you have no part in the other world (*das Jenseits*)?" the Hunter replies, with grand defensive irony:

> I am forever on the great stair that leads up to it. On that infinitely wide and spacious stair I clamber about, sometimes up, sometimes down, sometimes on the right, sometimes on the left, always in motion. The Hunter has been turned into a butterfly. Do not laugh.

Like the Burgomaster, we do not laugh. Being a single crow, Gracchus would be enough to destroy the heavens, but he will never get there. Instead, the heavens signify his impossibility, the absence of crows or hunters, and so he has been turned into another butterfly, which is all we can be, from the perspective of the heavens. And we bear no blame for that:

> I had been glad to live and I was glad to die. Before I stepped aboard, I joyfully flung away my wretched load of ammunition, my knapsack, my hunting rifle that I had always been proud to carry, and I slipped into my winding sheet like a girl into her marriage dress. I lay and waited. Then came the mishap.

"A terrible fate," said the Burgomaster, raising his hand defensively. "And you bear no blame for it?"

"None," said the hunter. "I was a hunter; was there any sin in that? I followed my calling as a hunter in the Black Forest, where there were still wolves in those days. I lay in ambush, shot, hit my mark, flayed the skin from my victims: was there any sin in that? My labors were blessed. 'The Great Hunter of Black Forest' was the name I was given. Was there any sin in that?"

"I am not called upon to decide that," said the Burgomaster, "but to me also there seems to be no sin in such things. But then, whose is the guilt?"

"The boatman's," said the Hunter. "Nobody will read what I say here, no one will come to help me; even if all the people were commanded to help me, every door and window would remain shut, everybody would take to bed and draw the bedclothes over his head, the whole earth would become an inn for the night. And there is sense in that, for nobody knows of me, and if anyone knew he would not know where I could be found, and if he knew where I could be found, he would not know how to deal with me, he would not know how to help me. The thought of helping me is an illness that has to be cured by taking to one's bed."

How admirable Gracchus is, even when compared to the Homeric heroes! They know, or think they know, that to be alive, however miserable, is preferable to being the foremost among the dead. But Gracchus wished only to be himself, happy to be a hunter when alive, joyful to be a corpse when dead: "I slipped into my winding sheet like a girl into her marriage dress." So long as everything happened in good order, Gracchus was more than content. The guilt must be the boatman's and may not exceed mere incompetence. Being dead and yet still articulate, Gracchus is beyond help: "The thought of helping me is an illness that has to be cured by taking to one's bed."

When he gives the striking trope of the whole earth closing down like an inn for the night, with the bedclothes drawn over everybody's head, Gracchus renders the judgment: "And there is sense in that." There is sense in that only because in Kafka's world as in Freud's, or in Scholem's, or in any world deeply informed by Jewish memory, there is necessarily sense in everything, total sense, even though Kafka refuses to aid you in getting at or close to it.

But what kind of a world is that, where there is sense in everything, where everything seems to demand interpretation? There can be sense in everything, as J. H. Van den Berg once wrote against Freud's theory of repression, only if everything is already in the past and there never again can be anything wholly new. That is certainly the world of the great normative rabbis of the second century of the Common Era, and consequently it has been the world of most Jews ever since. Torah has been given, Talmud has risen to complement and interpret it, other interpretations in the chain of tradition are freshly forged in each generation, but the limits of creation and of revelation are fixed in Jewish memory. There is sense in everything because all sense is present already in the Hebrew Bible, which by definition must be totally intelligible, even if its fullest intelligibility will not shine forth until the Messiah comes.

Gracchus, hunter and jackdaw, is Kafka, pursuer of ideas and jackdaw, and the endless, hopeless voyage of Gracchus is Kafka's passage, only partly through a language not his own and largely through a life not much his own. Kafka was studying Hebrew intensively while he wrote "The Hunter Gracchus" early in 1917, and I think we may call the voyages of the dead but never-buried Gracchus a trope for Kafka's belated study of his ancestral language. He was still studying Hebrew in the spring of 1923, with his tuberculosis well advanced, and down to nearly the end he longed for Zion, dreaming of recovering his health and firmly grounding his identity by journeying to Palestine. Like Gracchus, he experienced life in death, though unlike Gracchus he achieved the release of total death.

"The Hunter Gracchus" as a story or extended parable is not the narrative of a Wandering Jew or Flying Dutchman, because Kafka's trope for his writing activity is not so much a wandering or even a wavering but rather a repetition, labyrinthine and burrow-building. His writing repeats, not itself, but a Jewish esoteric interpretation of Torah that Kafka himself scarcely knows or even needs to know. What this interpretation tells Kafka is that there is no written Torah but only an oral one. However, Kafka has no one to tell him what this oral Torah is. He substitutes his own writing therefore for the oral Torah not made available to him. He is precisely in the stance of the Hunter Gracchus, who concludes by saying, "I am here, more than that I do not know, further than that I cannot go. My ship has no rudder, and it is driven by the wind that blows in the undermost regions of death."

* * *

"What is the Talmud if not a message from the distance?" Kafka wrote to Robert Klopstock on December 19, 1923. What was all of Jewish tradition, to Kafka, except a message from an endless distance? That is surely part of the burden of the famous parable "An Imperial Message," which concludes with you, the reader, sitting at your window when evening falls and dreaming to yourself the parable—that God, in his act of dying, has sent you an individual message. Heinz Politzer read this as a Nietzschean parable and so fell into the trap set by the Kafkan evasiveness:

> Describing the fate of the parable in a time depleted of metaphysical truths, the imperial message has turned into the subjective fantasy of a dreamer who sits at a window with a view on a darkening world. The only real information imported by this story is the news of the Emperor's death. This news Kafka took over from Nietzsche.

No, for even though you dream the parable, the parable conveys truth. The Talmud does exist; it really is an imperial message from the distance. The distance is too great; it cannot reach you; there is hope, but not for you. Nor is it so clear that God is dead. He is always dying, yet always whispers a message into the angel's ear. It is said to you that: "Nobody could fight his way through here even with a message from a dead man," but the Emperor actually does not die in the text of the parable.

Distance is part of Kafka's crucial notion of the negative, which is not a Hegelian nor a Heideggerian negative, but is very close to Freud's negation and also to the negative imaging carried out by Scholem's Kabbalists. But I want to postpone Kafka's Jewish version of the negative until later. "The Hunter Gracchus" is an extraordinary text, but it is not wholly characteristic of Kafka at his strongest, at his uncanniest, or most sublime.

When he is most himself, Kafka gives us a continuous inventiveness and originality that rivals Dante and truly challenges Proust and Joyce as that of the dominant Western author of our century, setting Freud aside, since Freud ostensibly is science and not narrative or mythmaking, though if you believe that, then you can be persuaded of anything. Kafka's beast fables are rightly celebrated, but his most remarkable fabulistic being is neither animal nor human but is little Odradek, in the curious sketch, less than a page and a half long, "The Cares of a Family Man," where the title might have been translated: "The Sorrows of a Paterfamilias." The family man narrates these five paragraphs, each a dialectical lyric in itself, beginning with one that worries the meaning of the name:

> Some say the word Odradek is of Slavonic origin, and try to account for it on that basis. Others again believe it to be of German origin, only influenced by Slavonic. The uncertainty of both interpretations allows one to assume with justice that neither is accurate, especially as neither of them provides an intelligent meaning of the word.

This evasiveness was overcome by the scholar Wilhelm Emrich, who traced the name Odradek to the Czech word *odraditi*, meaning to dissuade anyone from doing anything. Like Edward Gorey's Doubtful Guest, Odradek is uninvited yet will not leave, since implicitly he dissuades you from doing anything about his presence, or rather something about his very uncanniness advises you to let him alone:

> No one, of course, would occupy himself with such studies if there were not a creature called Odradek. At first glance it looks like a flat star-shaped spool for thread, and indeed it does seem to have thread wound upon it; to be sure, they are only old, broken-off bits of thread, knotted and tangled together, of the most varied sorts and colors. But it is not only a spool, for a small wooden crossbar sticks out of the middle of the star, and another small rod is joined to that at a right angle. By means of this latter rod on one side and one of the points of the star on the other, the whole thing can stand upright as if on two legs.

Is Odradek a "thing," as the bemused family man begins by calling him, or is he not a childlike creature, a daemon at home in the world of children? Odradek clearly was made by an inventive and humorous child, rather in the spirit of the making of Adam out of the moistened red clay by the J writer's Yahweh. It is difficult not to read Odradek's creation as a deliberate parody when we are told that "the whole thing can stand upright as if on two legs" and again when the suggestion is ventured that Odradek, like Adam, "once had some sort of intelligible shape and is now only a brokendown remnant." If Odradek is fallen, he is still quite jaunty and cannot be closely scrutinized, since he "is extraordinarily nimble and can never be laid hold of," like the story in which he appears. Odradek not only advises you not to do anything about him, but in some clear sense he is yet another figure by means of whom Kafka advises you against interpreting Kafka.

One of the loveliest moments in all of Kafka comes when you, the *paterfamilias*, encounter Odradek leaning directly beneath you against the banisters. Being inclined to speak to him, as you would to a child, you receive a surprise: "'Well, what's your name?' you ask him. 'Odradek,' he says. 'And where do you live?' 'No fixed abode,' he says and laughs; but it is only the kind of laughter that has no lungs behind it. It sounds rather like the rustling of fallen leaves."

"The 'I' is another," Rimbaud once wrote, adding: "So much the worse for the wood that finds it is a violin." So much the worse for the wood that finds it is Odradek. He laughs at being a vagrant, if only by the bourgeois definition of having "no fixed abode," but the laughter, not being human, is uncanny. And so he provokes the family man to an uncanny reflection, which may be a Kafkan parody of Freud's death drive beyond the pleasure principle:

> I ask myself, to no purpose, what is likely to happen to him? Can he possibly die? Anything that dies has had some kind of aim in life, some kind of activity, which has worn out; but that does not apply to Odradek. Am I to suppose, then, that he will always be rolling down the stairs, with ends of thread trailing after him, right before the feet of my children? He does no harm to anyone that I can see, but the idea that he is likely to survive me I find almost painful.

The aim of life, Freud says, is death, is the return of the organic to the inorganic, supposedly our earlier state of being. Our activity wears out, and so we die because, in an uncanny sense, we wish to die. But Odradek, harmless and charming, is a child's creation, aimless, and so not subject to the death drive. Odradek is immortal, being daemonic, and he represents also a Freudian return of the repressed, of something repressed in the *paterfamilias*, something from which the family man is in perpetual flight. Little Odradek is precisely what Freud calls a cognitive return of the repressed, while (even as) a complete affective repression is maintained. The family man introjects Odradek intellectually but totally projects him affectively. Odradek, I now suggest, is best understood as Kafka's synecdoche for *Verneinung*—Kafka's version (not altogether un-Freudian) of Jewish negation, a version I hope to adumbrate in what follows.

* * *

Why does Kafka have so unique a spiritual authority? Perhaps the question should be rephrased. What kind of spiritual authority does Kafka have for us, or why are we moved or compelled to read him as one who has such authority? Why invoke the question of authority at all? Literary authority, however we define it, has no necessary relation to spiritual authority, and to speak of a spiritual authority in Jewish writing anyway always has been to speak rather dubiously. Authority is not a Jewish concept but a Roman one and so makes perfect contemporary sense in the context of the Roman Catholic Church but little sense in Jewish matters, despite the squalors of Israeli politics and the flaccid pieties of American Jewish nostalgias. There is no authority without hierarchy, and hierarchy is not a very Jewish concept either. We do not want the rabbis, or anyone else, to tell us what or who is or is not Jewish. The masks of the normative conceal not only the eclecticism of Judaism and of Jewish culture but also the nature of the J writer's Yahweh himself. It is absurd to think of Yahweh as having mere authority. He is no Roman godling who augments human activities, nor a Homeric god helping to constitute an audience for human heroism.

Yahweh is neither a founder nor an onlooker, though sometimes he can be mistaken for either or both. His essential trope is fatherhood rather than foundation, and his interventions are those of a covenanter rather than of a spectator. You cannot found an authority on him, because his benignity is manifested not through augmentation but through creation. He does not write; he speaks, and he is heard, in time, and what he continues to create by his speaking is *olam*, time without boundaries, which is more than just an augmentation. More of anything else can come through authority, but more life is the blessing itself and comes, beyond authority, to Abraham, to Jacob, and to David. No more than Yahweh do any of them have mere authority. Yet Kafka certainly does have literary authority, and in a troubled way his literary authority is now spiritual also, particularly in Jewish contexts. I do not think that this is a post-Holocaust phenomenon, though Jewish Gnosticism, oxymoronic as it may or may not be, certainly seems appropriate to our time, to many among us. Literary Gnosticism does not seem to me a time-bound phenomenon, anyway. Kafka's *The Castle*, as Erich Heller has argued, is clearly more Gnostic than normative in its spiritual temper, but then so is Shakespeare's *Macbeth*, and Blake's *The Four Zoas*, and Carlyle's *Sartor Resartus*. We sense a Jewish element in Kafka's apparent Gnosticism, even if we are less prepared than Scholem was to name it as a new Kabbalah. In his 1922 *Diaries*, Kafka subtly insinuated that even his espousal of the negative was dialectical:

> The Negative alone, however strong it may be, cannot suffice, as in my unhappiest moments I believe it can. For if I have gone the tiniest step upward, won any, be it the most dubious kind of security for myself, I then stretch out on my step and wait for the Negative, not to climb up to me, indeed, but to drag me down from it. Hence it is a defensive instinct in me that won't tolerate my having the slightest degree of lasting ease and smashes the marriage bed, for example, even before it has been set up.

What is the Kafkan negative, whether in this passage or elsewhere? Let us begin by dismissing the Gallic notion that there is anything Hegelian about it, any more than there is anything Hegelian about the Freudian *Verneinung*. Kafka's negative, unlike Freud's, is uneasily and remotely descended from the

ancient tradition of negative theology and perhaps even from that most negative of ancient theologies, Gnosticism, and yet Kafka, despite his yearnings
for transcendence, joins Freud in accepting the ultimate authority of the fact.
The given suffers no destruction in Kafka or in Freud, and this given essentially is the way things are, for everyone, and for the Jews in particular. If fact
is supreme, then the mediation of the Hegelian negative becomes an absurdity, and no destructive use of such a negative is possible, which is to say that
Heidegger becomes impossible, and Derrida, who is a strong misreading of
Heidegger, becomes quite unnecessary.

The Kafkan negative most simply is his Judaism, which is to say the
spiritual form of Kafka's self-conscious Jewishness, as exemplified in that
extraordinary aphorism: "What is laid upon us is to accomplish the negative;
the positive is already given." The positive here is the Law or normative Judaism; the negative is not so much Kafka's new Kabbalah, as it is that which is
still laid on us: the Judaism of the negative, of the future as it is always rushing
toward us.

His best biographer to date, Ernst Pawel, emphasizes Kafka's consciousness "of his identity as a Jew, not in the religious, but in the national sense."
Still, Kafka was not a Zionist, and perhaps he longed not so much for Zion
as for a Jewish language, be it Yiddish or Hebrew. He could not see that his
astonishing stylistic purity in German was precisely his way of *not* betraying his self-identity as a Jew. In his final phase, Kafka thought of going to
Jerusalem and again intensified his study of Hebrew. Had he lived, he would
probably have gone to Zion, perfected a vernacular Hebrew, and given us the
bewilderment of Kafkan parables and stories in the language of the J writer
and of Judah Halevi.

* * *

What calls out for interpretation in Kafka is his refusal to be interpreted,
his evasiveness even in the realm of his own negative. Two of his most
beautifully enigmatical performances, both late, are the parable "The
Problem of Our Laws" and the story or testament "Josephine the Singer
and the Mouse Folk." Each allows a cognitive return of Jewish cultural
memory, while refusing the affective identification that would make
either parable or tale specifically Jewish in either historical or contemporary identification. "The Problem of Our Laws" is set as a problem in the
parable's first paragraph:

> Our laws are not generally known; they are kept secret by the
> small group of nobles who rule us. We are convinced that these

ancient laws are scrupulously administered; nevertheless it is an extremely painful thing to be ruled by laws that one does not know. I am not thinking of possible discrepancies that may arise in the interpretation of the laws, or of the disadvantages involved when only a few and not the whole people are allowed to have a say in their interpretation. These disadvantages are perhaps of no great importance. For the laws are very ancient; their interpretation has been the work of centuries, and has itself doubtless acquired the status of law; and though there is still a possible freedom of interpretation left, it has now become very restricted. Moreover the nobles have obviously no cause to be influenced in their interpretation by personal interests inimical to us, for the laws were made to the advantage of the nobles from the very beginning, they themselves stand above the laws, and that seems to be why the laws were entrusted exclusively into their hands. Of course, there is wisdom in that—who doubts the wisdom of the ancient laws?—but also hardship for us; probably that is unavoidable.

In Judaism, the Law is precisely what is generally known, proclaimed, and taught by the normative sages. The Kabbalah was secret doctrine but increasingly was guarded not by the normative rabbis but by Gnostic sectaries, Sabbatarians, and Frankists, all of them ideologically descended from Nathan of Gaza, Sabbatai Zvi's prophet. Kafka twists askew the relations between normative and esoteric Judaism, again making a synecdochal representation impossible. It is not the rabbis or normative sages who stand above the Torah but the *minim*, the heretics from Elisha ben Abuyah through to Jacob Frank, and in some sense, Gershom Scholem as well. To these Jewish Gnostics, as the parable goes on to insinuate: "The Law is whatever the nobles do." So radical a definition tells us "that the tradition is far from complete," and that a kind of messianic expectation is therefore necessary. This view, so comfortless as far as the present is concerned, is lightened only by the belief that a time will eventually come when the tradition and our research into it will jointly reach their conclusion and, as it were, gain a breathing space, when everything will have become clear, the law will belong to the people, and the nobility will vanish.

If the parable at this point were to be translated into early Christian terms, then "the nobility" would be the Pharisees, and "the people" would be the Christian believers. But Kafka moves rapidly to stop such a translation: "This is not maintained in any spirit of hatred against the nobility; not at all, and by no one. We are more inclined to hate ourselves, because we have not yet shown ourselves worthy of being entrusted with the laws."

"We" here cannot be either Christians or Jews. Who then are those who "have not yet shown ourselves worthy of being entrusted with the laws"? They would appear to be the crows or jackdaws again, a Kafka or a hunter Gracchus, wandering about in a state perhaps vulnerable to self-hatred or self-distrust, waiting for a Torah that will not be revealed. Audaciously, Kafka then concludes with overt paradox:

> Actually one can express the problem only in a sort of paradox: Any party that would repudiate not only all belief in the laws, but the nobility as well, would have the whole people behind it; yet no such party can come into existence, for nobody would dare to repudiate the nobility. We live on this razor's edge. A writer once summed the matter up in this way: The sole visible and indubitable law that is imposed upon us is the nobility, and must we ourselves deprive ourselves of that one law?

Why would no one dare to repudiate the nobility, whether we read them as normative Pharisees, Jewish Gnostic heresiarchs, or whatever? Though imposed on us, the sages or the *minim* are the only visible evidence of law that we have. Who are we then? How is the parable's final question, whether open or rhetorical, to be answered? "Must we ourselves deprive ourselves of that one law?" Blake's answer, in *The Marriage of Heaven and Hell*, was: "One Law for the Lion and the Ox is Oppression." But what is one law for the crows? Kafka will not tell us whether it is oppression or not.

Josephine the singer also is a crow or Kafka, rather than a mouse, and the folk may be interpreted as an entire nation of jackdaws. The spirit of the negative, dominant if uneasy in "The Problem of Our Laws," is loosed into a terrible freedom in Kafka's testamentary story. That is to say: In the parable, the laws could not be Torah, though that analogue flickered near. But in Josephine's story, the mouse folk simultaneously are *and* are not the Jewish people, and Franz Kafka both is *and* is not their curious singer. Cognitively the identifications are possible, as though returned from forgetfulness, but affectively they certainly are not, unless we can assume that crucial aspects making up the identifications have been purposefully, if other than consciously, forgotten. Josephine's piping is Kafka's story, and yet Kafka's story is hardly Josephine's piping.

Can there be a mode of negation neither conscious nor unconscious, neither Hegelian nor Freudian? Kafka's genius provides one, exposing many shades between consciousness and the work of repression, many demarcations far ghostlier than we could have imagined without him. Perhaps the ghostliest come at the end of the story:

Josephine's road, however, must go downhill. The time will soon come when her last notes sound and die into silence. She is a small episode in the eternal history of our people, and the people will get over the loss of her. Not that it will be easy for us; how can our gatherings take place in utter silence? Still, were they not silent even when Josephine was present? Was her actual piping notably louder and more alive than the memory of it will be? Was it even in her lifetime more than a simply memory? Was it not rather because Josephine's singing was already past losing in this way that our people in their wisdom prized it so highly?

So perhaps we shall not miss so very much after all, while Josephine, redeemed from the earthly sorrows which to her thinking lay in wait for all chosen spirits, will happily lose herself in the numberless throng of the heroes of our people, and soon, since we are no historians, will rise to the heights of redemption and be forgotten like all her brothers.

"I am a Memory come alive," Kafka wrote in the *Diaries*. Whether or not he intended it, he was Jewish memory come alive. "Was it even in her lifetime more than a simple memory?" Kafka asks, knowing that he, too, was past losing. The Jews are no historians, in some sense, because Jewish memory, as Yosef Yerushalmi has demonstrated, is a normative mode and not a historical one. Kafka, if he could have prayed, might have prayed to rise to the heights of redemption and be forgotten like most of his brothers and sisters. But his prayer would not have been answered. When we think of *the* Catholic writer, we think of Dante, who nevertheless had the audacity to enshrine his Beatrice in the hierarchy of Paradise. If we think of *the* Protestant writer, we think of Milton, a party or sect of one, who believed that the soul was mortal and would be resurrected only in conjunction with the body. Think of *the* Jewish writer, and you must think of Kafka, who evaded his own audacity, and believed nothing, and trusted only in the covenant of being a writer.

The Castle

The full-scale instance of Kafka's new negative or new Kabbalah is *The Castle*, an unfinished and unfinishable autobiographical novel that is the story of K., the land surveyor. What is written between its lines? Assaulting the last earthly frontier, K. is necessarily audacious, but if what lies beyond the frontier is represented ultimately by Klamm, an imprisoning silence, lord of the *kenoma* or cosmic emptiness, then no audacity can suffice. You cannot redraw the frontiers, even if the authorities desired this, when you arrive at the administrative center of a catastrophe creation, where the demarcations hold fast against a supposed chaos or abyss, which is actually the negative emblem of the truth that the false or marred creation refuses. *The Castle* is the tale of how Kafka cannot write his way back to the abyss, of how K. cannot do his work as land surveyor.

Part of K.'s burden is that he is not audacious enough, even though audacity could not be enough anyway. Here is the interpretive audacity of Erich Heller, rightly rejecting all those who identify the Castle with spirituality and authentic grace, but himself missing the ineluctable evasiveness of Kafka's new Kabbalah:

> The Castle of Kafka's novel is, as it were, the heavily fortified garrison of a company of Gnostic demons, successfully holding an advanced position against the maneuvers of an impatient soul. There is no conceivable idea of divinity which could justify those interpreters who see in the Castle the residence of "divine law and divine grace." Its officers are totally indifferent to good if they are not positively wicked. Neither in their decrees nor in their activities is there any trace of love, mercy, charity, or majesty. In their icy detachment they inspire certainly no awe, but fear and revulsion. Their servants are a plague to the village, "a wild, unmanageable lot, ruled by their insatiable impulses . . . their scandalous behavior knows no limits," an anticipation of the blackguards who were to become the footmen of European dictators rather than the office boys of a divine ministry. Compared to the petty and apparently calculated torture of this tyranny, the gods of Shakespeare's indignation who "kill us for their sport" are at least majestic in their wantonness.

On such a reading, Klamm would be the Demiurge, leader of a company of Archons, gods of this world. Kafka is too evasive and too negative to give us so positive and simplistic an account of triumphant evil, or at least of reigning indifference to the good. Such Gnostic symbolism would make Klamm and his cohorts representatives of ignorance and K. in contrast a knower, but K. knows almost nothing, particularly about his own self, and from the start overestimates his own strength even as he deceives himself into the belief that the Castle underestimates him. The Castle is there primarily because K. is ignorant, though K.'s deepest drive is for knowledge. K.'s largest error throughout is his desire for a personal confrontation with Klamm, which necessarily is impossible. K., the single crow or jackdaw, would be sufficient to destroy the authority of Klamm, but Klamm and the Castle of Westwest signify simply the absence of crows, the inability of K. to achieve knowledge and therefore the impossibility of K. himself, the failure of land surveying or of assaulting the frontiers, of writing a new Kabbalah.

Klamm is named by Wilhelm Emrich as the interpersonal element in the erotic, which seems to me just as subtle an error as judging Klamm to be the Demiurge, leader of a company of Gnostic demons. It might be more accurate to call Klamm the impersonal element in the erotic, the drive, as Martin Greenberg does, yet even that identification is evaded by Kafka's text. Closer to Klamm, as should be expected, is the negative aspect of the drive, its entropy, whose effect on consciousness is nihilistic. Freud, in his posthumous *An Outline of Psychoanalysis* (1940), says of the drives that "they represent the somatic demands on mental life." That approximates Klamm, but only if you give priority to Thanatos over Eros, to the death drive over sexuality. Emrich, a touch humorlessly, even identifies Klamm with Eros, which would give us a weird Eros indeed:

> Accordingly, then, Klamm is the "power" that brings the lovers together as well as the power which, bestowing happiness and bliss, is present within love itself. K. seeks contact with this power, sensing its proximity in love, a proximity great enough for communicating in whispers; but he must "manifest" such communication and contact with this power itself through a spiritual-intellectual expression of his own; this means that, as an independent spiritual-intellectual being, he must confront this power eye to eye, as it were; he must "manifest" to this superpersonal power his own understanding, his own relation with it, a relation "known" only to him at the present time; that means, he must make this relation known to the power as well.

Emrich seems to found this equation on the love affair between K. and Frieda, which begins, in famous squalor, on the floor of a bar:

> Fortunately Frieda soon came back; she did not mention K., she only complained about the peasants, and in the course of looking round for K. went behind the counter, so that he was able to touch her foot. From that moment he felt safe. Since Frieda made no reference to K., however, the landlord was compelled to do it. "And where is the Land-Surveyor?" he asked. He was probably courteous by nature, refined by constant and relatively free intercourse with men who were much his superior, but there was remarkable consideration in his tone to Frieda, which was all the more striking because in his conversation he did not cease to

be an employer addressing a servant, and a saucy servant at that. "The Land-Surveyor—I forgot all about him," said Frieda, setting her small foot on K.'s chest. "He must have gone out long ago." "But I haven't seen him," said the landlord, "and I was in the hall nearly the whole time." "Well, he isn't in here," said Frieda coolly. "Perhaps he's hidden somewhere," said the landlord. "From the impression I had of him, he's capable of a good deal." "He would hardly dare to do that," said Frieda, pressing her foot down on K. There was a certain mirth and freedom about her which K. had not previously noticed, and quite unexpectedly it took the upper hand, for suddenly laughing she bent down to K. with the words: "Perhaps he's hidden underneath here," kissed him lightly, and sprang up again saying with a troubled air: "No, he's not there." Then the landlord, too, surprised K. when he said: "It bothers me not to know for certain that he's gone. Not only because of Herr Klamm, but because of the rule of the house. And the rule applies to you, Fräulein Frieda, just as much as to me. Well, if you answer for the bar, I'll go through the rest of the rooms. Good night! Sleep well!" He could hardly have left the room before Frieda had turned out the electric light and was under the counter beside K. "My darling! My darling!" she whispered, but she did not touch him. As if swooning with love, she lay on her back and stretched out her arms; time must have seemed endless to her in the prospect of her happiness, and she sighed rather than sang some little song or other. Then as K. still lay absorbed in thought, she started up and began to tug at him like a child. "Come on, it's too close down here," and they embraced each other, her little body burned in K.'s hands, in a state of unconsciousness which K. tried again and again but in vain to master they rolled a little way, landing with a thud on Klamm's door, where they lay among the small puddles of beer and other refuse scattered on the floor.

"Landing with a thud on Klamm's door" is Kafka's outrageously rancid trope for a successful completion to copulation, but that hardly makes Klamm into a benign Eros, with his devotees lying "among the small puddles of beer and other refuse scattered on the floor." One could recall the libertines among the Gnostics, ancient and modern, who seek to redeem the sparks upward by a redemption *through* sin. Frieda, faithful disciple and former mistress of Klamm, tells K. that she believes it is Klamm's "doing that we came together there under the counter; blessed, not cursed, be the hour." Emrich gives full credence to Frieda, a rather dangerous act for an exegete, and certainly K. desperately believes Frieda, but then, as Heller remarks, "K. loves Frieda—if he loves her at all—entirely for Klamm's sake." That K., despite his drive for freedom, may be deceived as to Klamm's nature is understandable, but I do not think that Kafka was deceived or wished to be deceived. If Klamm is to be identified, it ought to be with what is silent, imprisoned, and unavailable in copulation, something that partakes of the final negative, the drive toward death.

Whether *The Castle* is of the aesthetic eminence of Kafka's finest stories, parables, and fragments is open to considerable doubt, but *The Castle* is certainly the best text for studying Kafka's negative, his hidden and subversive New Kabbalah. It abides as the most enigmatic major novel of our century, and one sees why Kafka himself thought it a failure. But all Kabbalah—old and new—has to fail when it offers itself openly to more than a handful. Perhaps *The Castle* fails as the *Zohar* fails, but like the *Zohar*, Kafka's *Castle* will go on failing from one era to another.

The Trial

"Guilt" generally seems more a Christian than a Jewish category, even if the guilt of Joseph K. is primarily ignorance of the Law. Certainly Kafka could be judged closer to Freud in *The Trial* than he usually is, since Freudian "guilt" is also hardly distinct from ignorance, not of the Law but of the reality principle. Freud insisted that all authority, communal or personal, induced guilt in us, since we share in the murder of the totemic father. Guilt therefore is never to be doubted, but only because we are all of us more or less ill, all plagued by our discomfort with culture. Freudian and Kafkan guilt alike is known only under the sign of negation, rather than as emotion. Joseph K. has no consciousness of having done wrong, but just as Freudian man nurtures the desire to destroy authority or the father, so even Joseph K. has his own unfulfilled wishes against the image of the Law.

The process that Joseph K. undergoes is hopeless, since the Law is essentially a closed Kabbalah; its books are not available to the accused. If traditional questers suffered an ordeal by landscape, Joseph K.'s ordeal is by nearly everything and everyone he encounters. The representatives of the Law, and their camp followers, are so unsavory that Joseph K. seems sympathetic by contrast, yet he is actually a poor fellow in himself and would be as nasty as the keepers of the Law if only he could. *The Trial* is a very unpleasant book, and Kafka's own judgment of it may have been spiritually wiser than anything its critics have enunciated. Would there be any process for us to undergo if we were not both lazy and frightened? Nietzsche's motive for metaphor was the desire to be different, the desire to be elsewhere, but Kafka's sense of our motive is that we want to rest, even if just for a moment. The world is our

Gnostic catastrophe creation, being broken into existence by the guilt of our repose. Yet this is creation and can be visibly beautiful, even as the accused are beautiful in the gaze of the camp followers of the Law.

I do not think that the process Joseph K. undergoes can be called "interpretation," which is the judgment of Ernst Pawel, who follows Jewish tradition in supposing that the Law is language. *The Trial*, like the rest of Kafka's writings, is a parable not of interpretation but of the necessary failure of interpretation. I would surmise that the Law is not all of language, since the language of *The Trial* is ironic enough to suggest that it is not altogether bound to the Law. If *The Trial* has a center, it is in what Kafka thought worthy of publishing: the famous parable "Before the Law." The dialogue concerning the parable between Joseph K. and the prison chaplain who tells it is remarkable but less crucial than the parable itself:

> Before the Law stands a doorkeeper on guard. To this doorkeeper there comes a man from the country who begs for admittance to the Law. But the doorkeeper says that he cannot admit the man at the moment. The man, on reflection, asks if he will be allowed, then, to enter later. "It is possible," answers the doorkeeper, "but not at this moment." Since the door leading into the Law stands open as usual and the doorkeeper steps to one side, the man bends down to peer through the entrance. When the doorkeeper sees that, he laughs and says: "If you are so strongly tempted, try to get in without my permission. But note that I am powerful. And I am only the lowest doorkeeper. From hall to hall keepers stand at every door, one more powerful than the other. Even the third of these has an aspect that even I cannot bear to look at." These are difficulties which the man from the country has not expected to meet; the Law, he thinks, should be accessible to every man and at all times, but when he looks more closely at the doorkeeper in his furred robe, with his huge pointed nose and long, thin, Tartar beard, he decides that he had better wait until he gets permission to enter. The doorkeeper gives him a stool and lets him sit down at the side of the door. There he sits waiting for days and years. He makes many attempts to be allowed in and wearies the doorkeeper with his importunity. The doorkeeper often engages him in brief conversation, asking him about his home and about other matters, but the questions are put quite impersonally, as great men put questions, and always conclude with the statement that the man cannot be allowed to enter yet. The man, who has equipped himself with many things for his journey, parts with all

he has, however valuable, in the hope of bribing the doorkeeper. The doorkeeper accepts it all, saying, however, as he takes each gift: "I take this only to keep you from feeling that you have left something undone." During all these long years the man watches the doorkeeper almost incessantly. He forgets about the other doorkeepers, and this one seems to him the only barrier between himself and the Law. In the first years he curses his evil fate aloud; later, as he grows old, he only mutters to himself. He grows childish, and since in his prolonged watch he has learned to know even the fleas in the doorkeeper's fur collar, he begs the very fleas to help him and to persuade the doorkeeper to change his mind. Finally his eyes grow dim and he does not know whether the world is really darkening around him or whether his eyes are only deceiving him. But in the darkness he can now perceive a radiance that streams immortally from the door of the Law. Now his life is drawing to a close. Before he dies, all that he has experienced during the whole time of his sojourn condenses in his mind into one question, which he has never yet put to the doorkeeper. He beckons the doorkeeper, since he can no longer raise his stiffening body. The doorkeeper has to bend far down to hear him, for the difference in size between them has increased very much to the man's disadvantage. "What do you want to know now?" asks the doorkeeper, "you are insatiable." "Everyone strives to attain the Law," answers the man, "how does it come about, then, that in all these years no one has come seeking admittance but me?" The doorkeeper perceives that the man is at the end of his strength and that his hearing is failing, so he bellows in his ear: "No one but you could gain admittance through this door, since this door was intended only for you. I am now going to shut it."

Does he actually perceive a radiance, or are his eyes perhaps still deceiving him? What would admittance to the radiance mean? The Law, I take it, has the same status it has in the later parable "The Problem of Our Laws," where it cannot be Torah, or the Jewish Law, yet Torah flickers uneasily near as a positive analogue to the negation that is playing itself out. Joseph K. then is another jackdaw, another Kafkan crow in a cosmos of crows, waiting for that new Torah that will not be revealed. Does such a waiting allow itself to be represented in or by a novel? No one could judge *The Trial* to be grander as a whole than in its parts, and "Before the Law" bursts out of its narrative shell in the novel. The terrible greatness of Kafka is absolute in the parable but wavering in the novel, too impure a casing for such a fire.

That there should be nothing but a spiritual world, Kafka once wrote, denies us hope but gives us certainty. The certainty would seem to be not so much that a radiance exists, but that all access to it will be barred by petty officials at least countenanced, if not encouraged, by what passes for the radiance itself. This is not paradox, any more than is the Kafkan principle propounded by the priest who narrates "Before the Law": Accurate interpretation and misreading cannot altogether exclude each other. Kafka's aesthetic compulsion (can there be such?) in *The Trial*, as elsewhere, is to write so as to create a necessity, yet also so as to make interpretation impossible, rather than merely difficult.

Kafka's permanent centrality to the postnormative Jewish dilemma achieves one of its monuments in *The Trial*. Gershom Scholem found in Kafka not only the true continuator of the Gnostic Kabbalah of Moses Cordovero but also the central representative for our time of an even more archaic splendor, the broken radiance of Hebraic revelation. Perhaps Scholem was right, for no other modern Jewish author troubles us with so strong an impression that we are in the presence of what Scholem called "the strong light of the canonical, of the perfection that destroys."

ANTHONY THORLBY

Kafka's Narrative: A Matter of Form

It is always hard to final words appropriate to commemorate a man. When the man is Franz Kafka, there is more than usual occasion to ponder the appropriateness of language to a life. He regarded his own life as a failure, to the point of feeling ashamed of it; to commemorate that must seem inappropriate and less than kind. Is it kinder to the man to commemorate his words? With Kafka, doubts arise here too.

It was because he had given so much of his life to writing that he felt guilt—something like that barely explicable "shame" which (in the phrase his novel, *The Trial*, ends with) he had good reason to believe "would outlive him." One reason perhaps why he did not want the novel to be published. It was still in fragmentary, unpublished form when he died, as was a very large part of what is today regarded as Kafka's works, which he asked his friend Max Brod to destroy. What Kafka actually published himself, in short-lived journals and limited editions of very slim volumes, amount when collected to some 300 pages. Brod took the publication of these as sufficient justification for publishing the rest, the bulk of Kafka's writing, thereby (it is said) ignoring the advice of a Viennese wag, whom he anxiously consulted about the propriety of such a step, and who said he was sure it would be all right, if only Brod destroyed some unwanted writings—why not his own?

From *Kafka and the Contemporary Critical Performance: Centenary Readings*, edited by Alan Udoff, pp. 30–40. © 1987 by Indiana University Press.

Brod saw no essential difference between what Kafka had been willing to publish and what he had not. Time has shown that he was wrong, though in no very subtle respect. Quite simply, the sheer extent of the Collected Works, including Kafka's Diaries and his Letters, has established him as a major writer worth commemorating, in a way that the pieces he alone prepared for publication, many of them not even stories, let alone novels in any recognizable sense, almost certainly would not have done. With the help of knowledge gained, thanks to Brod, of Kafka's life and personality, and above all of how he thought and wrote behind the scenes, as it were, where he tried out variations, which suggest he had a theme, and larger structures and generalizations, which suggest he had a purpose, a method, a philosophy even, it has proved possible to construct around those few original works a vast situation. Critics have found this situation inexhaustibly fascinating, and they have explained it in many ways: psychoanalytically, as an expression of Kafka's relationship to his father and to women; sociologically, as an expression of disgust and horror towards modern society; philosophically and theologically, as an expression of profound concern for human intelligence without God. To judge from the few things he did publish, this sounds like just the kind of situation which Kafka was hoping to avoid: namely, one in which precisely those aspects of his writing to which he did not want to call attention have nevertheless attracted all of it to themselves. The situation could hardly be more Kafkaesque.

Kafkaesque: the name has even entered the English language. What does the word mean, how is it used? Behind this question lurks the vaster one of how, or to what, any word relates; and I shall argue that the difficulties and even dangers which arise when we try to answer it, are what is Kafkaesque. Let me begin pedantically: the word is an adjective, it describes a quality, and it is almost invariably applied, as here, to a situation. Other writers have lent their names to rather more distinct things: Plato, to a kind of love; Machiavelli, to a kind of political behavior; and so on. In cases like these, we are familiar enough with the phenomenon in general, with love and politics, and so understand that it is a particular form of each which is to be designated as Platonic or Machiavellian. But what exactly is a situation "in general"? It is, I suppose, a recognition that a number of phenomena, factors of many different kinds, such as persons and places, wishes and thoughts, things that have happened and others yet to come, in some way belong together to form a whole. The word "situation" originally meant location or site, and it is now mostly used metaphorically to delineate an area or moment of experience. A situation, we might say, is not really there at all, except to the extent that we choose to experience a number of things in conjunction with one another. Thus, a situation can be resolved by introducing more factors, or eliminating some, or by rearranging them all.

When we speak of a situation as being Kafkaesque, we mean that we see this metaphorical activity going on—but without understanding what the connections are. For the (minor) characters in *The Castle* and *The Trial*, the situation is self-evident and normal; but for the protagonist and especially for Kafka's readers, it is not. He sees—and we see even more—a mass of bizarre details inexplicably brought together; but being a good hero, and we still more heroic readers, neither of us gives up. And neither of us succeeds, no matter how determined we may be, in making sense of this situation. But if we cannot make sense of it, is it really a situation? To speak of a Kafkaesque situation begins to sound like a contradiction in terms. Yet the linking power of language, especially its metaphorical resources, is inexhaustible. The array of phenomena in the hero's life, as in our own, may at first look limitless and therefore shapeless; as soon as we begin to take account of it, however, we become convinced that there must be a story in it somewhere, a necessary shape, a place for everything. We become aware, that is to say, of two opposite things at once, and are not let off the hook by arguing that this is a contradiction. What, after all, is a contradiction but a mere mental protest, which does not actually extricate us from life's quantities of sand? So, despite contradiction, we say a situation is Kafkaesque when we mean: Don't be silly, it can't be like that, while seeing all too plainly that it is. Indeed, while seeing something still odder: namely, that we have no idea *what* it is, the likeness of which we so plainly see.

The situation which criticism has constructed around the few works Kafka himself published is Kafkaesque in the extreme. It has argued that they are metaphors or similes of psychological complexes, and sociological alienation, and metaphysical despair—while leaving the reader who thought he had some idea of what these things are really like, exclaiming: Don't be silly, that can't possibly be what they are. And besides constructing ways of reading, criticism has also constructed actual stories. Editors, following Brod's example, have put several fragments into larger wholes, which constitute new situations for the most part a good deal more complicated than the original—but also more open to critical explanation. However, so long as none of this criticism is found to be entirely fitting—and so far there is not much agreement among critics—it only heightens the effect of impenetrability in Kafka's original, rather than explains it. This may even be what Kafka intended.

For it is possible, to judge from a few of Kafka's remarks about writing, that through it he hoped to liberate himself from the troubling illusion of there being a world to explain. Might he write in such a way so as to expose the illusoriness of the interpretative, metaphorical activity itself, into which language leads us in vain pursuit of the truth? If truly successful, the impenetrable text, sealed off from reality, would presumably no longer trouble us or him; it would not reflect the world's ills but offer escape from them into some pure lucidity and artistry all its own. It would cease to be what we now think of as Kafkaesque. But since we now do, of course, have every scrap of Kafka's writing, all the unsuccessful scraps as he judged them to be, we also know that he doubted the attainability of his own ideal. He must have doubted whether Brod would actually destroy the telltale bundles of undeniably Kafkaesque material. And would critics, if they had been confined to the work published by Kafka, ever have taken it at its face value, whatever that expression means? For what critics do is to probe the value of texts and the meaning of expressions, and they might have guessed anyway in the teeth of what adversity Kafka fought for his peculiar value, and over how deep an abyss of unfathomable meaning his seemingly watertight expressions float. Critics never leave well enough alone, and for better or for worse, we live now with this peculiarly Brodesque affair of the Kafkaesque.

We get a fair idea of Kafka's intention to isolate his texts from reference to the world, and thus escape the delusions generated by trying to situate them there, if we look at one of his most famous original pieces: "Before the Law." To retell it would be to spoil it, but we may recall at least the sublime rejoinder with which it ends. Here is this wretched little man, who has waited all his life before the Great Door, behind which lies, terrifyingly, all that is most important for him as for all men. The story does not actually say what this is (does anyone know, since no one is ever allowed through to find out?). Dying at last, the man asks why in all these years he has never seen anyone else ask for admittance to what all men must surely strive for. "No one else," comes the reply, "could gain admittance at this entrance, for this entrance was intended only for you. I am going to go now and shut it."

Kafka included this story in one of the provisional chapters for his unfinished novel *The Trial*. It is preached to the hero, K., in an almost totally dark cathedral by someone in some sort of holy orders. It is set in a context which looks more real than itself. This context purports to—but does not—explain the story by showing why it is told to K.: it is meant to disabuse him of delusions he has about the situation he finds himself in—namely, on trial. K. remains unenlightened. He assumes that if he is on trial, there must be a law according to which he is either guilty or innocent; there must also be judges to decide his case. The most important thing in his life is to confront them, but like the man in the story, K. never gains access to anything. He will never find out what his trial is about, in fact; he is misled by the way he thinks about it—misled by language. The nouns "law" and "court" sound as if they refer to real things; but these apparent substantives are (in German anyway) abstract concepts formed from verbs. In English, the word "trial" could be similarly misunderstood. Something is going on in K.'s life, as in the life of all of us, which may make it "a trial"; but it does not follow that this trial is a legal one or that any knowable law decides its outcome. It certainly does not follow in K.'s case (and the word "case" also does not refer to a specific thing, even though it seems to say it does; the noun, the thing, derives from a verb meaning "to fall"). Thus, Kafka describes K.'s case, indeed his whole story, with a word that means perhaps no more than that something is going on: namely, a *Prozeß*, a process; and with the similarly, dubiously metaphorical, or perhaps merely literal word, *ein Verfahren*.

K.'s mistake, then, is to suppose that his life constitutes a case, and his case a trial, that he is being tried for something, by somebody, and according to some code of law. He cannot see what he is guilty of, because all the bodies and things he expects to encounter are grammatical misunderstandings. He is guilty, you might say, of bad grammar: a guilt which Kafka felt he had incurred by writing at all. His basic mistake is a tiny, prepositional one. Prepositions are the smallest words which establish the most fundamental relationships: in this case, the relationship of these supposed things to K.—that is, what he is guilty "of," and what his trial is "about." He is warned of this error by the storyteller, who represents (in German) all things spiritual rather than any concrete doctrine. The law, as his story illustrates it, is empty of content; the word "law" (*Gesetz*) carries overtones that suggest something is only being "assumed." But take an assumption literally, as real, and it acquires the solidity of what is "laid down"—of what is the case, of law, in fact.

K. takes the story very seriously and tries to judge it by realistic and literal criteria. Ignoring the traditional phrase with which it begins, to the effect that this is what is said to be the case, that this is what it is called (*heißt*), he points to the mistake at once: The little man mistakenly waited all his life until it was too late. The storyteller then makes another altogether Kafkaesque rejoinder. No, there is no such mistake in the story at all. Though he previously said that the story was about a mistake, he now says there is no trace of a mistake actually in the story. A prepositional mistake, indeed—and one which rests in German on two different uses of the same preposition (*von*). This harmless little word contains and confuses a variety of different, even contrary, relationships. K. is therefore told he is changing the story—relating it differently—by trying to find out what is wrong with it. It never occurs to him that the mistake is one he is making in the way he looks for it in the story: that is, in the same literal-minded spirit in which he looks for it in life. And we are in some danger, of course, of making the same mistake ourselves. In pursuing a serious conclusion, based on Kafka's hilarious parody of Biblical midrash, practiced on a wittily fictitious text, we come close to toppling out of Kafka's boat into the abyss—and not without some suspicion that we may have been pushed by an author whose sense of humor we had underrated.

At all events, K. does not get the point, and the scene ends in total darkness. He is no longer anywhere near the great door and has to be shown the way out—unlike the man in the story, who so much wanted to be let in (Kafka amuses himself by using the same words in the world of the parable and the world of the novel). K.'s sense of right has been outraged by what he has heard from his spiritual mentor. For instance: that "a correct conception of a thing and misunderstanding of the same thing do not entirely exclude one another." That is not the sort of language K. is prepared to accept; it implies that the rules of understanding are not one and universal. Nor can he accept this remark by the unorthodox priest: "One does not have to hold everything to be true, one only has to hold that it is necessary." K. replies: "That's a dismal view—the lie is made into the ruling principle of the world."

Some critics cite this reply (about the lie) as Kafka's own last, pessimistic word. It is unwise to do so, however, for it is not even K.'s; he says it because he is tired and wants to put an end to the discussion. It is, in fact, the cliché of the age: the age of Nietzsche and Ibsen and Chekhov and Shaw with their so-called "life-lie." The age too of all their next of kin on the political left and right who have taken advantage of this principle of universal mendacity, in order to throw off the yoke of lies and unite the people, or else to yoke the people with new lies and unite them that way—a way that often looks much the same in practice.

The English tend to pride themselves on alone having the common sense to see what is wrong with absolute assertions made by less pragmatic nations. We like to remember Bertrand Russell's wit in showing why you cannot say that all language is a lie. It is one of history's grimmest ironies that a German-Jewish intellectual from Prague should also have understood, but to no avail, the dangers latent in a false use of language. Kafka distinguished between orders of language quite as wittily as Russell, seeing the different relationship to reality implied by different kinds of statement, and also the ultimate difficulty in knowing at all what it is that words are about. Language seems to be about "life"; at all events, it is a necessary part of what we mean by human life; but we cannot get outside it to see how well it fits. A very peculiar kind of problem begins once we do try to get outside it and do not take any fit for granted. We find then, like K., that this problem has us in its grip when we take it up, and that we are released from it when we do not. With these words, the chapter "In the Cathedral" ends—except that Kafka does not write "problem" but that mysteriously conceptual word for "court" (*Gericht*), about which K. is making his big mistake. The word, behind which lies the nightmare K. never penetrates, reveals what Kafka felt this unspeakable problem to be like. It was as if, in trying to see how well language (as we think) passes judgment on life, we come to suspect that someone or something is passing judgment on us. The situation seemed to him grotesquely hopeless; it was not life which was hopeless in his eyes, but language, because (like all intellectuals) he pinned to it an impossible hope. Max Brod, being much more like K. than K. is like Kafka, once asked his friend this very question: Did he see no hope—"Hope," replied Kafka, "infinitely much hope. But not for us."

Everything that Kafka wrote has to do with this most problematic of relationships: between language and reality and between language and itself. The problem preoccupied many of the best minds of the century, and Prague was to become renowned for work on the subject. Although Kafka's work is quite different in character, it is as profound as that of any contemporary. He reflected much on the sense in which we encounter reality at all outside the spiritual forms of language. He was drawn toward a belief as old as Christianity (and the heresy most persistently threatening to it), namely, the Manichaean one that "there is only a spiritual world; what we call the physical world is the evil in the spiritual one." Kafka's desire for a language that would liberate and transfigure was always matched by doubts about his actual writing, which he feared might be a kind of heretical reaching after an impossible, impermissible insight; as though a writer were a man looking on from somewhere outside life, from beyond the grave, being dead while still being alive; as though he were being rewarded for services rendered to the devil.

Kafka makes us notice the problem in which language engulfs itself and the world; he does this by blurring the distinctions we are used to: between thoughts and things, between literal and metaphorical usage, between the speaker's view and what he is speaking about. For many readers, the Kafkaesque is a quality they notice particularly in the blurring of this latter distinction, even more than in the confusions we have just examined between concepts and what they are supposed to be concepts of. Essentially, the confusion is the same in the case of the speaker and the spoken. Who is speaking to us about these things? Can't he see that the world he is looking at doesn't make sense? He seems to be a part of it and yet apart from it; he tries ever so thoughtfully to work it out, and so presumably has a point of reference outside it—that is what the logic of his as of all language implies—and yet he never succeeds. Indeed, his thoughtful narration is the world he is failing to make sense of. And it is this that lends to Kafka's narrations their nightmare character. For a nightmare too engulfs us, leaving us no independence of view or action, no possibility of escape or control. We cannot separate ourself from it: that *is* the nightmare, as we recognise on waking and half feel while we are in its grip.

Of course, that could be the way life is, that could be the lesson of dreams. Again, the thought is an ancient and a religious one, for it assumes we shall wake up from this dream one day into some other, after life. Is Kafka preaching this thought (as Max Brod believed), or parodying it (which seems more likely)? Those who preach it use the metaphorical potential in language in a serious, positive way, telling us we see now as in a glass darkly, but then face to face. Kafka's confusing play with the distinction between literal and metaphorical language is spiritually unnerving, not reassuring. In his prose, you cannot tell what is literal and what metaphorical; the two blur, you can no longer be sure what each is nor of the relationship between them. Kafka summed up this confusion in a narrative shorter even than "Before the Law"; it refers to the language in which that story is written, being called "On Parables (or Metaphors)," and it ends with a no less witty exchange of words. After a common-sense and unconfused account of how the metaphors spoken by the wise are only metaphors and of no real use amidst the cares of daily life, someone says:

> If you only followed the metaphors, you would become metaphors yourselves, and thus be rid of all your daily cares.
> Someone else says: I bet this is also a metaphor.
> The first says: You have won.
> The second persons says: But unfortunately only in metaphor.
> The first says: No, in reality; metaphorically speaking you have lost.

There is enough intellectual energy in this passage to put one's mind into perpetual orbit. This is no simple parable preached against those of little faith, who do not believe in metaphors or the language of the spirit. The advocate of the metaphorical life does not actually live it; he knows its value by reference to a reality where for him too it does not prevail and is not true. While the unbelieving realist knows that the value of his winning common sense is—albeit "unfortunately"—a metaphorical one. The two speakers are in the same boat and are merely arguing about the sense in which it is a winner or a loser. Neither of them inhabits the land about which he speaks: neither that of legend and poetry and scripture, the land where wisdom is lived; nor that of daily life, about which nothing much can be said other than that it is the opposite of the former, defined (in fact) by the loss of metaphor and meaning, and full of cares. And thus it is with Kafka's writing: it confines us to a linguistic boat, from which we can dimly perceive, like distant shores we never reach, dim mythic shapes of imagined meaning on the one hand, and on the other odd facts, inscrutable events, momentarily realistic perspectives, all of them inexplicably highlighted and pointlessly explained. He makes us aware of the unfathomable uncertainty which separates the one from the other shore, an uncertainty surrounding every word we use in the falsely confident belief that a word corresponds to something real.

Kafka's stories are like myths which discredit themselves in the telling. For they are told in non-mythological language, in a style which eschews figurative and poetic phrases, a prose so pedantically clear it would be plain dull were it not so startlingly inappropriate to what is being narrated. There is no need for us to ask what the meaning is of the inconceivable circumstances and subjects of his stories: his singing mouse and beetle-salesman, his dog researching canine habits and ape reporting on his progress toward man, his man who practices the suicidal artistry of transcending the human condition altogether. Kafka's narration itself explains everything, every noteworthy detail, every necessary development; and we listen rather like K. in *The Castle*, when he is granted an explanatory interview at last with someone competent to tell him what he wants to know: we are agog, but then grow tired, and finally fall asleep. Only to find our sleepy deafness to the narrator is not final: we start to dream, distorting the elements of the narration and imagining meanings in these which we have not actually heard. We behave like literary critics. We may be forgiven for dreaming over the text, though; for the one thing we, like K., really want to have explained never is and never will be—namely, why we are in this Kafkaesque situation at all.

What on earth is the point of reading Kafka's prose, then, if it fails to explain its own subject matter? The answer is that it makes clear the linguistic and psychological character of explanation: that continuous effort by the mind, not just when it is reading but all the time, to tell itself what it is doing, why it is doing it, and how this activity constitutes an appropriate response to its situation in life. The response generally does appear appropriate, since the situation is itself produced largely by this explanatory activity. Successful explanations fit the situation too well: they are not noticed. Kafka's do not fit, and so they are noticed; and so is a new kind of anxiety, compounded of funniness and fear, which ensues when explanations fail. Kafka knows there have been times when people did have a language, social and symbolic as well as verbal, which explained why things are as they are and what they should do about it. But those times are past, and the point of his writing is to show what life is like once they are; when the explanatory ideologies, as they are then called, of former ages are no longer credible or comprehensible.

For Kafka, then, and for us as we read him, the interest and pathos and humor of our situation resides not in our getting the point of it, but in our failing to do so. As, for example, when the message sent especially to us by the dying emperor never gets through (in another parable, included now in the larger story "The Chinese Wall," where it occupies a non-explanatory place similar to that of "Before the Law" in *The Trial*). We see the message on its way, we see all the signs of its great importance, the vast palace, and the valiant messenger; we even see why it is impossible that it should ever arrive. What we never see is the message. We have no idea what it is we fail to get. The more so since we do not even realize we have failed to get it. The parable ends with a beautifully Kafkaesque sentence: "But you sit at your window and dream the message to yourself as evening falls." Here is the experience of revelation without anything ever having been actually revealed. Likewise we, as readers, have the experience of understanding the parable without knowing what the parable is about, except that it clearly shows the absence of any real content or contact in the message we think we have got. Is this what thinking and understanding, hope, endeavor, and revelation, are always like? If it is, how could we be told, how would we ever find out? The answer is, of course, like this: by means of this form of writing, in which Kafka broke through to a peculiarly modern revival of something very like myth—except that it is only metaphorically speaking a myth. Literally, it is a parody.

For this reason, we must be careful to notice especially the form of Kafka's writing, rather than start interpreting at once its content. Interpretations in effect try to say what the message is; they supply the missing contact with the world. Philosophy, for instance, speaks of messages from the senses which are received in a moment of time that is always on its deathbed, and embark on a journey to the mind that can never be followed through. And theology looks for the message from the dying god, which got lost in secular obstacles but faith preserves. And then there is psychoanalysis, which tells us that libido is displaced onto surrogates, never reaches its goal, leaving the unconscious to dream of gratification as evening falls. Or there is value, alienated from labor, clogged in capital. . . . But no: we have only to make such silly suggestions to see again that Kafka was more interested in creating a gap between form and content than in closing it (as the rules of art traditionally demand). One last example: Kafka's story "The Stoker," which he published on its own and Brod then combined with other material to produce the novel *Amerika*. It even takes place on a boat at the moment when the hero is about to disembark—but does not, as though Kafka wanted to warn us too against hurrying off onto familiar dry land. The hero turns back, loses himself in the unfamiliar depths of the boat, and meets there the mysterious personage of the stoker. This man has a story to tell, which needless to say is never told—not to us. But whatever it is, it captures the hero's attention totally and rouses him to a state of interest and concern greater than he feels for his own story. And no wonder: for his own, which is told to us, is utterly banal and boring: son of the family, seduced by a cook with a heart of gold, he is emigrating to America in disgrace, where an uncle awaits him with more gold, this time in dollars. Eventually, the hero has to leave the stoker and submit to this trivial story:

sailors salute, everyone applauds, the Statue of Liberty presides. This is how American musicals end: everything explained, happiness in prospect. And then, Kafka writes one of his simple but devastating sentences:

> It was really as though there were no longer a stoker at all. Karl looked more keenly at his uncle ... and the doubt came over him, whether this man would ever be able to make up for the loss of the stoker.

Why was the stoker so important, then? As with the imperial message, we never find out; and even more plainly here, our sense of importance is due to our not finding out. Kafka stresses that the stoker cannot get his case across; it is one of grievance, deeply felt but incommunicable and incoherent, like the things we struggle to say in dreams. How monstrous that the world should be so deaf, so perverse, so inaccessible to such a plight! High time to protest on this stoker's behalf, show human solidarity, force the authorities to sit up and take notice. Here is a cause the hero would far rather embrace than any wealthy uncle; he does not need to know exactly what the cause is—it is having one that counts. That is why its representative is called the stoker: he fuels the ship—and he has had a good few other names since Kafka's time and before: stokers, stirrers, leaders, creeds. . . . Again we stand on the brink of an explanation, and again we must remind ourselves that we have found it in the form, not in the content, of the story. Or rather: in the relationship of the form to the content. If, after all, there is a lesson for us somewhere in Kafka, we have to take careful note of just where it lies, in order to see what kind of lesson it is.

A lesson, of course, meant originally an act of reading; one might even say it meant a lecture. Kafka's lesson calls attention to this act of reading by making the plain ordinariness of the text so strangely out of keeping with what the text says. His texts have something in common with the words of scripture—also regarded as "lessons"—which likewise announce messages they scarcely begin to explain; the circumstances of the announcement often are the message—a still, small voice that does not actually say anything. Has the content, has the explanation, been filled in by the scribe, the theologian, the critic, and the reader who sits and dreams it to himself? Is the relationship of words to a moment in life, and even to the most concrete, common objects present there, always impenetrable? Do explanations never explain, and only critics and theologians think they do? Higher criticism of the Bible—an art which is nowadays practiced on literature—looks for a point of reference outside and above the texts, from which to explain their meaning (and generally belittle it). Kafka produced texts one cannot get outside, as K. discovered when he tried some higher criticism on the parable "Before the Law."

Kafka's lesson is religious in this sense: it is as impossible to verify the truth of language as it is to verify the existence of God. The problem is the same in each case: the reality cannot be confronted; it has to be taken on trust. We are simply not in a position to know for sure whether we are using the right words or believing the right things. And once we try to find out, from motives of curiosity or insecurity, we become entangled, Kafka shows, in a most extraordinary situation: the one which bears his name. Nowadays, the text of our existence is no longer trusted; we suspect that it is arbitrary in all its manifestations—social and personal, psychological and spiritual, political and linguistic. And the impulse to protest against all forms of arbitrary imposition on life is very strong. Since Kafka's time, none have shown themselves more radical protesters than the critics of language. Not wishing, of course, to impose anything themselves, they are still waiting, and protesting, to know what life's message really is; rather like the higher theologians who transcended the literal content of the Bible and found they had nothing left to live on except their own complex critiques.

Kafka never does tell us, then, what would be the appropriate words in his case; he also does not know what the message is. He does know, however, what this state of ignorance and felt inappropriateness is like. His imagination is obsessed by the image of mad officialdom, cluttered with files among which the case that matters can never be traced and the rules that apply to it can never be fathomed. His obsession is not sociological but spiritual. He tells us nothing remotely plausible or useful or true about the faults of bureaucracy (which are doubtless many), but quite a lot about the spirit in which we are liable to interpret them and react to them: the radical spirit in which we approach not only bureaucracy but every institution and event in life. It is our approach which is inappropriate; we long for something far more than better treatment and a better deal—something more like a god and a dispensation beyond the limits of the possible. Kafka satirizes neither the approach nor the thing approached; satire implies the possibility of adjustment of the one to the other. His writing is not really satirical at all, but at once more serious and more humorous. In the situations he presents, adjustment either mental or practical is quite inconceivable. Even his own style, his form of words, is quite inconceivably inappropriate to what he is writing about.

We cannot say what would be appropriate in a Kafkaesque situation; that is what makes it Kafkaesque. What on earth is it appropriate to feel, think, do, and say, if you wake up one morning and find that you have turned into a big beetle? There is nothing very remarkable about the way Gregor Samsa, who is suddenly revealed in this literary form, then reacts or about the way his family reacts. Page after page of utterly ordinary, domestic sentiment and behavior ensue, which it would be excruciatingly boring to read about but for the extraordinary light we now see them in. It is all very bourgeois and full of the failings and fatuities one might expect. Heaven help us, there are critics who have swept up these crumbs and analyzed them to show what is wrong with domestic relations, petty bourgeois morality, and capitalist exploitation. They have, that is to say, tried to find some meaning in the content, without remarking that all the meaning lies in what has been done to the form. Like the hero's form, it has been transformed, metamorphosed; it no longer fits the person he is. *Metamorphosis* is a title which describes all Kafka's work; in it, content and form are always inappropriate to one another. They have been wrenched apart, and their disintegration is not relative—to some better form of family life or a better deal for beetles—but absolute. The result would be merely comic, were it not for the uneasy suspicion Kafka inspires: How on earth do we ever know that what we are feeling, thinking, doing, and saying is appropriate to the situation we are in? For instance, now.

To speak of the disintegration of form and content conjures up images of devastation which, looking back across this century, it is easy to imagine that Kafka foresaw. Personally, I doubt it and do not read him as a prophet of material terrors. Everyone knows those things are bad. Kafka's terrors are in the mind; like the ones behind the doors in the parable, it is only said that they are terrible; perhaps that is not the right word, perhaps no word is. Our life is no less devastated by not being able to say, by not knowing what matters and what does not, whether we should go on or wait, whether it is worth striving or not. If Kafka foresaw anything, it was the situation—still nameless then—of life that has no necessary form, not in art or science or morals, and above all not in language. "All things," Kafka once remarked, "are a matter of construction." They were susceptible therefore to deconstruction, as the fashionable euphemism of our day expresses it. Kafka discovered that writing might be used to bring that about; that was why he felt so guilty about it; it could result in a catastrophe of religious proportions. He was amazed, so he remarks in a letter, by the assurance with which people use ordinary language as though it were natural.

Language covers existence with a familiar and comprehensible surface. Beneath this exterior, there lay for Kafka magnitudes infinitely vast and unspeakably dangerous. The danger lay in learning to manipulate the laws of surfaces and signs by a linguistic technology that disintegrates all that once made human life supportable and civilisation possible. The price of man's learning this, Kafka wrote in a famous aphorism, is that he will turn his discovery against himself. The aphorism refers probably to his own writing, but of how much modern knowledge might we not now feel the same is true. We have broken through those doors of a world once screened by fairy tales, and found ourselves not face to face with truth, but, like K., in a limbo of impenetrable signs, an echo chamber of our own intelligence.

That too is no more than a metaphor; Kafka leaves us unable to speak otherwise. With him, all meaning becomes an unending process of verbal transference and transformation; like him, I will have now, a little arbitrarily, to break off. I fear I have not reached him or his work. For in what any words really originate, toward what they signal, are things he seems to have placed forever out of reach. Including himself. I hope I do not represent his case as worse than it is—nor ours. As an English reader of that parable of the gates before the Law, I am reminded of an image in Gray's "Elegy in a Country Churchyard"; the more so since Kafka's man who waits has come up from some simpler country, and his annals are certainly both short and poor. Perhaps it is better, after all, that he never did break through. Those who have done so, as Gray knew as well as Kafka, have tended to go and shut them on mankind. Gray called them "the gates of mercy."

WALTER H. SOKEL

Kafka and Modernism

A review of a recent biography of Kafka carried this title: "He (Kafka) Found Himself Transformed to a Giant Modernist" (Hafrey)—the latest proof that critical discussion of literary modernism has generally included Kafka. He has been ranked among the "high" or "classical" modernists (Quiñones 18), though any discussion of his relation to modernism must, of course, be preceded by the question, What was modernism?

The term *modernism* was first used in Anglo-American criticism in the late 1920s (Faulkner viii). By 1960, when Harry Levin's impassioned "necrologue" on modernism appeared, the use of the term was already well established. It denotes the wave of experimentation in the arts in general, and literature in particular, that agitated the first half of the twentieth century. With mock precision, Virginia Woolf set the date for its beginning: "'[o]n or about December 1910'" (Bradbury and McFarlane 33).

The concept of "the modern," however, as the revolutionary and unprecedented in the arts, long antedates the term *modernism*. It goes back to the French poet Charles Baudelaire, who invoked it in the middle of the nineteenth century. With Baudelaire, who in turn was decisively influenced by Edgar Allan Poe in this regard, the term *modern* acquired a meaning quite different from the merely modish or contemporary, with which *modern* had hitherto been synonymous. Henceforth *modern*, as applied to art and

From *Approaches to Teaching Kafka's Short Fiction*, edited by Richard T. Gray, pp. 21–34. © 1995 by the Modern Language Association of America.

37

literature, came to designate a deliberate and programmatic rupture with all preceding art, a revolutionary turn in aesthetics and poetics.

This break with tradition implied two somewhat different yet related tendencies. One was the inoculation of art with the bacillus of capitalist-industrial modernity, which serious art had until then tried to ignore. In this respect, modernism converged, to a significant extent, with the contemporary movement of realism. The two trends united in their thematic emphasis on modern urban life, highlighting not only its banality, sordidness, and hypocrisy but also the enormous broadening of experience and sensation its technological advances betokened. Furnishings and sceneries of realism and modernism were often indistinguishable, and the boundaries between the two movements were extremely porous. An outstanding example of their overlapping are the works of the novelist Gustave Flaubert. A pioneering figure in the development of consistent realism, he was also, together with Baudelaire, a fountainhead of modernism. Kafka took Flaubert as his model and, like the French author, placed his narratives in the locales of contemporary bourgeois and petty-bourgeois life, especially during his early and middle period, in works such as "The Judgment," *The Metamorphosis*, and *The Trial*.

In its purpose, however, modernism sharply diverged from realism. Realism extended the parameters of art toward contemporary life at its most banal and uninspiring, to record it, to present the "real truth" of life, free from the idealization inherent in traditional "high" art. Modernism performed the same movement but aimed to "create the sensation of the new" (Abrams 422). It sought a radical extension of the aesthetic dimension by exploring the possibilities of the ugly, the grotesque, the bizarre, to shake art loose from inherited restrictions.

A second tendency characterizing modernism involves the notion of the autonomy of art, whose roots go much farther back than Poe and Baudelaire. They lie in the eighteenth century: in Rousseau and Diderot, in Herder and Romanticism, and particularly in the philosophy of Kant. The theory of the autonomy of art is part of the general emancipatory movement, called the Enlightenment, that sought to free humankind from the unquestioned rule of authority and unreasoning obedience to tradition. Its aim was that self-government, that autonomy, by which human beings give themselves the laws according to which they wish to live, rather than uncritically accept what tradition and authority decree. Autonomous art is the extension into the aesthetic realm of the emancipatory idea of the Enlightenment. Kant, in his *Critique of Judgment* (1790), was the first to give systematic foundation to its theory (Sokel, *Writer* 9). The Romantics, with profound modifications, continued the call for an autonomous art, but Baudelaire was the artist who made it the foundation of the aesthetics that was to inform modernism. Baudelaire held that art has no purpose beyond itself (Abrams 130). It is autotelic. It has no obligation. It should consider itself free from the ancillary relation to nature and society to which it was consigned by traditional aesthetics, both in the Aristotelian doctrine of mimesis and the representation of nature and in the Horatian demand that art be morally useful as well as entertaining. In protest against both traditions, Baudelaire called teaching, truth, and morality the "heresies" of poetry (Abrams 130). Stéphane Mallarmé, following Baude-laire, claimed that only "reportage," not "literature" proper, aims to "narrate, instruct, even to describe" (Abrams 134). Literature should rid itself of the duty to represent reality or to deliver messages—moral, philosophical, or oth-erwise. It is beyond good and evil, as it is beyond true and false. The ultimate objective of autotelic art came to be called absolute, nonrepresentational, non-objective, or abstract art. Flaubert's wish-dream was to write a book without content, "a book about nothing" (Bradbury and McFarlane 25).

Autotelic art rarely went to such extremes. Most essential in modernist aesthetics, as begun by Baudelaire, was the conviction that art is not primarily a representation but a presentation, not the imitation of the actual world but the composition of a created world. The work had to obey no logic other than that imposed by its own expressive process. An artist would use elements of mimetic referentiality to the actual world not to offer a recognizable portrait of that world but to play their part in the composition of the work.

This idea, of a created rather than a represented world, does not imply formlessness; rather, form springs entirely from the work. The modernist critic Herbert Read called this concept "organic form," which is "self-chosen, inherent in the work, not imported from outside" (Faulkner 19). Internal function rather than relation to external factors became the decisive crite-rion for the elements of the work. Many of them were referential, borrowed from external reality, which imparted to the work echoes of the natural world. For Baudelaire, however, the point was to utilize these echoes to create a "counterworld," an "antinature," a composition that would compete with and constitute a superior alternative to the existing world. For this purpose, the poetic imagination "decomposes all of [natural] creation; then it gathers and organizes the parts according to laws springing from the innermost ground of the soul, and produces with them a new world" (Friedrich 41).[1] Creation might more properly be called transformation or recomposition. In the dis-tortion and deformation of elements of the natural world, Baudelaire saw the "power" of the creative imagination at work. That power manifested itself by its refusal to be bound by plausibility and habitual expectation.

This transformative operation of the imagination on elements of the empirical world closely parallels what Freud called "the work of the dream" ("Traumarbeit"). In dreams, too, the individual elements come from the empirical world but are deformed and transformed according to rules unknown to the dreamer's consciousness. Each dream element, even though taken from waking reality, functions according not to the rules of that reality but to the "thought" that the dream seeks to express. Independent of Freud's *Interpretation of Dreams*, the Swedish dramatist August Strindberg, under the spell of Nietzsche, applied the logic of the dream to the writing of his plays *To Damascus* (1898) and *A Dream Play* (1902), followed by others, and thus founded the line within modernism that came to be called expressionism. Kafka, by the time he wrote "The Judgment" (1912), the work of his "breakthrough," had become familiar with Freud's theory and was also extremely fond of Strindberg; "I read him not to read him—but to lie on his breast," he confided in his diary (*Diaries, 1914–1923* 126). Indeed, Kafka saw his "talent" as lying in his ability to portray his "dreamlike inner life" (*Diaries 1914–1923* 77). His writing can best be approached in terms of an oneiric functionalism.

Such an approach is particularly relevant in addressing the notion of character in Kafka's fiction. The fullest account of Kafka's poetics is to be found in his comments on "The Judgment," in which he wrote that the figure of the friend "is hardly a real person; he is perhaps rather that which the father and Georg have in common. The story is perhaps a walk around father and son, and the changing figure of the friend is perhaps the change of perspective in the relationship between father and son" (*Letters to Felice* 267; trans, modified). According to this statement, Kafka conceived of the friend not as the fictional portrait of an empirically possible person but as the mere function of a relationship. According to a diary entry (*Diaries, 1910–1913* 278), the friend must be seen as a counter in the struggle between father and son, as an indicator of the relative standing of the two combatants at the various points of their contest, and as a weight on the scale that helps decide the outcome. In the beginning, Georg, according to Kafka, thinks he has the friend on his side. As the story develops, however, Georg must learn that it is the father who really has the friend, while Georg has nothing and consequently suffers defeat. Since the friend is, as Kafka also notes, the connection between Georg and his father—their "common bond"—he also functions as a part of each. He is a projection like a figure in a dream. What matters is not his empirical existence, which the father at one point seems to doubt, but his signifying role in the battle.

A closer look at the text shows that the father, too, is less a mimetically conceived person than he is a function in the self-inflicted decomposition of Georg's adult self, his regression to a child who obeys parental commands and, beyond that, to nonbeing. The father functions as a projection of Georg's psyche. He accuses Georg of having attempted to displace and suppress him.

His charges originate, however, in Georg's own fleeting thoughts. Georg notes the terrible darkness of his father's room and the father's unclean underwear and reproaches himself for having relegated his old father to the dark back of the apartment while having reserved for himself the bright, spacious front room with its commanding view of the outside world.

Even earlier in the story, it occurs to Georg that "during his mother's lifetime his father's insistence on having everything his own way in the business had hindered him" (*CS* 78). Together with this acknowledgment of past frustration by and resentment of his father, Georg's triumphant satisfaction at the reversal of their positions since his mother's death is strongly implied, although not explicitly stated. The enormous physical strength of his father still impresses itself on Georg's mind when he sees his father, after a very long absence from his room, as "still a giant" (*CS* 81). This piece of inner monologue could be a sign of admiration, resignation, fear, or all three in one. It is an observation that could be made by a combatant evaluating his foe as well as by an admiring son proud of his father's undiminished strength. By entering his father's room, an unaccustomed act lacking apparent motivation, Georg literally goes to get his father's judgment. Georg is about to take a decisive step into full adulthood by sending off a letter in which he has at last announced his impending marriage. The recipient of the letter is to be Georg's distant friend, who is closely associated with permanent bachelorhood as well as with childhood and youth. The German word for bachelor, *Junggeselle*—literally meaning "young fellow"—emphasizes this association with a state preceding full adulthood. For Georg, who had for so long neglected his father and hardly communicated with him, there was no need to go into the father's room to tell him about this letter. Georg's act is unmotivated. In the light of what happens next in his father's room, however, this act is a literal, if unconscious, eliciting of his father's response to and judgment of Georg's declaration of adulthood.

In the scene that follows, the father reveals himself to be functioning as an emanation of, first, the son's guilt, anxiety, and murderous resentment and, ultimately, of Georg's childlike submissiveness. In the voice of his suddenly demonic father, what had been lurking in Georg's fleeting thoughts now confronts him from outside, with drastic explicitness. What happens in this story is thus the enactment of conflicting forces in the protagonist that never cross the threshold of consciousness to become reflective articulation. Instead, they are projected onto a seemingly autonomous antagonist, Georg's father, who articulates, in extreme form, the feelings the protagonist hinted at but never fully admitted.

The world presented in this text behaves analogously to the way dreams function according to Freud. Thoughts and emotions not admitted to the dreamer's conscious awareness appear disguised as external events, apparently independent of the dreamer's will but strange, surprising, grotesque, and enigmatic. In some of Kafka's later texts, the parallels to dreams and their implicit, indirect wish-fulfilling function is more obvious than in "The Judgment" and *The Metamorphosis*. In "In the Penal Colony," the penal apparatus collapses as if in response to the Explorer's unwillingness to support its continuance. In "A Country Doctor," the magic horses that appear from the doctor's pigsty, carrying him to his destination in a second, answer his urgent need to follow the call to his patient. Their emergence together with the groom, who then rapes the doctor's maid, pictorializes, with some obviousness, the division within the doctor between his calling—literally signified by the "alarm" of the bell (*CS* 225)—and his erotic desire, which, allegorizing a fundamental problem of Kafka's life, tragically awakens only at the moment when it has to conflict with his mission.

When Herbert Read speaks of the organic form inherent in the modernist work, "without consideration of the given forms of traditional poetry" (Faulkner 19), he has in mind above all the emancipation of such art from the restrictions improved by genre. One crucial effect of genre is satisfaction of the reader's expectation of finding the familiar in the new, an expectation that a text such as "The Judgment" shatters. In this story a violent, wrenching shift of focus tears the text apart into two radically discordant sections, producing a dissonance that severely upsets the reader's generic expectations.

The oneiric functionalism that I have traced so far is only one aspect of modernism. In Kafka, it combines with a quite different principle of modernist composition, one that Marjorie Perloff has called "the poetics of indeterminacy," or undecidability, of meaning and that she locates in a tradition of modernist poetry beginning with Rimbaud. In contrast to symbolism, this extreme branch of modernism eschews even hidden referential meaning and restricts itself to the "direct presentation" of the image, to pure description or evocation that discourages the reader's hermeneutical attempt to "understand" (Perloff 37). The search for referentiality, deeply built into habits of reading, is counteracted by the very luminosity of the images that language evokes. Nonreferentiality is helped by the withholding of contextuality. The artist presents images, narrates events, and makes statements outside any discernible context, such as the context supplied by causality.

The poetics of indeterminacy—or undecidability or, in the literal sense, meaninglessness—is consistent with a general modernist attitude toward the reader. Indeterminacy completes the alienation of the reader which the antimimetic, antididactic theory of autonomous art had initiated. The doctrine of autotelic art relates to society in two different ways. Seen in the context of the liberal view of history—extolling the progressive emancipation of the individual from authority at work—indeterminacy is a big step forward, extending to art the general principle of liberty. In a view of history such as that of Marxism, however, it is a leap in the growing alienation of the artist from society and is therefore seen as typical of bourgeois, capitalist modernity. And, indeed, a radical and deliberate alienation from the public characterizes important formal and thematic aspects of modernism. Alienation resides above all in the break of the "mimetic contract" (Barthes, "Introduction") between author and reader—a break fundamental for modernism. That familiarity between authorial narrator and reader, their "shared sense of reality" (Faulkner 1) so characteristic of Victorian novels, was shattered by modernism. The cozy chattiness of direct address of the reader by an interventionist narrator, typical of the older novel, was severely interdicted by Flaubert and Henry James.

Alienation accounts for two seemingly contradictory but in fact closely related elements of modernism: on the one hand, its aggressive provocativeness, which seeks to shock, outrage, and scandalize, and, on the other hand, its withdrawal from public comprehension into obscurity, difficulty, and hermeticism. Both tendencies are aspects of the same antagonism toward the bourgeois public. In the indeterminacy of meaning, which both angers and excludes the public, the two tendencies join. The undecidability of meaning frustrates readers in their most fundamental concern: the attempt to understand, to recognize, to empathize, and to translate the newly encountered into the familiar. The modernist work makes it extremely difficult for the reader to cross the chasm that separates a text from life. Modernism is the enemy of a hermeneutics that seeks to appropriate art to life.

Kafka's *Metamorphosis* conforms, in an almost exemplary manner, to both aspects of the modernist assault on the reader. The transformation of a human being into "a giant specimen of vermin" (the literal meaning of the form into which, as the text tells us, Gregor finds himself transformed) shocks and disgusts the reader, and it likewise baffles understanding. The initial event of the story could be, and has been, used as a textbook case of a modernist alienation effect. Above all, Gregor's metamorphosis contradicts the most basic premise of mimesis.

Mimesis has social foundations. It rests on the actual or imagined participation of work and public in a shared reality. Even if the reader does not believe in the mythology that forms the setting of Ovid's *Metamorphoses*, they are still mimetic in the Aristotelian sense because they describe sequences of causally connected, and thus explicable, events. Within the convention of belief in supernatural beings as causal agents, the transformations of human beings into animals and plants is perceived as natural. By sharp contrast, Gregor Samsa's metamorphosis occurs and remains unexplained. It thus breaks the mimetic contract. Samsa's metamorphosis falls outside even the context of what one might consider miraculous, if miracles are thought of as linked to supernatural agencies and so embedded in an order that, though transcending sensory and empirical nature, is an order nonetheless. Gregor's metamorphosis does not point to any cause at all, not even a supernatural one. Tzvetan Todorov ranks it in the genre of the fantastic. In that genre, readers can never know whether a natural or supernatural explanation applies. According to that definition, however, the fantastic applies only to the world of the reader. It does not apply to the world within Kafka's text. Within the text, no question arises as to the cause of Gregor's fate. Gregor himself seems to view his transformation as a misfortune that could befall anyone—for instance, the head clerk of his firm. He treats it as an accident, a sorry contingency, tough luck. No one within the represented world, including Gregor himself, ever speculates on possible causes.

Thus we find a remarkable discrepancy between the represented world and the world of the reader. The reader looks for a causality with which the characters are not concerned. No causality can be established on the basis of what the text explicitly communicates. In this way, Gregor's metamorphosis behaves according to the poetics of indeterminacy.

Yet Kafka's story follows this poetics only partway. A narrative of high realism succeeds the initial shock of alienation. *The Metamorphosis* presents a causally connected chain of events, a sequence of described thoughts, actions, and feelings that are made perfectly plausible, or at least empirically possible, in the milieu and the circumstances described. After the initial event, the plot stays consistently within the conventions of narrative realism. This singularity of the nonmimetic occurrence, which initiates the plot and gives the story its title, sharply distinguishes *The Metamorphosis* from a text of indeterminacy, such as Rimbaud's *Illuminations*, and from the tradition of surrealism that followed it. "A Country Doctor," comprising as it does a string of "magical" events, comes much closer to surrealism than does *The Metamorphosis*. The latter story has been compared to a fairy tale, and it has also been discussed as an "anti-fairy tale" (Heselhaus). The distinction here is a thematic one. That events for which no causes are given constitute a common structural denominator of Kafka's story and fairy tales is not at issue. What does prevent the generic expectations associated with fairy tales to maintain themselves for the reader of *The Metamorphosis*, however, is the radical consistency of the realistic style of representation following the initial event.

Here we come upon a bipolar tendency as typical of Kafka as it is of modernism in general. At one of the poles, we find hermetic nonreferentiality, a frustration of the quest for understanding. At the other pole, we encounter what Aristotle called mythos—that is, mimetic narrativity, a representation of human fate and action that elicits the reader's empathy with the represented world. Kafka is a storyteller as well as a modernist.

If we apply the principle of dreamlike functionalism, which we have observed in other texts of Kafka, to the initial event of *The Metamorphosis*, we find that it counteracts indeterminacy and meaninglessness and thus extends the reach of mythos. Gregor's transformation acquires a definite function in a plot that is mimetic in psychological and social terms, though not in physical ones. Near the beginning of the narrative, the text presents Gregor's memories and reflections about the onerous aspects of his job. The reader is informed that Gregor has been intensely dissatisfied with the dehumanizing conditions of his job and would have resigned with a rebellious flourish if his father's indebtedness to the firm had not forced him to delay this decision. His metamorphosis thus functions as a fulfillment of his wish to be rid of his job without his becoming responsible for deserting his financially dependent family. An inexplicable event has absolved him of deliberate revolt. It fulfills his wish while not only relieving him of responsibility but also punishing him, since it transforms him into a creature that elicits disgust. By presenting us with Gregor's reflections and memories, the text offers us the possibility, and even plausibility, of such a construction. We can deduce a functional rationale for the incredible happening.

Yet nowhere does the connection between Gregor's rebellious desire and his fantastic fate become explicit. Nowhere within the text does it emerge into consciousness. It remains a construction by the reader. Gregor, who is the sole registering consciousness in the largest part of the story, does not show any awareness of such a connection. Neither do the narrator or any of the story's other characters. This silence makes the text hermetic, since it withholds any referential, or mimetically understandable, meaning for Gregor's metamorphosis. That hermetic quality stands at what we might call the modernist pole of the text. At the opposite pole, in its hints of a possible connection between Gregor's thoughts and his fate, the text allows the possibility of establishing a meaning for Gregor's metamorphosis. It allows the reader to construct a mimetic representation of a causal link between the narrated facts and thus a mythos in the Aristotelian sense, a "story." Such a reading cannot account for the empirical impossibility of the crucial event, the metamorphosis itself, but merely by establishing a psychologically motivated link between the character's fate and his preceding intentions, this reading reintroduces a substantial element of mimetic representation. The designation "magic realism" would literally apply. For a realistic representation of human alienation and repression, in the circumstances of exploitative capitalism and the patriarchal bourgeois family, is coupled with the magic intrusion of empirical impossibility into the realistically described milieu. According to Freud's definition of magic as the "omnipotence of thought"—that is, the projection of inner-psychic constellations onto the external world—we can view Gregor's self-transformation as an unacknowledged application of magic, suspending the laws of physical plausibility (Sokel, "Freud").

Kafka's text presents itself on two levels. The literal or writer's level—the level of indeterminacy—withholds referential meaning and causal coherence. The second level, however, empowers the reader to discern functional roles in the elements of narration, which combine into a mimetic sequence. On this level, the text enables the reader to fill in missing links in the representation of an action that, though empirically impossible, achieves psychological and sociological plausibility and thus a meaningful connection with the world outside the text. Without officially consenting to it, the text—unofficially, as it were—invites the reader to reestablish referentiality. Fredric Jameson points out that the recommitting to mimesis—the translation of the alienating text into a mimetically explanatory mythos—is an integral feature of modernist works. They are "simply canceled realistic ones." When, as Jameson goes on to say, one "make[s] sense of" one of Kafka's texts, one inserts into it "the flux of realistic narrative" ("Beyond the Cave" 129). We must add, however, that at least in Kafka's case, the text itself suggests and directs the reader's procedure, provided the dreamlike functionalist structure is recognized as informing it.

Kafka himself set the example for such a reading of his texts. After he had written "The Judgment," he asked Felice Bauer, his future fiancée, whether she found "some straightforward, coherent meaning that one could follow" in "The Judgment" (*Letters to Felice* 265). He himself, he admitted, found no meaning and could not explain anything in it. Yet immediately upon this declaration of total indeterminacy, he reversed himself and began to interpret the story as an autobiographical allegory. He drew attention to the close relation of the names of the characters to his own and Felice's. He found much that he called "noteworthy" and thus potentially meaningful in the very story that he, in the preceding sentence, had declared devoid of sense. His initial impression of meaninglessness thus gave way at once to the attempt to find meaning, to translate the unknown code of his text into the codes of real life.

Kafka's strangely puzzled response to his own writing reflects a fundamental change of the traditional view concerning the relation between writing and reading. It was a change wrought by modernism and its antecedent, the theory of autonomous art. The theory of autonomous art runs counter to the sharp division between writer and reader that existed in traditional aesthetics. In particular, it militates against the idea that the relation between writing and reading is a one-way street on which all traffic flows from writing to reading, where the reader is the passive recipient of the writer's message. The theory of autonomous art changed that vision in two ways. First, it depersonalized the author, while functionalizing character and event within the work. Second, it made the reader the writer's collaborator in the creative process.

Since Diderot and Kant, the doctrine of the autonomy of art had held that the only law to be observed in a work was the law its creator, the genius, gives to it. Genius, however, came to be understood not as an empirical person but as the function that makes genius what it is—namely, the creative imagination. The symbolists increasingly came to see the creative imagination not as a personal property or quality of the empirical author but as a productive process; not as arbitrary personal planning but as the artist's opening and surrender to the powers inherent in the medium of the work. The poet, according to Mallarmé, disappears "in the poem," an insight Mallarmé calls "the discovery of our [the modern] time" (Abrams 134). The poet "cedes the initiative" in creation "to the words" (Abrams 120) and allows language to direct the production of the work. In one of the most important documents of modernism, Arthur Rimbaud's "Lettre du voyant" ("Letter of the Seer"), Rimbaud advocates the breakup of the conscious and deliberate self, the empirical ego, by a systematic "dérèglement de tous les sens" ("unhinging of all the senses") in order to let another, deeper self, a buried unconscious other, take over. The "I" speaking in his poetry is not the empirical I but "an other." His famous programmatic sentence "For I am an other" could serve as the motto of all modernism. Roland Barthes's structuralist diagnosis of "the death of the author" in the self-productive and self-perpetuating flow of language that is seen as the true agent of creation appears adumbrated in the poetics of the symbolists and even in the statement of their Romantic precursor Victor Hugo that "the word is a living being more powerful than the one who uses it" (Friedrich 22). At the same time Rimbaud published his "Lettre du voyant," Nietzsche proclaimed in *The Birth of Tragedy* (1872), "The subject—the striving individual . . . can be thought of only as an enemy of art, never as its source . . . to the extent that the subject is an artist he is already delivered from individual will and has become a medium . . ." (41). What Nietzsche, the French symbolists, and the structuralist Roland Barthes hold in common is the conviction that it is not the conscious, planning, empirical person, the "subject," that is essential in the writing process. The process of creation emancipates itself from the personal author. This strong belief in depersonalization is an integral part of the "dehumanization" that the Spanish philosopher José Ortega y Gasset saw as the dominant tendency of modern art and literature, a tendency that lies at the foundation of modernism. In Rainer Maria Rilke's avant-garde novel *The Notebooks of Malte Laurids Brigge*, Malte, wrestling with the task of becoming a poet, identifies the moment of his (possible) breakthrough with the passive voice: "I shall be written" (52). His birth as a poet would be the reduction of his person to point zero, to a mere medium, a mere instrument.

Such a depersonalizing unification of the empirical self with the creative process is what, according to a diary entry, Kafka felt he had experienced in writing "The Judgment"—the only one of his works with which he was and remained fully satisfied. He had, he confides in his diary, composed the story in a trancelike state,

> at one sitting, during the night of the 22nd–23rd, from ten o'clock at night to six o'clock in the morning. I was hardly able to pull my legs from out under the desk, they had got so stiff from sitting. The fearful strain and joy, how the story developed before me, as if I were advancing in water. (*Diaries, 1910–1913* 275–76)

And, enlarging his report into a program, a poetics, he adds, "Only *in this way* can writing be done, only with such coherence, with such complete opening of the body and the soul" (*Diaries, 1910–1913* 276). Conscious planning and intention have nothing to do with such writing. Kafka reported that he had intended an entirely different plot when he started to write, "but then the whole thing turned in my hands" (*Letters to Felice* 265). The story that emerged was not the result of his intention. Emphasizing his role in its creation as that of a medium, he compared himself to a mother giving birth to her child (*Diaries, 1910–1913* 278). This absorption of the self in the writing process remained Kafka's ideal even though, after the writing of "The Judgment," he never again attained it to his satisfaction (Sokel, "Kafka's Poetics").

Kafka's ideal of depersonalized writing has an important bearing on the relation of writing to reading. Since writing is not the product of conscious plan and intention, writers cannot know the "meaning" of their own work. A writer thus occupies an interpreter's, a reader's, position in regard to the work produced. Using E. D. Hirsch's equation of meaning with authorial intention, we can see that there is indeed no meaning in a text written without intention (46–48). According to the aesthetics of autonomous art, literary language can have no meaning in the ordinary sense, since it is free of the intent to inform, which launches mimetic representation and description as well as didactic instruction. Its only purpose is to stimulate the mind's or soul's activity. At the time this vision was forming, Kant distinguished the language of aesthetic from that of logical ideas: The former "does not . . . represent what lies in our concepts . . . but rather something else—something that gives the imagination an incentive to spread its flight . . ." (Sokel, *Writer* 11). Lacking meaning, such language engenders a search for significance. Writing provides merely the opportunity for this search to come into being. It is literally a pre-text for reading.

In Kafka's later work, writing itself, having ceased to be the flow carrying the writer, becomes the search for significance that makes it a kind of reading. Writing and reading become interchangeable, a circular continuum, without a break between them. Kafka expressed this relation in his parable "Prometheus" (January 1918). Here Kafka tells four highly idiosyncratic variants of the Prometheus myth. Together they describe a development of the myth, which Kafka's text calls legend, from its traditional version to a last one in which all the actors of the original myth have grown weary and bring the "*meaningless* affair" (my italics) to an end. "There remained the inexplicable [shape of] the rocky mountain range," which had given rise to the original myth. The "legend" had been the attempt to explain the puzzling shape of the mountain. It "tried to explain the inexplicable. As it came out of a ground of truth, it had to return to the inexplicable" (*CS* 432; trans, modified).

Here the desire to narrate forms a continuum with the need to understand—that is, to read. Representation is inextricably enmeshed with interrelation. It is the wish to read meaning into enigmatic givenness that begets the myth (i.e., narration or "writing," which are the same prior to the bifurcation of telling and writing). In terms of the parable, "writing" is inseparable from reading. Together they form the attempt to understand what is simply there—the strangely shaped mountain range. The telling of tales is presented as an attempt to produce meaning.

As in *The Metamorphosis*, we see a movement from indeterminacy to the telling of a mythos, here in the literal form of a Greek myth. The puzzling mountains function not only like the enigmatic event of Gregor's metamorphosis but also like the enigmatic text that Kafka found his "Judgment" to be. All three stimulate a reading and interpreting process that seeks to give birth to understanding. In "Prometheus," however, the movement evident in *The Metamorphosis* is reversed, or at least made circular. *The Metamorphosis* begins with the inexplicable, then supplies hints of an explanation, and finally narrates a mimetic story, a mythos. In the last section, the mythos actually turns into a kind of myth. It tells the rebirth of hope in the Samsa family after Gregor's self-imposed death, by which he liberates his family from himself. In the light of this ending, Gregor's metamorphosis takes on the character of a redeeming self-sacrifice and thus becomes a version of the myth of the scapegoat-savior that James Frazer's *The Golden Bough* had made popular in turn-of-the-century Europe (Trilling 14). Kafka was thoroughly dissatisfied with this mythic ending of his story. He called it "unreadable . . . imperfect almost to its very marrow" (*Diaries, 1914–1923* 12).

In Kafka's legend, the text begins with the mythos, in its original for-mulation as an actual Greek myth, then moves toward its cancellation. Here mythos functions as a temporary detour around the inexplicable "ground of truth." Storytelling is a provisional attempt to explain what permanently bears no explanation. In the end, we must realize that the ground of truth returns us to the meaningless, the literally unmeaning. The unmeaning gives birth to the reader and, with the reader, to the writer. Their joined mythmaking search is a series of displacements in which one version follows another on the road to exhaustion. In the end, the mythopoeic process is wearisome and has to be given up. However, mimetic mythos, by which we seek to explain the inexpli-cable, is a need in human beings that forever seeks fulfillment. Literature is that search. Its road is circular—shades of Nietzsche's "eternal return"?—and the attempt to read, which is writing, might begin ever anew.

Presenting such relationships, Kafka reveals himself to be the "giant modernist" he was called in the book review title I began by quoting. He was linked to modernism mainly for two reasons—first, because modernism was the response to a fundamental rift between the notion of truth or reality and the notion of meaning. In late-nineteenth- and twentieth-century philoso-phy the view became increasingly prominent "that the very object of realism . . . objective reality no longer exists" (Jameson, "Beyond the Cave" 122) and that a thing can be considered to exist "only with reference to the act of see-ing" it (Ryan 11). In accordance with this fundamental skepticism concerning the very ideas of truth and reality, modernist literature could no longer abide by the mimetic convention. Where an objective reality cannot be determined, it cannot be imitated or represented either. Modernist art thus adhered to a radical perspectivism that abolished the omniscient narrator. The "unimental" perspective, a narrative structure in which the reader does not receive more, but usually even less, information than is available to the protagonist—a dis-tinctive element of Kafka's narratives—dovetails perfectly with the epistemo-logical relativism or perspectivism that typifies modern thought.

This severe restriction of the reader's traditional cognitive privilege leads us to the second reason we may call Kafka a true modernist: namely, that the work confronts readers as a challenge forcing them to participate in and, in a sense, continue the writer's activity. Provocation of art's addressee was, as we have seen, a fundamental feature of modernist practice. Its antecedents lay in the very idea of autonomous art. In sharply distinguishing aesthetic from logical discourse, Kant and his immediate successors saw the aesthetic effect residing not in orientation and information about either the phenom-enal or the moral world but in the stimulation of the imagination, in the production of the most multifarious and variegated emotional and mental activity. According to Kant, an "aesthetic attribute" broadens the range of thoughts and feelings, quickens their flow, accelerates psychic metabolism (Sokel, *Writer* 11–12). In modernist literature, the contact between reading and writing lies not in "understanding" but in a kind of "magic suggestion" (Fokkema 19). Respect for the reader's freedom, independence, and "idiosyncracies ... became a Modernist convention," dictating "the very organization of [modernist] texts" (Fokkema 18). The text was not structured to provide authoritative meanings directing as well as binding the reader. Instead, the text was to serve merely as a springboard, a possibility for the play of interpretation. That situation did not make reading an easy task, for along with dependence on an "official" line of understanding, the reader lost the comfort of authorial guidance and the opportunity of easy identifications. Without the author's "author-itarian" steering, reading became a hazardous venture on which no certainty beckoned as a reward.

"To unsettle ... that is my role." André Gide's definition of the authorial function, which sums up the modernist attitude toward the reader (Fokkema 24), leads straight to Kafka. "A book," he said, "must be the axe for the frozen sea inside us" (*Letters to Friends* 16). With this programmatic statement, made in 1904, at the very beginning of his literary life, Kafka showed that, for all his isolation, he finally belonged in a tradition, stretching back to Diderot and to Kant—the tradition of autonomous or nonmimetic art, in which art is not a representation of the world but a tonic for the soul.

NOTE

1. Unless otherwise indicated, all translations are mine.

HENRY SUSSMAN

The Text That Was Never a Story: Symmetry and Disaster in "A Country Doctor"

Although organized, perhaps, by an intense oedipal pain, Kafka's "A Country Doctor" never becomes what might be properly called a story. The results are so inconclusive, the characters so blurred as to deny any pretense to narrative cohesion on the part of this brief work. Twice the peasants who receive the doctor's judgments break out into incantations that, like the music throughout Kafka's writing, exemplified by Josephine's piping, are refrains of fugitive and unfulfilled desire. The doctor may indeed be stripped and placed beside the ailing young patient as the chants exhort, but he is "only a doctor, only a doctor" (*CS* 224). The peasant song, which lends the text the air of an anthropological encounter, declares the limits of its own expectations, as well as those of the patient.

But for all the tale's declared and dramatized inconclusiveness, it is a suggestive allegory of how texts configure themselves. There is no lack of structure here. The text begins and ends in the forbidding winter landscape to which an aging doctor no less harsh and forlorn has been summoned by his vastly inferior clients. The scenic and thematic symmetry of the two scenes constituting the narrative framework is duplicated within the dramatic core. The text dramatizes not one diagnostic scene but two. Only after an initially unsympathetic examination of the sick boy—on the basis of which the doctor concludes that "the boy was quite sound, something a little wrong with his

---

From *Approaches to Teaching Kafka's Short Fiction*, edited by Richard T. Gray, pp. 123–34. © 1995 by the Modern Language Association of America.

circulation, saturated with coffee by his solicitous mother, but sound"—is the doctor persuaded to admit "that the boy might be ill after all" (*CS* 222, 223). A reexamination, which the doctor undertakes almost whimsically, reveals the extent and nature of the illness as it affects both patient and healer.

At the end of the narrative the doctor sits in the same coach that brought him to his appointment, no longer wearing his coat, perhaps, but facing the same climatic and personal bleakness with which the text began. If anything, the framework and organization of the narrative suggest structure: mirrored endpoints bracketing a doubled scene. And this structural symmetry, at least on the level of the text's widest components, is well suited to the doubling that takes place between characters and that is discussed more fully below. "A Country Doctor" is not reticent to admit the place of structure within its own encoding and decoding. Structure, however, does not so much account for or determine the allegory of the text as support or facilitate it. As I show, associations of a far more shifting nature disclose the qualities of this text but within the format that structure provides. The text gathers its resonance at the point where its structure embraces something other, something transformational and anomalous. And here, as throughout Kafka's fiction, the image bonding structure to theme, but precluding the narrative cohesion of a story, is nothing more than a metaphor.

The symmetry that so strikingly frames and colors this story places it in the nexus of Kafka's long-standing interest in doubling—as a narratological, psychological, and even phenomenological feature. Kafka's fascination with doubling, deriving from his most beloved literary sources, among them E. T. A. Hoffmann and Dostoyevsky, transcends the particular uses to which doubling can be put. Kafka began his exploration of this phenomenon in such brief works as "The Knock on the Manor Gate," in which the nearly undefinable guilt of the sister is displaced and irrationally magnified as it rebounds on the brother, and "A Crossbreed [A Sport]," in which an uncanny commiseration links the family son to his biologically and logically anomalous legacy. In stories even as late as "The Burrow," Kafka's artistic burrowing rodent projects the image of a predator, his semblable, who stalks him and deprives him of his supplies in the subterranean deep.

The title character in "A Country Doctor" finds unlikely doubles in the groom with whom he wages battle over Rose and in the twice-examined, twice-dismissed wounded little boy. The story thus reverberates off Kafka's brief masterpiece of doubling, "The Judgment," which Kafka believed to have been his breakthrough piece of fiction.[1] "The Judgment" records and dramatizes the undermining of a son's best-faith narrative of his own achievements, qualities, and prospects by a discourse of the other that turns out to emanate from his uncannily hostile father. The narrative voice is a willing conspirator in this confusion. It subliminally sides with and rationalizes the son's position until the father attacks him—not with heaved apples, as in "The Metamorphosis," but with accusations: that the son tricked the friend in Russia (toward whom he feels condescendingly protective), allowed himself to be seduced by his fiancée, and violated the better interest of the family business.

"The Judgment" resides at a benchmark in the systematicness of the kinds of doubling it entertains. The excruciating dialectical tension between the discourse of the son and the father's debunking cynicism corresponds to the "split consciousness" that for Freud, at the time of Kafka's writing, constituted the very structure of repression (indeed, the vast majority of the manifestations Freud interpreted between 1893 and 1910 were conditions of repression, above all hysteria). In writing so penetratingly on ambivalence, whether Gregor's toward the family that takes his sacrifices so much for granted or the country doctor's toward the groom and the sick boy, Kafka performs Freudian acts of undermining the divisions that segment the divided consciousness. The systematic duplication structuring "The Judgment" is narratological and characterological as well. Georg Bendemann watches in horror as the friend in Russia, whom he regards as a subordinate, supplants him as his father's son; indeed, the letters by means of which Georg has attempted to control the relationship are duplicated and disqualified by the counter-correspondence that his father has maintained with his double. With regard to the relentless doubling that structures and informs "The Judgment," "A Country Doctor" may well be the countertext sharing the closest affinities.

In the very first episode of "A Country Doctor," we see already the major structural and thematic elements that will serve as a setting for the story's metaphoric transformation. When Rose, the maid who will become the source and object of the doctor's anxiety throughout the text, offers her comment on the scene—"You never know what you're going to find in your own house"— she touches on the narrative's key psychoanalytic and sociological concerns. The well-equipped and generally efficient country doctor—"I had a gig, a light gig with big wheels, exactly right for our country roads"—is in a frustrated rage. He cannot begin a house call to a neighboring village because his horse died the previous night: "Muffled in furs, my bag of instruments in my hand, I was in the courtyard all ready for the journey." The bleak weather in which he waits with impotent anger only reinforces the sense that he is a man without a horse, a man who has lost his horse, or his kingdom for a horse, a victim of his own horse: "but there was no horse to be had, no horse" (*CS* 220).

The motif of psychological repression in this text is reinforced by the dreamlike quality of its movements and transitions. The doctor arrives instantaneously at the remote hamlet he is visiting: "I was already there" (*CS* 221). Just as suddenly, the apparent solutions to his predicament emerge from an abandoned pigsty on his property that he kicks open in his desperation: a man whose open, blue-eyed face is reminiscent of other servants in Kafka's fiction (notably, Barnabas of *The Castle*), and two horses, whose steaming bodies and powerful buttocks evoke a power that contrasts sharply with the doctor's present frailty. The doctor is well conditioned to make optimal use of this unexpected man—and horsepower. He commands Rose to help the groom (*Knecht*) hitch the horses to his wagon (the groom has emerged from the pigsty ready to serve), and he threatens the *Knecht* with whipping when the latter inexorably turns his attentions to Rose. This pugnaciousness turns to anxious despair when it becomes clear to the doctor that Rose is fated to serve the groom's sexual whims, that his own home is to be the setting for the vigorous sexuality figured in the splitting and bursting of the door. The doctor's tormenting vision of the groom's sexual victory over Rose and himself haunts him throughout the text with the force of obsessional thought as Freud defined it.[2] Until the groom declares, "I'm not coming with you anyway, I'm staying with Rose," the doctor has treated her indifferently as "the pretty girl who had lived in [his] house for years almost without [his] noticing her" (*CS* 221, 223). In many senses, then, the narrative's first scene may be said to investigate repression as it operates in psychoanalytic theory. Distinctly sexual beings emerge from a repository on the property, a long-abandoned hiding place. Late-oedipal competition stimulates a previously stunted desire for the girl. The psychological locus of the pigsty is repression in the unconscious.

This first scene is reminiscent of another repression, the sociopolitical sort dramatized and subverted in the section of *Phenomenology of Spirit* that Hegel entitled "Herrschaft und Knechtschaft" ("Lordship and Bondage"; 104–19). The doctor is not oblivious to his bullying and threatening his *Knecht*, even though, as he acknowledges, the groom is "a stranger . . . I did not know where he came from, and . . . of his own free will he was helping me out when everyone else had failed me" (*CS* 221). The groom is described as the sibling of the two horses, which he calls Brüder (Brother) and Schwester (Sister). The groom's conquest of Rose thus completes a series of substitutions set into play by the upheaval of the doctor's authority. The groom's sexual displacement of the doctor results in a deflection of the threatened whipping from the horses to the groom. The ultimate victim in this sequence of power-mongering is Rose, but the narrative, curiously, does not pursue that result.

The quick reversal of the doctor's mastery over his servants signals an ambiguity in characterization. Why does the doctor develop such a sudden, intense attachment to Rose? The contest over her may be between two distinct male characters or, as occurs at other points in Kafka's fiction, may represent a conflict within a single fictive subject, a conflict here between active heterosexual lust and repressive asexuality. More than any other major writer dealing in twentieth-century aesthetics, Kafka exploited the ambiguity between the intra- and intersubjective representations of dramatic interaction.[3] In the context of the intertwining and reversal of roles that will prevail between the doctor and the sick boy, it is perhaps not unreasonable to suggest that the doctor and the *Knecht* also exist as doubles in relation to each other. The doctor's doubling is doubled: he merges with his servants and patients. Doubling in characterization coincides with the doubling already observed in the scenic construction. "A Country Doctor" dispenses double medicine, but doubling, as Freud applies it to Hoffmann's tale "The Sandman," is a mark of the uncanny as well as of the familiar.[4] In Kafka's fiction, as in familial relations, it is sometimes difficult to ascertain where one identity begins and another ends. This soft border between fictive subjects becomes a major issue in the doctor's interaction with the peasant family.

For indeed, having arrived instantaneously at his patient's peasant cottage (this immediacy questioning again the status of distance and scale in the narrative), the doctor remains secure in the superiority and authority that have just been battered by the groom's conquest. In deference to the doctor, the patient's sister sets a chair out for his instruments and takes charge of his fur coat. No higher honor does the family pay the doctor than the precious glass of rum the father pours out for him.

Throughout Kafka's fiction siblings are implicated in one another's guilts and torments. The air in the Kafkan familial scene is stifling. Not only can the siblings exchange identities, but the horses get into the act as well, the same horses to which the groom referred as Brother and Sister: "each of them had stuck a head in at a window and, quite unmoved by the startled cries of the family, stood eyeing the patient" (*CS* 222). Throughout "A Country Doctor," but especially in the family setting, identities merge, making totemic distinctions useless. The highly visible horses in this text, at play in every aspect of the country doctor's interaction with the family, belong to a unique category of characters in Kafka's fiction: the mute and reactive figures who do not add to the action but comment on it with their silent gestures.[5] The horses' status as animals in no way impedes their serving this metacritical function. Their siblings in the world of Kafka's writing include K.'s servants, Arthur and Jeremias, in *The Castle*; the astonished villagers in "The Knock at the Manor Gate"; and the onlookers who witness Joseph K.'s arrest in *The Trial*.

Yet just as the doctor's mastery is undermined in the opening scene by the groom's (or his own) vibrant sexuality, so too does his encounter with the sick boy dissolve his air of superiority, his clinical detachment, his complacency, and his indifference. Intellectually, the doctor grasps the limits of his position when he thinks, "To write prescriptions is easy, but to come to an understanding with people is hard" (*CS* 223); this formulation, however, is only the weakest form of the lesson that the boy teaches him. During his initial examination of the boy, the doctor vacillates between two postures: contempt for the entire family, buttressed by a kind of self-aggrandizing rationalization, and a compulsive, morbid interest in Rose's current status:

> I am no world reformer and so I let him lie. I was the district doctor and did my duty to the uttermost, to the point where it became almost too much. I was badly paid and yet generous and helpful to the poor. I had still to see that Rose was all right, and then the boy might have his way and I wanted to die too. What was I doing there in that endless winter! My horse was dead, and not a single person in the village would lend me another. I had to get my team out of the pigsty; if they hadn't chanced to be horses I should have had to travel with swine. That was how it was. (*CS* 222–23)

This passage intertwines the doctor's two roles as aggressor and victim. Having conceded his lack of philanthropic interest, the doctor dramatizes his self-sacrifices to himself in the way that a manipulative parent would attempt to induce guilt in his or her family. The climate is terrible, the pay is not good, he constantly makes concessions to his patients. The humor in the passage is that of uncontrollable self-indulgence. The doctor suggests that if he hadn't found horses to transport him, pigs would have had to do. The doctor thus places himself in the role of a temporary paterfamilias whose bad conscience spurs him on to increasingly outrageous assertions of benevolence. But the doctor's martyrdom would not be real unless he faced some immediate and dire threat. The loss of Rose is not only like death; it is death itself ("I wanted to die"). The form, if not nature, of the doctor's fear is hypochondriacal. What threatens him is not a condition but the self-representation of a condition. It is no accident that he ends up beside his patient. In all this posturing, Kafka does not allow the aggression, bad faith, guiltmongering, and hypochondriacal cries for help to remain implicit: "And I nodded to the family. They knew nothing about it, and, had they known, would not have believed it" (*CS* 223). The doctor protects his posturing by endowing it with the aura of superior knowledge.

Thus far, then, we have a story structured to favor its themes of jealousy, displacement, ambivalence, ambiguity of character, and social conflict. The most prominent themes also lend themselves to interpretation through two readily available models of repression: the psychoanalytic model and the Hegelian undermining of mastery through the more direct relation to material (including words) in labor. Yet only when the doctor, casually and almost by chance, condescends to review his diagnosis does the text crystallize an emblem for its own operation as a text. The text locates its image only as the practitioner concedes some small margin of error. And, just as important, the insignia that the text inscribes upon itself (as the punitive apparatus of "In the Penal Colony" writes its sentence on the human body) is the external manifestation of a disease:

> And this time I discovered that the boy was indeed ill. In his right side, near the hip, was an open wound as big as the palm of my hand. Rose-red, in many variations of shade, dark in the hollows, lighter at the edges, softly granulated, with irregular clots of blood, open as a surface mine to the daylight. That was how it looked from a distance. But on a closer inspection there was another complication. I could not help a low whistle of surprise. Worms, as thick and long as my little finger, themselves rose-red and blood-spotted as well, were wriggling from their fastness in the interior of the wound toward the light, with small white heads and many legs. Poor boy, you were past helping. I had discovered your great wound; this blossom in your side was destroying you. (*CS* 223)

Unapparent during the initial examination, the wound opens itself like a hitherto undisclosed secret, like a groom hiding in a neglected part of one's estate, like the desire for a servant girl that has lain dormant under daily ceremony. The wound announces itself like a secret to the doctor, who discovers it and, as a competent practitioner, examines it both at a distance and in proximity.

Although located on the flank of a local boy, the wound is a metaphor for the secrets that have been disclosed to the doctor about himself. The festering wound, embellished with twisting parasitic worms, is an image of the doctor's own festering sexuality. These worms, for all the revulsion that they might inspire, consummate an intensity of narrative description rare in Kafka's work. Like certain tumors and growths encountered by practicing physicians, the boy's wound radiates a peculiar beauty—in this case, the beauty of vividness.

The wound is a displaced image for the doctor's sexual conflicts. While its color, "Rose," causes some syntactical ambiguity by virtue of its placement at the head of a sentence, the choice of hue relates the wound to the doctor's apparent competition with the groom over Rose. Kafka underscores the incorporation of the source of desire into the wound; he places in relief the inscription of desire as the wound's very nature. The wound is rosy. The doctor describes it explicitly as a flower in the boy's side. The bloody worms have white heads. They thrive on red fluid but are themselves consumptive. In different ways, the doctor and patient are both consumed.

The wound is the flower of desire. Desire here, as in Proust, is a disease. The boy, because he is affected with the festering wound of the doctor's desire, is the doctor's unlikely double. The bystanders are thus not being provincial when they place the two in the same bed, when they connect the doctor to his disease by means of metonymic contiguity. An aging man and an adolescent boy share a longing-sickness.

In the course of the story, then, the doctor is twice doubled, first in relation to the surprising groom, then with the sick boy. The image of the wound is both the mark and the agent of this doubling. It is that which connects the doubled framework to the doubled scene of medical speculation. The wound takes Rose out of the narrative's external shell, where she appears as a semiautonomous bone of contention, and internalizes her within a scene of subjective ambivalence. As Rose passes from exteriority to interiority, so too does the narrative as a linguistic wound fold on and consume itself. This text structures a desire for the resolution between its outside and inside, between its structure and its material. And the binding that it offers for its conflicts is the image of a wound. But a wound is traumatized tissue; it is the locus where the body capitulates to rather than resists dismemberment.

By virtue of its bruised texture, "A Country Doctor" may be taken as an instance of that weak cohesion that characterizes a literary work. It demonstrates that what binds texts need not be as tangible as themes, as abstract as ideas, or as systematic as logical schemes. The somewhat crumbly coherence of this text concentrates around the signifier rose, which functions simultaneously as the name of a character, the color of a wound, and the name and color of a flower. The character, wound, and color are depicted within the text's representational field, while the flower hovers beyond the textual margins as a metaphoric icon, insignia, caption, or shorthand for the narrative's "events." The boy's wound becomes allegorical of the text because of the shifting permitted, even solicited, by rose. Rose marks the spot, precisely, where the text's dramatic scenario, structure, semantics, and thematic underpinnings intertwine. By closely implicating a persona, Rose, within the metaphoric economy of a text, Kafka comes as close as any author has to admitting the semiological rather than substantive nature of fictive "characters." Characters do not exist (or even act) so much as play within an ultimately deranged exchange of positions demarcated by Hegel as the speculative limit of the notion of force. They gather and abandon meaning in texts as signifiers pursue chains of displacement in the Lacanian imaginary (see Lacan, *Ecrits* 146–78; *Fundamental Concepts* 42–52).

The overdetermination of the role of rose within the text helps account for the pronounced duplicity of the characterization and thematics. The self-referentiality dramatized by this signifier also serves as a precedent for the allegory of parasitism. A consumptive boy devoured by consumptive worms is a narrative representation of a metaphor that can both consume and fragment itself.

The boy is indeed correct, then, when he asserts, "A fine wound is all I brought into the world; that was my sole endowment" (*CS* 225). For this brief work as well as for the sick character, a wound constitutes the total equipment and production. The wound in the work as well as in the boy constitutes the fissure in the Möbius strip describing the text's configuration. Crowned by a rose, the wound is the site where the text endlessly folds and feeds on itself.

It is therefore no accident that any departure from this domain must be abrupt and arbitrary. If the narrative framework results in an unresolved conflict over a woman between the doctor and his double, then in the core of the text the doctor's link to his second double, the sick boy, is ultimately complicitous:

> "Do you know," said a voice in my ear, "I have very little confidence in you. Why, you were only blown in here, you didn't come on your feet. Instead of helping me, you're cramping me on my deathbed. What I'd like best is to scratch your eyes out." "Right," I said, "it is a shame. And yet I am a doctor. What am I to do? Believe me, it is not too easy for me either." "Am I supposed to be content with this apology?" . . . "My young friend," said I, "your mistake is: you have not a wide enough view . . . and I tell you: your wound is not so bad. Done in a tight corner with two strokes of the ax. Many a one proffers his side and can hardly hear the ax in the forest, far less that it is coming nearer to him." "Is that really so, or are you deluding me in my fever?" "It is really so, take the word of honor of an official doctor." And he took it and lay still. (*CS* 224–25)

As this consultation commences, the boy has no confidence in the doctor, and the latter shows no sign of deviating from his general contempt for the surroundings. By the end of the interchange, the practitioner has been roused out of his indifference and the patient is calm, reassured, and perhaps prepared for death. The motive for this double reversal of positions may well come from the potentials offered by the ax and its relation to the image of the wound. If the wound figures the ambiguous textual intertwining afforded by the movement of the shifter between structural, thematic, and semantic levels, the ax promises release from the uncertainty by the excision of the function that loosens while it binds. A wound is all the text brings into the world to hold itself together, yet precisely as a function of textuality, the wound marks the side of repression, desire, and internal and external conflict. It delimits the extent of life with surgical precision.

At the end of "A Crossbreed [A Sport]," both the marginal kitten-lamb and the narrator, the son for whom the creature and its intellectual conditions are an inescapable legacy, eye the butcher's knife as a possible escape from their despair. The execution of Joseph K. in *The Trial* may be described as the application of a penetrating instrument to the victim after it has playfully shuttled back and forth between the henchmen. In "A Country Doctor" as well, a sharp blade holds out the promise of resolution and acquires the thrust of a poignant wish. A double blow of the ax in a tight corner can free the patient from his inherited mark of Cain. Only in conceptually offering this instrument does the country doctor serve as a healer. The prescribed treatment involves, however, not a regeneration of tissue but an amputation. Two decisive strokes of an ax can release the prisoner from his double bind, can free him, perhaps, from the narrow path on which Oedipus meets his father. The ax strikes outward, beyond the confines of a constricting familial space, but, to complete its task, also strikes inward, penetrating the superficial layers of the flesh.

The image of the ax is the sum total of the country doctor's reassurance. The wound is not so severe ("übel"): done ("geschaffen") "with two strokes of the ax," both dispatched and created by the healing-incising ax. The ax is a messiah (or avenging angel) of resolution. Those who offer their sides to it, in reverence, may not hear it in the forest, but eventually its work is done, silently and implicitly ("geschweige"). The silent ax in the forest recalls the falling tree whose status is so crucial to ontology and to the hypothetical status of God. The ax, were there only an ax, would clarify, resolve, amputate, the duplicity and ambiguity whose locus is language and whose form is that of a congenital wound. But the closure provided by the ax may still be described only in terms of inscription: incision, marking, scarring. The poignant wish for a termination of involution and complexity is expressed by several of Kafka's characters; it hovers at the horizon in much of his fiction. This end-wish or wish to end wishes can be articulated only in writing, through the textual economy that writing both promises and renders bankrupt. The ax is only one moment of the wound that is both the flower and disease of writing.

The mere invocation of the ax is sufficient to release the patient from his tension. To terminate a text whose insignia assumes the form of a Möbius strip is, however, not so simple. The country doctor's exit from the narrative stage necessarily takes the form of a desperate escape. Only the fall of an ax can truncate this text. Like his arrival at the patient's house—"as if my patient's farmyard had opened out just before ["unmittelbar"] my courtyard gate, I was already there" (*CS* 221)—the doctor's departure is abrupt. These movements are as sudden as the shifts of location that Freud finds characteristic of dreams, but the doctor's concerns are hardly dreamlike. The narrative ends as the doctor helplessly reaches for his fur coat at the back of his gig. He remains naked, having been stripped by the peasants and placed in bed next to his patient. He despairs of ever reaching home, fears seeing his medical practice collapse as he is usurped by a successor—and, of course, he despairs at the sacrifice of Rose and at the groom's successful rage. "Betrayed! Betrayed!" moans the doctor as the text ends. "A false alarm on the night bell once answered—it cannot be made good, not ever" (*CS* 225). The betrayal that the country doctor suffers is systematic and not merely sexual. Events are simply out of control. The arbitrary truncation of this text is merely one further manifestation of the loss of control that it has embellished. The losses and concerns that the text dramatizes are not to be recuperated. Betrayal cannot be undone. The "false alarms" that will disturb the doctor's sleep forever are the tones of absence whose textual manifestation is the figure of a wound.

Related contrapuntally to the rhythm of the eruption and amputation of ambiguity that may in fact constitute this text's only story is the music that twice breaks forth from the peasants. Although the text provides some psychosocial context for this singing, its very outbreak in the text possesses a shock value that cannot be reduced or assimilated. The peasants' incantations shift the narrative's setting to a world of primitive, obsessive, and ritualistic thought.

A school choir with the teacher at the head of it stood before the house and sang these words to an utterly simple tune:

"Strip his clothes off, then he'll heal us,
If he doesn't, kill him dead!
Only a doctor, only a doctor." (*CS* 224)

The performative dimension of this chant consists of two imperatives and a judgment. The logic of the exhortations is the simple causality characteristic of infantile obsession. The stripping of the doctor is the initial phase of a sacrificial act. If we prepare the doctor for sacrifice, the logic runs, he will spare our martyr. If this effort fails, we will sacrifice him. The narrative rationalizes the singing in terms of the sociopolitical wish it expresses: to cut the doctor down to size, to strip him, literally, of his authority and paternalism. The song's prescriptions intertwine him with the boy. The doctor will suffer what he fails to cure. Because the doctor has been inscribed within the peasants' obsessive reasoning, the outcome of the boy's case is already fated to be his own condition. The peasant's final incantation celebrates the events that the initial one announces and, with inexorable logic, fulfills: "O be joyful, all you patients, / The doctor's laid in bed beside you" (*CS* 225).

The music in the text not only intensifies the arbitrariness of its events but also breaks free of the thematic networks that would seem to reinforce a sense of cohesion. The gestures celebrated by the music are precisely arbitrary: command, soothsaying, judgment, exaltation. The incantations become a counterpoint of arbitrariness arising from the text but then floating above it with impunity, only tangentially related. The music hovers above the text as the doorbell tone floats beyond the confining domestic setting of "A Fratricide," "right over the town and up to heaven" (*CS* 403). In Kafka's fiction music diacritically annotates the directional aspirations of his writing. Though of the text, the music hovers above it, uncommitted to the apparent trends in which the thematic level has invested. Music underscores the constitutive role played by the metaphor in Kafka's writing: a fleeting refrain that sings of the difference between texts and stories.

NOTES

1. In *Diaries, 1910–1913* Kafka writes of "[t]he fearful strain and joy, how the story developed before me, as if I were advancing over water. . . . How everything can be said, how for everything, for the strangest fancies, there awaits a great fire in which they perish and rise up again" (276).

2. A good general introduction to Freud's thought regarding obsessional ideas is to be found in the theoretical section of the "Rat Man" case history (*Standard Edition* 10: 221–49).

3. This ambiguity in characterization may be said to structure such major works as "Description of a Struggle" and "A Hunger Artist." Kafka rehearses its potentials in "First Sorrow." For a full treatment of "Description of a Struggle" as an exercise in scenic construction based on a play between intersubjective and intrasubjective conflict, see Sussman 61–74.

4. Freud develops his notion of the uncanny in a 1919 essay, "The 'Uncanny,'" whose major instance of this phenomenon derives from E. T. A. Hoffmann's "Sandman." Initially, Freud situates the uncanny at the end of primary narcissism, when a child's self-image of benevolent omnipotence is partially eclipsed by its opposite. Freud realizes, however, the inadequacy of a developmental explanation in accounting for the full literary potentials of doubling (*Standard Edition* 17: 232–45).

5. Of all critics, Walter Benjamin provides the best account of the allegorical gestic language in Kafka's fiction, an illustration of his broader notion of shock. For a discussion of Kafka's gestic language, see Benjamin, "Franz Kafka."

STEPHEN D. DOWDEN

The Impossibility of Crows

T he turn of Kafka studies into cultural criticism has helped to make Kafka
more intelligible in two main ways: first, by situating him better than ever
before with respect to his own historical, social, and intellectual context, and
second, by positioning him with respect to the contemporary interest in race
and ethnicity, community and individuality Even if it remains difficult to
translate the specific details of his fiction (imagery, allusion, form) directly
into social meanings, his own manifest interest in Judaism, coupled with
contemporary critical interest in questions of multiculturalism and social
identity, authorizes the approach offered by cultural studies. Still, cultural
criticism has its limits. It cannot contain all of Kafka; his fiction remains too
subversive. Certain questions slip through the nets of cultural critique.

Why, if Kafka was principally interested in giving imaginative form to
his cultural roots, is his fiction so unforthcoming about it? The works rarely
refer to Jews or Judaism and its rituals. Moreover, the language of his fiction
is purged not only of any hint of Jewish speech but of practically all distinguishing features of class, region, and ethnicity. Even children, barbarians and
animals use the same neutral idiom that the adults do. The reason, I think,
is that Kafka was interested in achieving in his writing a sense of universal
timelessness and placelessness. This is not meant to suggest that the "topic"
of Judaism is excluded from his fiction, only that Kafka meant the fiction

From *Kafka's Castle and the Critical Imagination*, pp. 119–42. © 1995 by Camden House.

to encompass even more. He had an abiding fascination for what might be called the anthropological absolute. By this I mean a piece or level of human reality that inhabits but also transcends the contingencies of institutions such as state and religion and ethnicity.

When Kafka wrote in his diary about "storming the last earthly border" by means of his writing, it certainly sounds as if at least he believed his fiction had some capacity to resist the contingencies of time and circumstance. On December 25, 1917, he wrote that works of his such as "Ein Landarzt" gave him a modicum of satisfaction but that happiness would come only if he succeeding in elevating the world into "the pure, the true, the unchanging." These words disclose his deepest point of artistic departure. There is every indication that Kafka regarded this task as the supreme challenge to his literary gift, even if there is no indication that he thought he ever measured up to it fully. Even Josefine, his most affirmative artist figure, achieves at best an ambiguous success. No one can tell how her "piping" differs from that of any other mouse's. Indeed, it may not be her piping at all that so delights the mouse-folk at her recitals but the "feierliche Stille," the ceremonial silence that envelops and unites them as they listen to her. Josefine's song is an art beyond concept and reference. It is an art that *does* something rather than *saying* something.

Kafka's achievement in *Das Schloß* is in principle similar, as should be evident at this late date in Kafka criticism. It is not so much what he says as the forum that he has provided for discussion, debate, exchange, and disagreement. His book is not an act of communication so much as the scene of it. Early in his career he wrote that we need books that affect us like a sharp blow to the head. *Das Schloß*, historically, has turned to be a blow to our collective heads. It is news that stays news, inexhaustible not because it appeals directly to the emotions—indeed, its undercoooled style hardly appeals to emotion at all—but because it appeals to the imagination, the sense of mystery and the sublime. The last category is especially pertinent. *Das Schloß* is deeply concerned with that which lies above and beyond mimetic expression, inspires awe and fear, and is all but lost to K., the prototypically alienated modern. I want to conclude this study of castle criticism by pursuing this last, insufficiently explored aspect of *Das Schloß*.

Kafka's Anthropological Absolute

In September 1917, after Kafka's tuberculosis was diagnosed, he took a leave of absence from his job and went to the northwestern Bohemian village of Zürau (called Siřem in Czech) for a rest cure. He stayed there several months, until April 1918. It is the received view that this sojourn marks a final renewal of Kafka's creativity. He did not turn away from earlier interests so much as he experienced a new and vigorous development in his way of seeing the world. During this period he turned his hand to writing brief parables and aphorisms, literary miniatures that should be regarded as finger exercises in preparation for *Das Schloß*.

In Zürau he read widely, including works by Buber (with little appreciation), Kierkegaard, Tolstoy, and Schopenhauer; he also read in the Hebrew Bible. In his afterword to *Das Schloß*, Max Brod claimed that Kafka's reading of Kierkegaard was decisive for the novel, supplying Kafka with the basic conception of the earthly and divine as incommensurable. This could be true, though no commentary of Kafka's supports Brod's contention. It seems likely that Kafka's dualism, expressed in many of his aphorisms, was generated out of his own strangely unique resources of creativity and owes little to Kierkegaard or even to Jewish mystical traditions. Kafka was indeed interested in the Jewish myth and folklore, but the evidence (or rather the lack of it) suggests that his actual, specific knowledge was haphazard and limited. What knowledge he did possess has left no clear trail in his fiction and aphorisms. Consequently the critics have been left to speculate. Robertson guesses the aphorisms to have been vitally shaped by the Kabbalah, and he offers an extensive exegesis of them on this basis, yet he produces no objective evidence in support of the conjecture (1985:195ff).

Nevertheless, the emphasis on the Zürau aphorisms as an imaginative achievement central to Kafka's understanding of the world is on target. Apart from any specifically Jewish component, they also belong to an identifiable European tradition, as Richard Gray (1987) has shown. Finally, even if they are not directly inspired by the Kabbalah—and it seems unlikely that Kafka knew much if anything about it—the character of the aphorisms is distinctly kabbalistic (Alter 1993b).

One such element that is decisive for Kafka's writing, the aphorisms as well as *Das Schloß*, is the gnostic-like, kabbalistic distinction between the earthly here-and-now and a transcendent realm. Kafka often calls it "das Geistige," the spiritual, though it has other names. He sets it above and beyond "die sinnliche Welt," or the sense world, a choice of words that suggests that his background in empirical psychology is also in play here. The sense world is loosely identified with evil ("das Böse"), as in the distinction between sensual love and heavenly love but also more abstractly:

Es gibt nichts anderes als eine geistige Welt; was wir sinnliche Welt nennen ist das Böse in der geistigen und was wir böse nennen ist nur eine Notwendigkeit eines Augenblicks unserer ewigen Entwicklung. (NS2:124, §54)

[There is nothing other than a spiritual world; what we call the sensuous world is only the evil within the spiritual one, and what we call evil is only a necessity of a moment in our eternal development.]

The rift between the earthly and the transcendent is complete: "Es gibt ein Ziel, aber keinen Weg," a goal but no pathway that leads there. The resemblance between this last aphorism (§26) and K.'s attempts to get into the castle has often been noted but never adequately clarified. It seems to me that the correspondence is important, but in need of deeper exploration.

Kafka's novel presents a world that is divided into two irreconcilable halves, village and castle. Yet to be in the village, in a certain sense, is to be in the castle, as Schwarzer points out to K. Moreover, bureaucratic officials evidently travel back and forth between the castle and the village. This suggests an arrangement rather like that in aphorism §54, in which the spiritual contains, yet also transcends, the sensual. The distinction between the two is an illusion, but one that is inescapable.

Yet we who are marooned in the realm of the senses are not without recourse. Art may have some modest access to the transcendent realm, though not unproblematically. It is the classic problem of language that Kafka addresses in aphorism §57: language can be used only to intimate (*andeutungsweise*) the things of the spiritual world. Language and fiction cannot render them mimetically. The language aphorism brings us to the brink of *Das Schloß*, which enacts as parable a dilemma that is cognate.

The danger in relating the aphorisms to *Das Schloß* lies in exaggerating the correspondence of details, especially conceptual ones. What strikes me as crucial is not so much a precise resemblance as a general one, a similarity of structural framework. Moreover, *Das Schloß* is truer to Kafka's radically uncompromising vision than the aphorisms. By Kafkan standards they are surprisingly blunt in the provisional naming of ineffable, unknowable things. Kafka talks about "das Unzerstörbare" (the indestructible) in human nature, refers longingly to paradise, (also indestructible, according to §74), and "das Geistige" (the spiritual). This reliance on conceptual abstraction is new and uncharacteristic for Kafka. His more usual mode is parable and image.

That he may have felt uneasy about this quasi-philosophical style can be inferred from the aphorism about language, which we have already discussed, but which needs further elaboration with a new inflection:

Die Sprache kann für alles außerhalb der sinnlichen Welt nur andeutungsweise, aber niemals auch nur annähernd vergleichsweise gebraucht werden, da sie entsprechend der sinnlichen Welt nur vom Besitz und seinen Beziehungen handelt. (NS2:59)

[Language can only be used to intimate things outside the sensory world. It can never be used comparatively, not even approximately, because language in its correspondence to the sensory world deals only with property and its relations.]

This is Kafka's secular reworking of the traditional Jewish Bilderverbot, the biblical prohibition that forbids the depiction of God or paradise. It seems likely there are other points of reference for Kafka as well. The lessons of empirical psychology would have stayed with him, as we have seen, because it persuaded him that the inner life, contra Proust and Joyce, is beyond representation. In the Zürau period, as we have noted, he was reading Kierkegaard, whose distinction between telling and showing may have impressed him. He was also reading Schopenhauer, whose doctrine of representation as it relates to the will bears a family resemblance to Kafka's notion of language and the spiritual. We may reasonably suppose that Kafka's attitude toward representation and the spirit were thus overdetermined. The failure of language is an ancient topos, the ultimate expression of which is in the decalogue. That the ancient Hebrew source was uppermost in Kafka's mind is suggested by the abundance of biblical allusions to paradise, the tree of knowledge, and original sin in his Zürau aphorisms and in the "Er" pieces of 1920.

In addition, the messianic idea—conditioned by Kafka's growing interest in the need for Jewish solidarity and nationhood—was on his mind, as it was on the minds of many Jews, hard-pressed as they were by the worsening of European nationalisms and attendant anti-Semitism. In the May 1921 issue of *Der Jude*, Martin Buber's Jewish monthly, there appeared an essay on Jewish messianism. Its author, Zionist Elfride-Salome Bergel-Gronemann, writes programmatically of the rigorous, traditional Jewish insistence on the absolute otherness of God and Paradise. She is referring to the *Bilderverbot*. Christianity, by contrast, offers earthly consolation to man's sin-battered soul in the form of symbolic images, especially that of Christ crucified, meant to seal the certainty of man's continuity with the divine. Art is thus an earthly resting place for the spirit. It is otherwise in Judaism. Since Jewish redemption has not yet occurred, it remains an indistinct and undefinable prospect, the object of uncertain longing. Therefore, in Judaism the spirit cannot and does not rest in this world. The infinite and absolute must remain infinite and absolute, beyond all earthly representation. The Messiah cannot be compelled into aesthetic form. Any such embodiment is idolatrous falsification.

Even the secret name of God is not to be spoken. This is the taboo that K. breaks when he speaks aloud the name of Count Westwest, for which the horrified schoolmaster rebukes him. This does not mean Count Westwest personifies God; far from it. It only means that the traditional structure of the taboo remains intact, if misapplied, in the degraded world of the castle. Westwest is something more along the order of secular deity, a false god for the benighted villagers.

The point that Bergel-Gronemann insists on is that the messianic event cannot be depicted because it has not occurred. The Jewish tradition presents redemption above all as a task that remains to be completed. The idea that redemption is a task and not a gift of grace also distinguishes Jewish messianism from the Christian version. Christ redeems the worst sinner, no matter how abject. The sinner is passive and must only desire to be redeemed. In the liberal Western tradition of Judaism that Kafka inhabited, it is the task of all Jews to prepare the world for the coming of the Messiah. However, as Bergel-Gronemann explains, he will come only when the preparations are complete—that is, when he is no longer needed. This is a social and political messianism. Interestingly and significantly, Kafka himself is explicit about this in his aphorisms:

Der Messias wird erst kommen, wenn er nicht mehr nötig sein wird, er wird erst nach seiner Ankunft kommen, er wird nicht am letzten Tag kommen, sondern am allerletzten. (NS2:57)

[The Messiah will not come until he is no longer needed. He will come only after his arrival. He will come not on the last day, but on the very last day.]

In a more secular vein, the same thought is transposed as follows:

Der entscheidende Augenblick der menschlichen Entwicklung ist immerwährend. Darum sind die revolutionären geistigen Bewegungen, welche alles frühere für nichtig erklären, im Recht, denn es ist noch nichts geschehn. (NS2:114, §6)

[The deciding moment of human development is everlasting. That is why the revolutionary spiritual movements that declare null and void all that has gone before them are in the right. For nothing has yet happened.]

The decisive moment is everlasting because the earth is continually being prepared, so to speak, for the coming of the messiah—that is, for a state of perfection that will never be reached. It is for the same reason that K. will never achieve his aim. It cannot be achieved. Crossing over from the realm of suffering, deception, and incompletion into the absolute is not possible:

> Er fühlt sich auf dieser Erde gefangen, ihm ist eng, die Trauer, die Schwäche, die Krankheit, die Wahnvorstellungen der Gefangenen brechen bei ihm aus, kein Trost kann ihn trösten, weil es eben nur Trost ist, zarter kopfschmezender Trost gegenüber der groben Tatsache des Gefangenseins. Fragt man ihn aber, was er eigentlich haben will, kann er nicht antworten, denn er hat—das ist einer seiner stärksten Beweise—keine Vorstellung von der Freiheit.

> [He feels himself imprisoned in this world. He feels closed in. The sadness, the weakness, the sickness, the delusion of the imprisoned break out in him. No consolation can comfort him, simply because it is only consolation, the tender headachy consolation versus the brute fact of imprisonment. But if you ask him what he wants, he cannot answer, because—and this is one of his most solid pieces of evidence—he has no idea (*Vorstellung*) of freedom.]

The "he" in this aphorism is not K., since it is a piece from the "Er" collection of 1920. But it may as well be K., for it describes his situation exactly. He knows that he is suffering, that he wants something better than what he has, but does not even know what that something better is. In the aphorism it is given as freedom. In the novel, that something, the object of K.'s vague longing, is left utterly unnamed.

I am suggesting that Kafka's secularized perception of the messianic ideal took an anthropological turn. It is an insight of Kafkan imagination that the individual contains an indestructible element of spirituality, a tiny, imperishable bit of the paradise that was lost and is yet to come, toward which K. falteringly strives.

> Der Mensch kann nicht leben ohne ein dauerndes Vertrauen zu etwas Unzerstörbarem in sich, wobei sowohl das Unzerstörbare als auch das Vertrauen ihm dauernd verborgen bleiben können. Eine der Ausdrucksmöglichkeiten dieses Verborgen-Bleibens ist der Glaube an einen persönlichen Gott. (NS2:124, §50)

> [The human being cannot live without a lasting trust in something indestructible within himself. Both the indestructible and the trust

can remain perpetually hidden from him. One of the possibilities for the expression of the concealment is the faith in a personal God.]

It is a condition of life, then, that the individual have a lasting confidence in the anthropological absolute, even if he is unaware of it. That the indestructible component of human being is simultaneously present to the imagination yet permanently absent to life lived in time and space is evident from the various invocations of biblical paradise in the Zürau aphorisms. This one is characteristic:

> Die Vertreibung aus dem Paradies ist in ihrem Hauptteil ewig: Es ist also zwar die Vertreibung aus dem Paradies endgiltig, das Leben in der Welt unausweichlich, die Ewigkeit des Vorganges aber macht es trotzdem möglich, daß wir nicht nur dauernd im Paradies bleiben könnten, sondern tatsächlich dort dauernd sind, gleichgültig ob wir es hier wissen oder nicht. (NS2:127, §64)

> [The expulsion from Paradise is, in the main, eternal: So the expulsion from Paradise is final, life in the world ineluctable, yet the eternity of the process makes it nevertheless possible that we not only could remain continuously in Paradise but actually are there continuously, regardless of whether we know it here or not.]

The language problem is evident. No language has a verb tense that expresses eternity, so Kafka must resort to strategies of parody and paradox to intimate the possibility of a moral dimension beyond time and space. Paradise is indestructible, hidden within—not lost at all, just unknown to us. Paradise is continually present, even if we remain estranged from it and unaware of it. I take the aphorism to be understood not as a philosophical truth but as an exploratory expression, one of many, concerning the essential dividedness of human nature, its lack of unity with itself, especially with a higher element that is always emergent yet never finally achieved.

The upshot of such passages—together with many more that could be offered in evidence—is that Kafka senses the presence of an ideal world outside the sensuous realm of time and space. That explains why the spatiality of his metaphors is unstable, sometimes internal (the indestructible), sometimes external ("Paradise"), but always a human universal that eludes conventional representation. It is a way of thinking that has an identifiable messianic tradition regardless of Kafka's intention, and it offers itself as a clue to understanding the peculiarities of *Das Schloß*. However, it would be a mistake to take the aphorisms too literally. Indeed, the categories with which they proceed (the indestructible, Paradise, the spiritual world) are flawed by self-contradiction. Abstract and metaphorical as they are, they offend the commandment forbidding images; they say too much. They transgress against the postreligious *Bilderverbot* by making the absolute contingent, the infinite finite.

Kafka's massive and supremely discreet parable, *Das Schloß*, corrects the error. It does so precisely because it does *not* offer any image that represents the infinite. All indications suggest that the opposite is true: the castle represents falsehood, idolatry, reification as one of the besetting problems of thought and imagination. The castle and its bureaucracy mask the infinite, concealing it behind a veil of quixotic misapprehension.

Error and the Sublime

We turn first to a crucial passage. The image of the castle and its main feature, the tower, is measured in the text against the implied norm of a lost world. In his mind's eye, K. remembers the church tower of his old hometown and judges the castle tower unfavorably by the standard it sets. In so doing, he comes closest to revealing the novel's ineffable center. The church tower soars confidently, youthfully upward. It unfolds its rooftop in a flash of bright red tiles. This catches the eye because it is one of the novel's only patches of color. Then the narrator adds, "ein irdisches Gebäude—was können wir sonst bauen—aber mit höherem Ziel. . . ." Kafka's mode here is negative affirmation. The building is only terrestrial (that is, not spiritual) but its aim is loftier (but not named). K.'s eye and the narrator's language move on to explore the crow-encircled castle tower. It is crumbling, shabby; it even has an "insane" look about it. It shows little sign of spiritual purpose.

The contrast between church tower and castle tower sets Kafka's theme. It is the earthly, which can be named, and something higher, which cannot, but which the church tower intimates. The contrast should help to confirm the view that the castle stands as an emblem for the modern, secular, postreligious era. It is important to note that K. shows no sign of nostalgia for the past. The past is gone, K. has come here to stay, a point about which he is emphatic. Emphatic too is K.'s striving toward an unnamed goal, which we should take to mean a future that is better. This does not make K. a messianic figure, but it does show that the messianic idea is at work in the novel. It is the idea of a fallen world in need of redemption, but not a redeemer in the form of a personal deity. K. is just an ordinary uprooted soul, aggressively seeking something he wants and needs yet hardly understands and cannot name. He has no clear idea how to fulfill the uncertain longing that drives him forward.

It is reasonable to wonder why Kafka chooses the image of a church rather than a synagogue as his point of comparison. The sense of it has to do with what might be called, orienting our perspective on the novel from the aphorisms, Kafka's anthropological absolute. The aphorisms deal not with the interests and spiritual problems of Jews alone, even though Kafka's own Jewishness certainly helped to shape his perception of basic human nature. When he talks about what is indestructible in people, he means all people, not just Jews. The church in *Das Schloß* refers to the average run of European reality, which is Gentile. If Kafka had added a synagogue, or used one instead of a church, it would have created confusion by giving the false impression that he is writing about the special problems of European Jews. The novel is about the human spirit in the postreligious era of the European mind.

Kafka's clues to this effect are plain enough. The castle tower is residential, not ecclesiastical. The village has no church, only an insignificant little chapel, suggesting the merest vestigial remnants of a once mighty but now defunct religious tradition. In the village the usual stock figures are present: schoolmaster, innkeeper, peasants, and so forth; but there is no priest, pastor, or rabbi. The role of spiritual leader, though still an official presence in *Der Proceß*, has simply disappeared from the world of the castle. K. himself could be a Jew, as his pariah status suggests, and the same holds true for the Barnabassian clan. As Suchoff and Robertson have shown, various elements of Judaism figure into Kafka's imaginary world.

Still, I believe the point is this: Kafka imagines a syncretic setting in which spiritual beliefs and practices have withered into senseless and oppressive parodies of spiritual observance. Religious leadership has been supplanted by a secularized caste of officials who parody the responsibilities and prerogatives of traditional spiritual leaders. And K. himself epitomizes the homeless, faceless, rootless stranger—Jew, Gentile, or anybody—in search of a sense of orientation. He will not find it because he does not know how or where to look. In orienting himself on Klamm (whose name, as noted earlier, means "delusion" in Czech), K. deceives himself. Klamm is the mere semblance of a godlike or priestlike figure, an illusion that K. shares with the villagers, who are in awe of him.

The castle itself is ugly and run-down, in fact not a castle at all but a huddle of low buildings surrounding a tower. The absence of beauty is conspicuous and significant. The castle lacks the symbolic power that is associated with beauty in the sense of the European Christian tradition of symbolization. K. actually dwells on this point in the passage in which he compares the church tower of his hometown to the castle tower. Back home, he recalls, the church tower rose confidently upward, seeming to become more youthful as it did so and then finishing with a flourish of red-tiled rooftop. K. remembers that it had a "loftier purpose" than the secular buildings around it, and he notes that the castle is quite different. It calls forth no sense of a superior purpose. K. notes too that the church tower was just an "earthly building" yet justly laid claim to its higher, spiritual identity. The church tower has symbolic power for K. because it compels into material form an intimation of a spirituality that is beyond the mere material. The castle, squat and dilapidated, does the opposite. It blocks spirituality, the fulfillment of self and of community.

Kafka presents a world in which beauty is absent. The beautiful symbolized the continuity of the earthly and the divine. The classic aesthetic expression of this continuity in European culture is the Roman Catholic tradition of ecclesiastical art, and its ultimate doctrine is that of transubstantiation. God's divine plan guarantees the coherence of the universe, and beauty is the visible sign of transcendence, guarantor of continuity between the earthly and the divine. K.'s ugly, snow-frozen world is one in which transcendence is impossible. The line of contact between this world and the fuller one that lies deeper has been broken. The castle, with its jagged battlements, "as if drawn by someone who is frightened or by a child's hand," is the allegory of the failed transcendence.

The castle and its somnolent army of bureaucrats are Kafka's comic image for the diminished state of modern spirituality. This is a confirmation and expansion of Ingeborg Henel's fundamental insight that the castle is a projected counterworld to the protagonist (Henel 1967:259–69). But whereas Henel refers the counterworld only to the protagonist, it seems to me that it should be referred to all the other villagers as well. It is the displaced embodiment of the human frailties of everyone, but especially K. It reflects not the true human spirit, which I am calling Kafka's anthropological absolute, but its reified simulacrum.

The castle and its bureaucrats, whose grotesque and comic aspect is not often enough chuckled over by Kafka critics, reflect the frozen spiritual lives of K. and the villagers. The bureaucrats—Klamm, Sortini, Sordini, Erlanger, Galater, Bürgel, and the rest—satirize bourgeois power and respectability extrapolated to the nth degree. They stand for the spirit congealed into static, stolid, false forms. The castle and its grotesque, bureaucratic apparatus are not symbols that reach outward toward transcendence. They are instead emblems of the blockage that prevent K. and the villagers from finding a way out of the eternal winter of the soul that imprisons them. Olga's nightly degradations and Barnabas's futile activities as a courier are telling examples of the castle's falsity. That both of them willingly undertake these activities suggests that their misery may well be self-imposed. The castle never demanded absolution from Amalia's family (S 328–29).

This view of the castle does not return us to long-discredited religious interpretations of Das Schloß. Brod sought to recover Kafka for a conventional Judaism, and writers such as Ong (1947) and Muir (1930) and, more recently,

Jens and Küng (1985) have sought to bring Kafka into a position compatible with ecumenical Christian theology. More persuasive are perhaps Harold Bloom (1987) and his precursor Gershom Scholem, who have explored what they regard as Kafka's spontaneous reinvention of Jewish mysticism. But I would like to suggest, building on Ingeborg Henel's reading of Kafka as a thinker (1980) and in partial agreement with Ritchie Robertson (1985), that Kafka's sense of spirituality has a secular cast, distant from traditional religious dogma and doctrine, distant even from theism itself.[1] Robertson rightly and persuasively identifies Kafka's spirituality not with the supernatural but with the "collective being of mankind united in 'das Unzerstörbare'" (201) and adduces this aphorism:

> Das Unzerstörbare ist eines; jeder einzelne Mensch ist es und gleichzeitig is es allen gemeinsam, daher die beispiellos untrennbare Verbindung der Menschen.

> [The indestructible is whole; it is every individual human being and at the same time all collectively, therefore the unexampled indivisible solidarity of the human race.]

By intellectual disposition and by his training in empirical psychology, Kafka is closer to the antidogmatic pragmatism of William James's *Varieties of Religious Experience: A Study in Human Nature* (1902) than to the theological minds that have claimed him as a kindred spirit. The notion of spirituality adumbrated in Kafka's aphorisms and more subtly and fully explored in *Das Schloß* has more to do with his sense of human nature than with the dogmas of temporal religious institutions. The image of castle and its bureaucracy, as I have been arguing, represents a final institutional petrification of the human spirit in Europe and nearly its death sentence. The aphorisms make it clear that Kafka had not entirely given up on the human spirit, that he sought a sign of something ahistorical and noncontingent, something that might elude the Midas touch of official codification in religion and even in literature and art.

Naturally there are traces of familiar religion, and one seems to me particularly important. The specifically Jewish component of Kafka's sober mysticism links his writing to the perdurable tradition of the sublime. Its decisive component is the Mosaic *Bilderverbot*, the biblical prohibition that underlies Kafkan negation, his endlessly refined tactic of not-naming. In Kafka, the infinite and absolute remain infinite and absolute.

For example, in comparing the church tower to the castle tower, Kafka's K.-like narrative voice talks about the church tower's loftier purpose, but without naming that purpose. And, as Ritchie Robertson shrewdly observes, a similar strategy informs the strange and obscurely metaphorical passage that describes the castle tower (Robertson 1985:203–4). It is "mercifully hidden" by ivy, which has the effect of calling forth feelings that a taboo is being transgressed here, that something better left unseen has greeted the light of day. That hidden something remains unsaid. It evokes in his readers a feeling of the Kafkan sublime. The effect is parallel to Josefine's song. The text does not tell us something. Rather, it causes us to sense the presence of an occulted reality, something uncanny, beyond the threshold of ordinary experience.

The link between the sublime and the *Bilderverbot* is strong. "Perhaps the most sublime passage in the Jewish Law," writes Kant in his *Critique of Judgment*, "is the commandment: Thou shalt not make unto thee any graven image, or any likeness of any thing that is in heaven or on earth, etc. This commandment ... holds also for our presentation of the moral law, and for the predisposition within us for morality" (1790:135). Kafka has no theory of the sublime, only its experience, which in *Das Schloß* is largely but not entirely blocked by the castle and its obfuscatory bureaucracy. The traces of this momentary experience in his fiction and aphorisms, occasionally figured conceptually (as in his notion of the indestructible within man), offer themselves as an Archimedean point from which to view *Das Schloß*.

Let us look first at light imagery, which is paradigmatic for the sublime. The defining passage in this instance occurs not in *Das Schloß* but in *Der Proceß*. In the parable of the man from the country, who waits a lifetime at the open door of the law yet never musters the courage to enter, light is the crucial image. Just before he dies, at a time when his eyesight is failing (the waning of the bodily senses points toward a waxing of the spiritual one), a radiance (*Glanz*) breaks forth inextinguishably (*unverlöschlich*) through the door of the law. It is the sublime epiphany of the unnameable, indestructible happiness that awaited the man. If we are justified in taking the aphorisms as a guide to the parable, then the fact that the light is inextinguishable is of central importance, pointing toward the undiscovered radiance that was simultaneously within the man (a finite being) but also transcends him as a common property, "the law" of human nature. While the man's life can be extinguished, the light in us all cannot.

As various critics have noted, K. bears some resemblance to the man from the country. We should not bear down on the analogy, however, because K. tries with all his ingenuity to penetrate the castle, whereas the man sits by the open door, not daring to enter. The man from the country is more like Amalia's father. After his daughter's insolent rebellion, he stations himself on the road to the castle begging for absolution for his family, never daring to think that they do not need any, even though castle officials repeatedly tell him they know of no offense. Nevertheless, there is some structural similarity between K.'s castle and "the law" of the man in the parable. The castle and the law function to obstruct passage. The sublime moment comes when the obstruction is momentarily pierced by the light.

In *Das Schloß* the light imagery is just as crucial but more ambiguously subtle. As K. stands eyeing the castle, its weird aspects come into view:

> Der Turm hier oben—es war der einzige sichtbare—, der Turm eines Wohnhauses wie sich jetzt zeigte, vielleicht des Hauptschlosses, war ein einförmiger Rundbau, zum Teil gnädig von Epheu verdeckt, mit kleinen Fenstern, die jetzt in der Sonne aufstrahlten— etwas Irrsinniges hatte das—und einem söllerartigen Abschluß, dessen Mauerzinnen unsicher, unregelmäßig, brüchig wie von ängstlicher oder nachlässiger Kinderhand gezeichnet sich in den blauen Himmel zackten. Es war wie wenn irgendein trübseliger Hausbewohner, der gerechter Weise im entlegensten Zimmer des Hauses sich hätte eingesperrt halten sollen, das Dach durchbrochen und sich erhoben hätte, um sich der Welt zu zeigen.

> [The tower up above—it was the only one visible—turned out now to be residential, perhaps the living quarters of the main castle. It was uniformly round, in part mercifully concealed by ivy and with small windows that now glinted in the sun—this had something insane about it—and was surmounted by a garret-like top whose crenelated wall, unsure, irregular, fragile as if drawn by the fearful or careless hand of a child, jutted into the blue sky. It was as if some wretched occupant, who justifiably ought to have kept himself locked up in the most remote room of the house, had broken through the roof and risen up to show himself to the world.][2]

The image of those little sunstruck windows flashing in the daylight, to which Kafka calls our special attention by insisting that there is something insane about their glint, is a more threatening transformation of the radiance. This time the passage leaves the reader with conflicted feelings, fully in the tradition of the sublime, inspiring both awe and terror.

The bizarre and striking imagery that continues the passage underscores the feeling of some fearful taboo that is near to being transgressed by K.'s gaze. In any event the passage discloses to the reader that the literal horizon of the understanding is outstripped by the metaphoric vision. The tiny windows, apertures through which some knowledge of the other side may pass, catch the light of the sun. The flashing prevents K. from seeing through them, presumably, but also signals that something violent, uncanny, possibly demonic is afoot. The image of the repressed giant bursting through the roof gives body to affect. In bursting forth through the rooftops into the deep vault of blue sky, Kafka's image enacts the power of the sublime moment to crash through the material obstacle into a kind of liberation that is not otherwise accessible to representation.

The ambiguous force that the giant represents is indestructible and irrepressible, a permanent feature of human nature that is simultaneously in K. and in every other individual in the village. The Kafkan sublime is within and beyond the individual, both at the same time. It rises up in both K. and Frieda when they lose themselves in the spontaneity of erotic bliss on the tavern floor. When I cited this passage in the section on the feminist reception of *Das Schloß*, it revealed Kafka to be a man of his era, at least with respect to the construction of feminine sexuality. The fuller view of sexuality, however, is linked to the experience of the sublime as being suddenly freed of time and space. Frieda lies next to K., as if rendered powerless by love, in a state of ecstasy and K. too gives himself over to the voluptuous pleasure that is, emphatically, shared with Frieda:

> Dort vergiengen Stunden, Stunden gemeinsamen Atems, gemeinsamen Herzschlags, Stunden, in denen K. immerfort das Gefühl hatte, er verirre sich oder er sei soweit in der Fremde, wie vor ihm noch kein Mensch, eine Fremde, in der selbst die Luft keinen Bestandteil der Heimatluft habe, in der man vor Fremdheit ersticken müsse und in deren unsinnigen Verlockungen man doch nichts tun könne als weiter gehn, weiter sich verirren. (*S* 68–69)

> [Hours passed there, hours of shared breath, shared heartbeat, hours in which K. continuously had the feeling he was losing himself or had strayed farther into foreign parts than anyone before him, into a foreign world in which even the air was nothing like the air at home, in which one might suffocate on the foreignness and within whose mad enticements one could do nothing but continue on, continue to lose oneself.]

As it happens, one of the Zürau aphorisms conceptually glosses the relation of erotic pleasure to spirituality. "Die sinnliche Liebe täuscht über die himmlische hinweg, allein könnte sie es nicht, aber da sie das Element der himmlischen Liebe unbewußt in sich hat, kann sie es" (NS2:130, §79): Sensual love deceives us of heavenly love; but it could not do so alone. Because it unknowingly contains heavenly love within it, the deception is possible.

Erotic experience is one of the moments in which a rift opens up in the material world, a sudden and sublime dislocation in the merely material that introduces K. into a more rarified atmosphere of human being. The superiority of the fictional passage over the aphoristic one should be plain. The metaphorics of the novel are more gripping, more truly in the spirit of Kafka's powerful imagination than the conventional, imaginatively weak metaphors of heavenly and sensual love.

When the sublime releases him from its grip, K. regains his calculating self-possession. Passionate experience cannot last, of course, but the problem is not that it does not last but that it fails to leave its mark on his imagination or moral life. K. resists the experience entirely, refusing to allow it to affect his conscious thought and deeds. He thinks not of Frieda but only that his "lapse" must have harmed his plans to master the castle. So he retreats into the rational, instrumental self and begins to treat Frieda as if he possessed her as he might possess a tool. She is now a pawn in what he thinks is his duel with Klamm.

But Klamm is K.'s double: uncanny, grotesque, and comic all at the same time. He represents the reified, alienated image of K.'s own sorry spirit. That is why K. shares the initial "K" with him, makes love to his woman, sits in his coach, drinks his cognac, and thinks about him all the time. He is to Klamm as Jekyll is to Hyde. But Klamm is also everyone's double. And if Klamm always looks different, depending on time and place and who the observer is, it is because the inner life is temporal, unfixed, permanently unreconciled.

From the perspective of the sublime, then, K. is mistaken about everything. Contrary to his fears, the surrender to human spontaneity was not a moment of contemptible weakness but a true victory over Klamm, both for him and for Frieda. They defy his deadening authority. The stayed bureaucrat embodies the anti-instinctive impulse toward planning, ordering, and rational exploitation. For K. it is as if Frieda were a natural resource. But the ecology here, as K. does not realize, is spiritual, not material. However briefly, Frieda liberated something in K. that needed to be set free. The lordly gentleman Klamm personifies a bureaucratization of the soul. He is the antithesis of spontaneity and submission of self to other. K.'s postcoital recovery of his usual scheming self, the self that exploits Frieda's honest affection for him, signals Klamm's victory over K., the strangulation of love freely offered and given (air and breathing are metaphors linked to life itself). Still, the experience has opened up a sudden crack in the unbroken surface of K.'s prosaic reality, giving him a perspective on his own soul that he, though not the reader, chooses to reject.[3]

There are other such moments in which the sublime tears a hole in the empirical to intimate what lies beyond. One occurs near the end of the first chapter, during K.'s failed attempt to ride up to the castle in Gerstäcker's little pony-drawn sled:

> Das Schloß dort oben, merkwürdig dunkel schon, das K. heute noch zu erreichen gehofft hatte, entfernte sich wieder. Als sollte ihm noch zu vorläufigem Abschied ein Zeichen gegeben werden, erklang dort ein Glockenton, fröhlich beschwingt, eine Glocke, die wenigstens einen Augenblick lang das Herz erbeben ließ, so als drohe ihm—denn auch schmerzlich war der Klang—die Erfüllung dessen, wonach er sich unsicher sehnte. (*S* 29)

> [The castle above, which was already strangely dark and which K. had hoped to reach today, withdrew again. As if a sign of temporary leave-taking were being given to him, a bell pealed, merry and bright, a bell that at least for a moment made his heart tremble as if he were being threatened—for the sound was also painful—with the fulfillment of that for which he uncertainly longed.]

What "fulfillment" can this be? The "vague longing" strongly recalls Bergel-Gronemann's explanation of Jewish messianism. The object of longing must remain unnamed because it obeys the prohibition against images of the messianic, what Kafka would more likely call the pure, the true, the indestructible.

The bell passage offers a fine and characteristic example of the operation of Kafkan sublimity. The protagonist is suddenly taken by surprise, momentarily torn out of his prosaic world. Terror, pain, merriment, and longing intermingle, temporally encapsulated in an epiphanic experience. And the narrator tactfully declines to name the hidden and forbidden object of desire ("unsicher" because its object is an unstable kenesis beyond fixed naming or unmediated apprehension). The sound of the bell does not define the unnamed but merely points to its unsuspected proximity. The experience does not last. The sublime call gives way to an ordinary tinkling of ordinary bells.

Immediately after the bell scene, K. meets the uncanny twins, his "helpers" Artur and Jeremias. Significantly, the otherwise mirthless K. laughs when he first sees them. Jeremias later points out to K. that it was their assignment to cheer him up; Galater dispatched them expressly for that purpose (*S* 367). The assistants, funny and creepy at the same time, are the living return of the repressed, and K. treats them accordingly. He beats them cruelly, ultimately driving them away. The twins doubly embody K.'s repressed capacity for mirth, play, and sensual pleasure. That is why they are present during K.'s lovemaking with Frieda and not, as Kundera supposes, because K. is under surveillance by the state. In this capacity they too are signs of Kafka's anthropological absolute, odd creatures who come from the castle but belong also to K. The absolute is individual and common to all, simultaneously within and without, immanent and transcendent.

My final example of the Kafkan sublime combines elements of all the others: light, the body, silence. When K. goes to visit Olga, he meets Amalia and has a conversation with her. The frosty Amalia is less than forthcoming, but it turns out that speech is not her most revealing mode:

> Amalia lächelte und dieses Lächeln, trotzdem es traurig war, erhellte das düster zusammengezogene Gesicht, machte die Stummheit sprechend, machte die Fremdheit vertraut, war die Preisgabe eines Geheimnisses, die Preisgabe eines bisher behüteten Besitzes, der zwar wieder zurückgenommen werden konnte, aber niemals mehr ganz. (*S* 265)

> [Amalia smiled and this smile, even though it was sad, illuminated her grimly drawn face, made her silence speak, made the foreignness familiar, was the giving away of a secret, the giving away of a possession that up to now had been carefully guarded and could be taken back again, but could never again be taken back completely.]

This passage gives the scale of the Kafkan sublime. It has nothing of the cataclysmic, monumental scale associated with Romanticism and its preoccupation with natural disaster and revolution. Kafkan sublimity has to do with human identity, a bond that is individual and common. Amalia's smile breaks through the hard shell of ice that surrounds her, and it gives off a light that clarifies her face and establishes a humane contact with K. that exceeds words. It does not last. She retracts the smile, to be sure, but the narrator is at pains to point out that once made, the contact cannot be broken entirely. As with the ivy-covered castle tower, some secret has been betrayed, and something hidden has now seen the light of day.

Amalia's smile requires no elaborate exegesis. Its human meaning is straightforward. The light of her smile is the sublime of human intimacy. What requires explanation is its place in the larger setting of the novel. It reiterates Kafka's non-mimetic strategy of intimating rather that describing the object of his narrative effort. That object is the transcendent, spiritual realm that lies beyond words and individuality. But it is not the divine, completely other realm of religion. It is the human contact that Kafka had so much trouble establishing during his lifetime, but that he was keenly aware of. It has a utopian, even messianic dimension that dictates Kafka's elaborately meta-phorical indirection in dealing with it in the language of fiction.

Kafka's fiction as a whole and the aphorisms in particular demonstrate unmistakably that the transcendent remains permanently out of reach. The exception to this rule, as I have been arguing, are the few rifts opened up by the scattering of sublime moments throughout the text. They do not offer themselves as a highroad to transcendence but serve only as an assurance that something is there in the nontime and nonspace of the human soul, something worth aspiring to even if it remains out of reach. K.'s unnamed ambition, his motive for wanting to penetrate the castle, is utopian. There is no method and no theory and no eschatology associated with it. Its literary corollary is mean-ing, which remains always present, always ahead, and always other.

K. aims for the good life but goes about achieving it in ways that make it even more distant. His exploitation of Frieda and his abuse of his assistants, which he supposes will further his interests, only alienate him more deeply from what he most ardently desires. He is like one of the crows from a Kafka aphorism who want to smash the heavens.

Die Krähen behaupten, eine einzige Krähe könnte den Himmel zerstören. Das ist zweifellos, beweist aber nichts gegen den Himmel, denn Himmel bedeutet eben: Unmöglichkeit von Krähen.

[The crows claim that a single crow can destroy the heavens. That is beyond doubt, but it proves nothing against heaven, for heaven simply means: impossibility of crows.]

Utopia means the impossibility of K. His repressed, self-absorbed, abusive nature is the castle that prevents him from achieving his own aim. But seen rightly, Kafka's pessimism is not so dark as it has traditionally been perceived. It has an uncompromising moral edge that has seldom come into view.

Ethics and Irony
What are the cultural politics of Kafkan sublimity? Is Kafka's anthropology the sign of a political culpability, a failure of liberal, democratic instincts? I do not think that Kafka's literary exploration of the soul compromises him ethically any more than Robert Musil's similar explorations do him (in *Vereinigungen* and the latter parts of *Der Mann ohne Eigenschaften*), or than William James's scientific exploration of mysticism compromises James.

Kafka does not offer his anthropological absolute as an article of politi-cal commitment, and it is not likely to be applied as one, not even in the clamorous political subculture of contemporary literary theory and criticism. Harold Bloom may be right when he claims that Kafka has had a lasting impact on the shape of modern Judaism, or at least among intellectuals, but such influence is not charged with a politically measurable, ideological valence. This is true at least partly because Western political culture remains currently stable. It was otherwise in Kafka's time.

In the Weimar era, mysticism and reaction were closely allied, especially in Germany. Ernst Jünger's thought, also an anthropology of sorts, carries with it a heroic, more or less Nietzschean ethic with plainly political implications. Kafka's does not. Nor does Kafka in any way suggest or imply that mysticism is a more profound alternative to public thought and action than politics. He is distant from the quasi-religious cult of art associated with Stefan George and his acolytes, and he is distant from the apolitical aesthetic snobbery of the early Thomas Mann. But he is also distant from Brecht's exaggerated insistence on a direct, didactic link between art and politics. Kafka's fiction is the vehicle of autonomously imaginative exploration. As Adorno has shown, Kafka is not easily co-opted by any ideological agenda, which would include, we might add, even the cultural Zionism that was closest to his indecisive heart.

Moreover, Kafka did not claim for himself or his writing a revolutionary social role. Art's place in politics is modest, which means that Lionel Trilling was right when he fretted that Kafka was probably indifferent to the kind of liberalism that undergirds the cultures in which his books are read, admired, and discussed. It was not the world in which he lived. In addition, he never said anything about creating a new kind of human being or a new kind of society. He was interested in exploring the spiritual depths of the versions that he knew, trying to understand them better. There is no point in his fiction at which his mystical anthropology threatens to reverse dialectically into a political expression. His fiction points neither toward activism of commitment nor toward the quietism that passively awaits the coming of the Messiah. Our activities in public life are likely to remain unaffected by Kafka, even though his influence on our collective imagination has been substantial.

If anything, Kafka's cultural politics resemble Freud's. Just as Lionel Trilling feared, neither of them shared our confidence in the liberalism upon which Western democracies are based. They were living and writing at a time and in a place in which liberal culture, the cornerstone of Jewish emancipation in the Habsburg lands, lay in ruins. Kafka's turn to a mystical anthropology probably shares its deepest motive with Freud's turn to psychoanalysis. The latter's *Interpretation of Dreams* (1900) carries with it an epigraph that applies to Kafka as well: "If I cannot shake the higher powers, I will stir up the depths." Together, Freud and Kafka have turned out to be our century's preeminent stirrers of the depths.

The retreat from politics in favor of art and psychology was, as Carl Schorske has shown (1980), characteristic for the dissolution of the Habsburg era. Kafka's unwillingness to put his faith in a new politics (or an old religion) is no more remarkable than Freud's parallel impulses. Both of them shunned the treacheries, uncertainties, and compromises of political engagement for what, from their perspective at least, seemed realms of spirit that were ahistorical, noncontingent. Even if they could not transform the status quo, they at least converted their generation's experience into powerful myths, visions of the world that, if not exactly reassuring, could be lived with: one poetic, the other scientific (more or less), both great narrative achievements.

Both Kafka and Freud were pessimists. They did not expect much in the way of improvement, least of all in human nature. But the myths they offered were and remain a consolation simply by transforming shared experience into objective aesthetic form. In thus transforming shared experience they lift it into a realm that makes it manageable by making it discussable, putting it on a human scale. If Gregor Samsa in particular has achieved the status of cultural icon—and still does not need the artificial life-support system of university teaching to survive in the public imagination—it must be because practically everyone can at some time identify with his experience. One gets the irrepressible feeling that Kafka has somehow hit the nail right on the head.

But what about the cultural politics of *Das Schloß* now, in a post–Cold War age that is politically stable yet extraordinarily conscious of ideological tensions within the overarching consensus? The features that define the moral identity of *Das Schloß* and Kafka in general when interrogated from the perspective of his sociopolitical meaning are the novel's irony and skeptical detachment from both culture and politics. Perhaps the irony is clearest in *Josefine, die Sängerin*, a communitarian reverie in which the artist's gift and social role are respected but in which her claim to exemption from average mouse responsibilities (for example, political responsibility) are treated with skepticism. Politically the mouse-folk is on its own, without direction from a charismatic figure. Each mouse must contribute. The artist is not its Führerin and is not exempt from responsibility.

As I noted earlier, there is no spiritual leader in *Das Schloß*, no priest, pastor, or rabbi. Another stock figure conspicuous in its absence from the novel is the artist. There is no figure in the village comparable to Titorelli of *Der Proceß*. But even if there were (and some critics take the secretary Momus as a diminished writer of sorts), it would make no difference. Art too tends to obey the law of reification. Titorelli's pictures are all the same: simple, dreary, lifeless landscapes. As Titorelli points out to Josef K., everything belongs to the court; there can be no escape from its law, least of all in what passes for art within its sphere of influence.

Likewise, in K.'s world everybody and everything must obey the law of the castle. Momus simply records what he hears. No imagination is involved. The castle's "law" is its all-consuming bureaucratic order, a deadening calcification of the human spirit. Reification, doctrine, dogma, conformism—all name the law that ideology obeys. It is worth remembering that Kafka was deeply alienated by the biblical Abraham, whose dogmatic faith was such that he was ready to kill his son for God the way a waiter might fill a customer's order. Kafka may not have had a politics, but his ethical sensibilities, his response to doctrine and dogmatic authority, is compatible with liberal habits of mind. With a supremely deadpan gaze, Kafka satirizes conformism in *Das Schloß*, which is to say that he distances himself and his reader from it by depicting it at its worst. To take that image as Kafka's view of reality too seriously, or seriously in the wrong way, as if it were social realism without the piercing comic irony that gives it its penetrating insight, underestimates the power and nature of his imagination. He offers *Das Schloß* as an ironic perspective on the world, not as its mimetic likeness.

In contemporary political life—that is, in the transactions that occur daily in our Western, middle-class, liberal culture—the "message" of *Das Schloß*, if it can be said to have anything as crude as a message at all, might sound something like this: the good life remains at all times both within us and ahead of us; it cannot be hurried or forced into submission but must be courted gradually, and above all with attention to the anthropological absolute that, when allowed to break through the bureaucratic encrustation that bears down on the human spirit like snow on cottage roofs, will join us wholesomely to others.

Admittedly, to extract a flat-footed moral like this from a Kafka novel is grotesquely reductive, both diminishing the text and implicitly attempting to co-opt the experience of the prospective reader by steering her or his response. But neither is the simplification completely wrong-headed. It is in error simply because it names what is incommensurable with language and therefore falsifies everything that Kafka intimated, with infinite tact and imaginative resource, without ever resorting to fixed concepts and static names.

Notes

1. I am skeptical about Robertson's view that K. is best understood as a messiah figure, false or not, and that *Das Schloß* is a critique of messianism. I will be arguing that Jewish messianism and the Jewish tradition of not depicting God and Paradise are decisive for the novel and that both are tied to Kafka's utopian belief in a last, indestructible core of pure humanity that inheres in and transcends each individual.

The common core is an anthropological universal that, for Kafka at least, accounts for the possibility (but not the achieved actuality, for it is at all times only emergent, never realized) of human community. This everlasting state of incompletion, modeled on the Jewish messianic ideal, is the foundation of Kafka's humane pessimism. Indeed, Kafka's vision of human nature is as pessimistic as the one Freud develops in *Civilization and its Discontents*, but on different grounds. Freud sees reason and instinct locked in perpetual, irreconcilable conflict. It is reason's task to hold rapacious instinct in check so as to make civilized life possible. At first glance Kafka's dualism (the spiritual versus the sensory world) seems parallel. But Kafka's opposition is actually quite different from Freud's. Like Freud, Kafka sees human nature in a state of irreconcilable conflict. But Freud offers instinct as the core of human nature, the source of evil that must be overcome by the exercise of reason. Kafka more optimistically offers a core of indestructible goodness as the basis of human nature. It is a state of spiritual innocence from which we have fallen yet which still exists in us, a condition that remains permanently desired though permanently out of reach. Reason and the senses want to recover this lost state of bliss but cannot because, belonging to this world, they are intrinsically flawed. Reason degenerates inevitably into self-serving connivance, and the senses give themselves over to self-indulgence. K. embodies both failures.

2. The Willa and Edwin Muir translation of this passage mutes the weird ambiguity that is expressed in Kafka's German, which I have tried to render in my version. The Muirs' ivy "graciously mantles" the tower, whereas Kafka's point is that something has mercifully been hidden from view. There are other such inadequacies in the Muir translation, in the same passage and throughout the novel. It is unfortunate that no new translation of *Das Schloß* has appeared in English. The critical edition of the manuscript has been in print in German since 1952. See *The Castle*, trans. Willa and Edwin Muir (New York: Knopf, 1992), 10.

3. K.'s refusal to see and accept what is most obvious is a trait shared with his predecessor Josef K. The trick of reading both novels involves grasping what the protagonist fails to grasp, understanding what Kafka is showing rather than what he is saying. In passing, we should also note that the sublime undergirds *Der Proceß* as well. Kafka's touch with it is ironic in a comic sense, beginning with the failure of his breakfast to appear in the novel's second line. As the text puts it (with sublime understatement): "Die Köchin der Frau Grubach, seiner Zimmervermieterin, die ihm jeden Tag gegen acht Uhr früh das Frühstück brachte, kam diesmal nicht. Das war noch niemals geschehn." It is the first shocking rift of many to open up in Josef K.'s thoroughly and inhumanly bureaucratized existence. Kafka's observance of the Bilderverbot in *Der Proceß* is as rigorous as in *Das Schloß*. Josef K.'s trial is best understood as a man's reluctant confrontation with his own conscience; and the conscience, spiritual site of the knowledge of good and evil, transcends representation (Dowden 1986).

ROBERT ALTER

Franz Kafka: Wrenching Scripture

At first thought, it would seem that Kafka's relation to the Bible is strictly analogous to his relation to Judaism: a concern that urgently engaged him in his private writings and that he rigorously excluded from his fiction. The analogy, however, does not entirely hold, for the first of his three novels, as I shall try to show, invokes an elaborate network of conflated allusions to Genesis and Exodus, which are thematically imperative, for all their transmogrification in a fantasized American setting. This use of biblical materials in a modern setting, at once playful and thematically serious, reflects both the afterlife of authority and the altered standing of the Bible in modernist writing.

Kafka's effort to make something for his inner life of Jewish tradition was first catalyzed, as is well known, by the visit to Prague of a Yiddish theatrical group in 1911 (just a few months after he began work on his American novel). It is thus a preoccupation of the last dozen years of his brief life. These are also, of course, the years when he produced his most compelling fiction. During this period, he began to read about Jewish history, Yiddish literature, Hasidism, and related topics in German, and from 1917 onward he devoted some of his already failing energies to learning Hebrew. He would achieve sufficient knowledge of the language to work his way arduously, with the help of a dictionary, through a recent Hebrew novel by Y. H. Brenner, to read

From *New England Review: Middlebury Series* 21, no. 3 (Summer 2000): 7–19. © 2000 by *New England Review: Middlebury Series*.

passages in the Hebrew Bible, and to look into Rashi's commentary on the Pentateuch. Toward the end, he made some attempt to study the Talmud as well. In any event, the component of Jewish tradition that would have been most directly accessible to his intense scrutiny was its founding text, the Bible, chiefly read by him, of course, in Luther's translation.

There is something almost uncanny about Kafka as a reader of the Bible. Midrash, Talmud, and Kabbalah were certainly not part of his formative cultural experience, and even his late acquaintance with them was rather marginal. Yet the way he read the Bible reflected a spiritual kinship with these classical vehicles of Jewish exegesis. Such kinship, which may look like a kind of spontaneous intellectual atavism, defies any simple causal explanation. My guess is that it has a good deal to do with Kafka's habitual concentration on the idea of revelation, and on the notion of the Law that in the Jewish view is the principal consequence of revelation for human praxis. That is to say, if you begin with the working assumption that this particular text, which as a canonical text is compact, enigmatic, and charged with a sense of authority, may be divinely revealed, you then proceed to exert terrific interpretive pressure on the text in order to unlock the truth, or multiple truths, it holds for you. Stating the case in this way, I do not presume to know very much about Kafka's actual beliefs. The evidence suggests that he was prone to radical skepticism, but it is equally clear that he found the hypothesis of Scripture as revealed truth alluring, and that he generally adopted that hypothesis in his practice as a reader of the Bible. One might think of it as a continuing thought experiment which Kafka undertook, a thought experiment which both afforded an expression to his theological searching and nourished his imaginative work as a writer of fiction.

Kafka is famously a disruptive modernist in regard to both his handling of literary form and his sense of the world, and so it is hardly surprising that his treatment of Scripture should be paradoxical—at once traditional and iconoclastic. The traditionalism is manifested in the pitch of spiritual tension and acuteness with which he scrutinizes the canonical text, in the midrashic adroitness with which he fleshes out the meanings of the text, endows its relevance to him with narrative palpability. The iconoclasm is reflected in his propensity to spin the text around one hundred and eighty degrees, to wrest from it ideas and values antithetical to its own ostensible intentions, and certainly antithetical to the interpretive consensus of tradition. If Kafka is a midrashic reader of Scripture, what he often proposes is a heretical midrash. It is this trait that led Gershom Scholem, in the last of his "Ten Ahistorical Theses on the Kabbalah," to compare Kafka's reflections on the Garden of Eden with those of an eighteenth-century radical antinomian, a follower of

Jacob Frank, and to conclude that "Kafka gave expression to the borderline between religion and nihilism, and so his writings possess . . . in the eyes of certain readers of our era [Scholem is clearly thinking of himself and kindred spirits], something of the rigorous light of canonicity."[1]

Before considering in detail the boldness and verve with which Kafka integrated biblical motifs into his American novel, let us look at the sort of radical midrash he constructed on one biblical text. It was Genesis, the book of origins, that engaged him more than any other in the biblical canon, and he was especially drawn to three topics: the first paradise, Abraham the first father, and the Tower of Babel. On the Tower of Babel he wrote four different midrashic reflections. There were, I think, two different features of that very brief and resonant story which spoke to his imagination. One was the human aspiration it recorded to reach up to the realm of the divine, to transgress eternally fixed boundaries: "Come, let us build us a city and a tower with its top in the heavens," the builders of Babel proclaim. The other aspect of the Tower of Babel that may have addressed a deep concern in Kafka, though he gave it no explicit expression in his readings, was its account of the origins of linguistic division. The biblical notion of the multiplicity of languages as a curse, a loss of primordial unity, surely would have haunted him, troubled as he sometimes professed to be (whatever the actual facts of the matter) that German was not really his language, a language he perfected in his own idiosyncratic way in predominantly Czech Prague, while often thinking about Yiddish antecedents and then struggling to acquire Hebrew.

Kafka's most quizzical reflection on the Tower, actuated by the same impulse to spiritual paradox that informs his musings on the Garden of Eden, is this brief sentence: "If it had been possible to build the Tower of Babel without ascending it, the work would have been permitted."[2] This paradox takes for granted, as a traditional reading would, the immutable authority of the biblical tale: its canonicity is not called into question. But it also reads the biblical text against the grain, teasing out of it an idea that contradicts the explicit condemnation in Genesis of the effort of the builders as an act of overweening presumption. This reader of the Bible sees the vision of a human edifice touching the heavens as a compelling aspiration, man in a perhaps Nietzschean fashion reaching beyond his own limits, striving to become more than himself. If the idea of human self-transcendence could have been nurtured without the transgressive act of its implementation, the Tower would have been no sin. Thus the imperative force of Scripture is left in place while the interpreter's twist of perspective on the biblical tale opens up a horizon of values that the biblical writer is not likely to have envisaged.

A second brief variation on the Tower story, entirely in dialogue, vividly etches that responsiveness to "the comic aspects of Jewish theology" which

Walter Benjamin, in a late letter to Scholem, identified as one of Kafka's defining features[3]: "What are you building?" an anonymous questioner calls out. To which the person interrogated responds: "I want to dig a passage. Some progress must be made. My station up there is too high. We are digging the pit of Babel" (p. 35, translation modified). This droll exchange is, of course, a precise rotation of the biblical story from up to down, but it also accords a certain respect to the biblical text, seeking, as the classical midrash does, to bridge the yawning gap between the interpreter and the text. The heroic, or presumptuous, stretch for transcendence of the builders of the Tower, admired in the previously cited text, is simply beyond the imaginative reach of this post-heroic personage, who instead, like the mole of Kafka's story, burrows into a hole in the ground (the term translated as "pit," *Schacht*, could also mean "mine shaft" in German). The idea, it should be stressed, of a mine shaft of Babel is funny exactly in Benjamin's theological sense, rather than silly. The story in Genesis 11 reflects the powerful yearning of the human creature to achieve impossibly great things. Kafka's reversal of the canonical tale sustains the perception of that yearning, assumes it as an essential trait of man, yet tries to imagine how the age-old impulse would play out in a fallen reality, where man is scared of the heights, content to push forward his concerted projects in the shelter of the underground, with transcendence turned into a negative or perhaps a parody of the original. The textual image of the canonical is refracted in a fun-house mirror, yet it continues to challenge the life of the interpreter.

Of Kafka's two somewhat longer reflections on the Tower, the one that comes closer to a midrashic model of reading Scripture is the piece that Kafka English editors have entitled *The City Coat of Arms* (*Parables and Paradoxes*, pp. 37, 39). The opening lines share with the Midrash an impulse to flesh out the spare biblical tale and to make it intelligible in more or less contemporary terms:

> At first all the arrangements for building the Tower of Babel were
> characterized by fairly good order; indeed the order was perhaps
> too perfect, too much thought was taken for guides, interpreters,
> accommodation for the workmen, and roads of communication, as
> if there were centuries before one to do the work in.

A single word slipped into this contemporary realization of Genesis 11 drastically shifts the grounds of the canonical story—*Dolmetscher*, "interpreters," that is, translators. The division of languages is no longer a consequence of human presumption, a divinely inflicted punishment, but a given of the human condition, which itself will be adduced to explain the failure of the

Tower. First, the building does not go forward because of collective procras-
tination: through the constant progress—*Fortschritt*, the same goal to which
the digger of the Pit of Babel is committed—of technology, in a century or
two the work will be completed far more swiftly and more soundly, so why
build the Tower now? "Such thoughts," the narrator observes, "paralyzed
people's powers, and so they troubled less about the tower than the construction of a city for the workmen." The building of the city, exploiting the very
advances in technology on which the builders had banked, becomes a source
of conflict, as each ethnic or national group (*Landsmannschaft*), fighting for
the best quarters, violently clashes with the others.

In one crucial respect, this reading radically reverses Genesis. Biblical
"after" turns into Kafkan "before"—divisiveness is not the consequence of the
aborted attempt to build the Tower but the very cause of its abortion, and a
naturalistic explanation replaces the supernatural one in which God's intervention (divine descent symmetrically answering human ascent) confounds
the builders. But for all this shifting of grounds, Kafka's reading retains a
firm grip on the thematic core of the biblical story. "The essential thing in
the whole undertaking is the idea of building a Tower that will reach the
heaven" (translation modified). Kafka steadily sees that the Babel story is an
urgent parable of the allure for the human spirit of overreaching aspiration:
"The idea, once seized in its magnitude, can never vanish again; so long as
there are men, there will also be the powerful desire to complete the building"
(translation modified). This ringing declaration is qualified by a dialectical
countermove toward the end of the parable: the would-be builders, trapped
in the internecine strife of the city, begin to think that the building of a
tower to the heavens is actually pointless. Here at its conclusion, Kafka's reading embraces a second urgent theme of the original biblical story—its anti-
urbanism. The ancient Hebrew writer, from his perspective in a little nation
of pastoralists and agriculturalists, viewed the urban concentration of power,
technology, and population of the great surrounding empires as an expression
of humankind's morally dangerous grandiosity. Kafka, writing in an urban
and technological environment three millennia removed from the setting of
Genesis 11, shares this fundamental perception of the biblical text. Indeed,
he amplifies its resonance by concluding his reflection on an apocalyptic note:
the intolerable conflicts of urban existence engender a longing for release
through destruction, "for a prophesied day when the city would be destroyed
by five successive blows from a gigantic fist." (The image of the menacing
clenched fist, no doubt psychologically derived from the looming power of
the paternal body, is quintessential Kafka.) In this fashion the biblical Babel,
upon which modern Prague or any counterpart elsewhere in Europe has been
superimposed, also becomes a medieval city that "has a closed fist on its coat

of arms." The paradoxical effect is that the authority of the canonical text, its universal relevance, is confirmed even as it is drastically revised.

There is no single, consistent relation to Scripture in Kafka but rather a shifting variety of takes on the biblical text, the one constant being the fact that the Bible grips his imagination, however he twists and turns it. In "The Great Wall and the Tower of Babel" (*Parables and Paradoxes*, pp. 25, 27), he sets the biblical tale in a broad web of scholarly conjecture that sounds more like an anticipation of Borges than a reminiscence of the Midrash. Here, in contrast to the collective voice of the Midrash, we have a first-person narrator—or rather, conjecturor ("I say this because in the early days of building a scholar wrote a book in which he drew the comparison [between the Tower and other construction projects] in the most exhaustive way."). The canonical story retains a certain imperative power but that power is now highly mediated: the story is a text in a vast library, the point of departure in a universe of exegesis (which is the Kafka universe par excellence), where inferences are drawn, documents and other proofs cited, arguments and counter-arguments proposed. In this universe, one of the scholars cited makes the daring proposal "that the Great Wall alone would provide for the first time in the history of mankind a secure foundation for a new Tower of Babel." The first-person conjecturor, however, is bothered by the fact that the Great Wall of China is very far from forming a complete circle and so could scarcely serve as the foundation for a tower. This perception leads him to the conclusion that the joining of the two monumental building enterprises must be meant only in "a spiritual sense" and that no actual tower need be built. At the end, he passes from the wild multiplicity of scholarly projects to the violent divisiveness of the human spirit that subverts all grandiose undertakings: "Human nature, essentially changeable, unstable as dust, can endure no restraint; if it binds itself it soon begins to tear madly at its bonds, until it rends everything asunder to all points of the compass, the wall, the bonds and its very self" (translation modified). Again, Babel turns into apocalypse.

This somber view of human nature picks up an emphasis from Genesis, implicit in the Tower story and explicit in the story of the Flood when God declares, "the devisings of the human heart are evil from youth." The odd turn that Kafka gives to the canonical tale, what may chiefly make it seem an anticipation of Borges, is the conflation of the Tower of Babel in the Mesopotamian Valley of Shinar with the Great Wall of China. Even as Kafka's lavishing of exegetical speculation confirms the authority of the biblical text—the measure of the canonical is that the interpreter assumes truth must be derived from the text through the labor of interpretation—biblical canonicity is also quietly compromised because its claim to be the exclusive source of truth is tacitly set aside. A canon in the strict sense is what Moshe Halbertal calls a "sealed text"[4]: "Turn it and turn it," as Ben Bag-Bag says in the Mishnaic Teachings of the Fathers, "for everything is in it." The universalism of Kafka's perspective, on the other hand, in which the Great Wall and the Tower of Babel may be variants of the same idea, or in which one is necessary to make sense of the other, suggests that the biblical text and the biblical history must be open to other texts and other histories, that Scripture is not the ultimate source of truth but one cultural instance among many of the truths of the human predicament. Kafka's interest in Chinese lore, in the Chinese idea of wisdom (compare Walter Benjamin's similar interest), is in one sense strictly coordinate with his interest in the Hebrew Bible. What attracts him is less a definite canon than the phenomenon of canonicity, the allure of the compact, enigmatic tale steeped in tradition that is a constant challenge to exegesis. Indeed, Kafka anticipates or perhaps actually inspires his great admirer Gershom Scholem in seeing endless interpretability rather than absolute truth as the principal criterion of the canonical. Thus, the dynamic of the canonical is retained but its authority is compromised. This double relation to the canonicity of the Bible, at once an imaginative allegiance to its compelling address to the reader and a readiness to open it to unfamiliar horizons, is reflected in Kafka's fantastic fusion of Genesis and Exodus with a contemporary New York and Oklahoma in the novel he provisionally called *The Man Who Disappeared* and that his literary executor Max Brod entitled *Amerika*.

As if to offer a clue to the biblical background of the novel, Kafka makes sure to include among the few items mentioned that are packed in Karl Rossmann's suitcase a pocket edition of the Bible (no doubt, in Luther's translation). The Bible lies at the bottom of the suitcase next to the photograph of Karl's parents that so mesmerizes him. It is thus associated by contiguity with parental authority in the person of the father, as we would expect in Kafka, a menacing, violent authority. Karl turns over the pages of the Bible without actually reading, then fixes his gaze on the image of his father, standing with clenched fist—like the fist in "The City's Coat of Arms"—behind his mother, whose mouth seems to him twisted in pain. The pocket Bible, leafed through as a kind of talisman but left unread, is a token of dramatic irony, for Karl remains oblivious to the contents of the text he holds while the alert reader will have been aware from the first page of the novel that this very text provides much of the thematic definition of Karl's story.[5]

When Karl Rossmann's ship sails into New York harbor in the first paragraph of the novel, a sudden burst of sunlight reveals to him what any new arrival around 1910 would have noticed: the looming figure of the Statue of Liberty. This Statue of Liberty, however, formally announcing at the very beginning that actual America is to be reconfigured as psychologically resonant fantasy, raises on high something other than a torch: "The arm with the sword rose up as if newly stretched aloft, and round the figure blew the free winds"[6] (p. 3, translation modified). The Freudian edge of the unexpected sword cuts an obvious swathe through Karl's story. The three sexually impelled women Karl encounters in the course of the novel all threaten him: Johanna Brummer (her last name means "grumbler"), the hulking servant girl back in Prague, rapes him; young Clara Pollunder uses jujitsu to fling him around like a rag doll; and the corpulent Brunelda crushes him with the overwhelming abundance of her flesh. It is hardly surprising, then, that the first figure of a woman in the novel should be brandishing a phallic sword, neatly assumed by the narrator to be her well-known accoutrement ("the arm with the sword"). But this sword also has a biblical provenance. America offers the possibility of being a new Eden for Karl Rossmann: in one of the novel's two Dickensian intertexts, *Martin Chuzzlewit*, the phony real estate located in swampland is called Eden and at the gates of Eden in Genesis God sets fearsome cherubim and "the flame of the whirling sword to guard the way to the tree of life."

The biblical image at the beginning, in nice accord with subsequent uses of the Bible in the novel, is an aggressive oxymoron: Karl has been banished from his father's house, but the indications of the harsh paternal regime suggest it was no Eden; in turn, his moment of entry into the Eden of the New World invokes a reminiscence of the primordial banishment. (This allusion to the Garden story, together with its unsettling ambiguities, has also been noted by John Hollander, who aptly observes that the sword-wielding statue "implicitly cancels and replaces the figure of a guardian angel assigned to seal up the eastern gate of lost, emptied Eden."[7]) This fusion of contradictory biblical allusions is an essential reflection of Kafka's location in existence—forever a creature in-between[8], wandering in the liminal zone of the Wilderness, equally excluded from the Eden of family origins and from the Promised Land of marriage, Zionism, and spiritual fulfillment. The biblical narrative tells a linear story of banishment from a particular place, eventual wanderings, and entering into another particular place. In Kafka's conflation of biblical places and themes, the linearity is dissolved, and we cannot be sure whether the hero is coming or going.

Karl's ill-fated sojourn in the fabulous New York apartment of his rich and powerful American uncle becomes the stage for still another banishment that harks back to the scriptural one. Uncle Jacob showers kindnesses on Karl, promises him a brilliant future, but also confronts him with seemingly capricious prohibitions. Karl's first temptation is the excitingly intricate American writing-desk with its combinations and permutations of shifting drawers and compartments. These are controlled by a delicate mechanism called a "regulator," which Karl's uncle repeatedly warns him not to touch, lest he put it out of order. "It was not hard to guess that these remarks were merely pretexts, though on the other hand it would have been quite easy to lock the regulator and yet Uncle Jacob refrained from doing so" (p. 42). The analogy with the divine prohibition in Genesis against eating from the tree of knowledge good and evil is piquant because of its very transposition into the distinctively Kafkan realm of modern gadgetry. Karl manages to resist this temptation, but, like the first humans in the Garden, he continues to find himself surrounded by interdictions he scarcely knows of and cannot fathom. When he takes the seemingly innocuous step of accepting a dinner invitation outside New York from his uncle's business associate, Mr. Pollunder, he is given, that very night at midnight, a peremptory letter from Uncle Jacob dismissing him forever from his presence for this act of betrayal. The echo of the first banishment is underscored when Karl then promptly leaves the Pollunder estate, making his way "out of the garden" amidst the barking of angry dogs into an unfamiliar and perhaps unfriendly world (p. 8).

If Uncle Jacob plays the role of God in the Garden story, he is also aligned with his biblical namesake because Jacob is, after all, Joseph's father, and, as we shall see, Karl Rossmann is very much a Joseph figure, not merely in relation to this surrogate father. When Karl first notices on board the ship the man he does not yet realize is his uncle, Jacob "was in civilian clothes and carried a thin bamboo cane which, as both his hands were resting on his hip, also stood out like a sword" (p. 13). The psychoanalytically inclined will immediately connect the swordlike cane with the weapon held on high by the Statue of Liberty, but the cane, which will be mentioned several times more, also has a biblical source: Jacob, recalling his arduous journeyings, tells God, "For with my staff I crossed this Jordan; and now I have become two camps." That trajectory from poverty through adversity to great wealth is shared by Uncle Jacob in the novel, who also participates in an archetype of modern European folklore, *mon oncle d'Amérique*, the rich uncle from America fantasized as the providential force in the life of a struggling nephew in the Old World.

Karl on his part would like to cut a Joseph figure in the new land to which he has been abruptly shipped off by his family. He is sixteen upon his arrival, but later the manageress at the hotel where he is employed will take him for seventeen—exactly Joseph's age when he is sold down into Egypt. He nurtures visions of working his way to the top in the New World, achieving a ringing success, vindicating himself in the eyes of the parents who rejected him. The biblical story of Joseph, one should keep in mind, is the great rags-to-riches story in Scripture, the tale of a brilliant career from abject beginnings that corresponds to a familiar plot in the nineteenth-century novel. In the event, Karl's story will correspond most of all to the moments of humiliation and defeat in the Joseph story. He is subjected to three different versions of Genesis 39, the tale of Joseph and Potiphar's wife. In Genesis, of course, Joseph manages to resist the sexual assault of the older concupiscent woman, leaving his garment in her grasping hand and fleeing naked, to be thrown into prison on the accusation of attempted rape. Kafka's more feeble protagonist is locked in the bedroom by the sex-starved Johanna and helplessly succumbs to her as she "pressed her naked belly against his body, felt with her hand between his legs, so disgustingly that his head and neck started up from the pillows, then thrust her body several times against him" (p. 29). Although it seems to him "as if she were a part of himself," this is by no means the becoming "one flesh" of Genesis 2: he is left with "a terrible neediness" (*Hilfsbedürftigkeit*) and with a sense that almost nothing has really happened to him. There is a reprise of this scene, and of the biblical one, in his nocturnal tussling with Clara: as she tosses him around with great gusto, an undercurrent of sexual invitation is visible in the wave of physical assault, though of course the intimidated Karl will not respond. The previous encounter with a latter-day Lady Potiphar led directly to Karl's disgrace and banishment. That banishment in turn takes him in the New World to a fate of imprisonment, like Joseph in Genesis 39. When he is dismissed from his post as elevator boy at the Hotel Occidental, the head porter actually threatens him with imprisonment. Then, in the claustral apartment of Robinson and Delamarche, squeezed against the railing by the copious flesh of Brunelda, who in her overripe sexuality is the novel's third avatar of Potiphar's wife, "he was literally a prisoner" (p. 254).

Imprisonment as threatened fate and metaphor is a central focus of what I would call the spatial thematics of the novel, which moves along a path of progressive constriction: Karl is constantly getting squeezed, crowded, hemmed in until the final reversal with its liberation into vast spaciousness in The Nature Theatre of Oklahoma. Joseph's Egyptian prison cell in Genesis is conceived here as an adumbration of the early chapters of Exodus, in which all Egypt, "the house of bondage," becomes a prison for the Hebrew people. The boldest paradox in the play with biblical materials in Kafka's novel is that America, alternately the New Eden and the Promised Land, proves to be a modern manifestation of the Egyptian house of bondage.

This correspondence with Exodus is more than one interpreter's fanciful analogy, for Kafka makes a point of giving the town where Karl goes to work the most un-American name Rameses, which is of course one of the two store-cities that the Hebrew slaves were forced to build for Pharaoh. Compulsive, incessant work is in general a topic that preoccupied Kafka. Indeed, it is a theme he attaches to the building of the Tower of Babel. Most prominently in *The Castle*, he offers a series of memorable representations of the frantic whirl of activity, the restless shuffling of dossiers and documents and memoranda, of bureaucratic labor. It is chiefly in *Amerika*, however, that he turns work into a species of enslavement. Therese, Karl's fellow employee at the Hotel Occidental, by way of introducing him to the regimen there, explains that she "wasn't equal to the heavy work. They expect a lot from you here." When she goes on to report how she literally collapsed under the strain, Karl, just having observed an elevator boy asleep on his feet, remarks, "The work here must really be tiring" (p. 140). This is the moment when he goes on to ask the name of the town and is told that it is Rameses. There are no literal pharaonic taskmasters with whips at the Hotel Occidental but we are repeatedly made aware of the gargantuan proportions of the enterprise—thirty-one elevators and an incessant flow of passengers managed by boys standing through twelve-hour shifts—as we are reminded of "the stupendous hierarchy of the hotel staff" (p. 165). And when Karl, inadvertently and quite helplessly, ends up transgressing the strict code that governs the behavior of the hotel labor force, he is confronted by a head waiter and a head porter as harsh and vindictive as any ancient taskmaster, and is threatened, as we have noted, with imprisonment.

Therese, who is an immigrant from Pomerania and thus, like Karl, a "Hebrew" worker displaced from her homeland to this latter-day house of bondage, tells him the sad story of her mother's accidental death in the new land: a pile of bricks with a heavy plank at a building site came tumbling down on her. The bricks recall the huge quantities of bricks the Israelites were compelled to make for Pharaoh's construction projects, and the burial by bricks might conceivably suggest the midrash in which the Hebrew slaves are forced to bury their infants among the bricks in the walls of the pyramids. (Kafka, with his distinctive eye for the farcical and bizarre, turns the death into a kind of burlesque rape by the building materials, as Therese describes her mother "lying there in her checkered skirt, which had come all the way from Pomerania, her legs thrown wide, almost covered by the rough plank atop of her" [p. 157].) The other biblical story in which brick-laying is prominent is of course the Tower of Babel. Given Kafka's fascination with the idea of reaching for the heavens in that project, he may be intimating that when humankind's fever of labor lacks a horizon of transcendence, as in biblical Egypt and in his version of modern America, it turns into sheer enslavement.

Karl, expelled in disgrace from the Hotel Occidental, is immediately yanked into the bizarre ménage of Delamarche, Robinson, and Brunelda. He quickly realizes that this new situation is a smaller-scale version, more claustrally restricting, of the bondage he experienced at the hotel: "So far as I can tell from your account of it," he remarks to Robinson, "and from what I have seen myself, this isn't service here, it's slavery. Nobody could endure it" (p. 242). In this penultimate episode of the novel, the Exodus theme of enslavement fuses with the Joseph-story theme of imprisonment. The tiny apartment with its locked door is literally a prison for Karl, and within that prison, the imposing body of the sexually demanding woman becomes a second prison as Brunelda crushes Karl against the railing of the balcony: "he flinched in an involuntary but unsuccessful attempt to escape from the pressure of her body" (p. 248). Kafka's novel thus describes an ingenious interpretive loop around the biblical story of Joseph: in place of the prison to which Joseph is condemned for an alleged sexual crime (as Karl has been sent off to what proves to be the prison-house of America for a supposed sexual transgression), the physical presence of the aggressive woman itself becomes the ultimate prison.

How can he get out? It was surely Kafka's difficulty in imagining this necessary extrication that led to the incompletion of the novel. At the end of the Brunelda episode, Karl goes to sleep dreaming once again of how, when he escapes, he will make his way through assiduous effort up the rungs of the American hierarchy. The last, ominous image of the chapter, however, is of the imperious Brunelda tossing and turning in her sleep. In the concluding fragment, "The Nature Theatre of Oklahoma," across the hiatus of the narrative transition that Kafka was unable to imagine, we have moved from Exodus 1–5 to Exodus 12–15, from the tale of oppressive enslavement to the story of liberation. The placard that invites all comers to join the great theater urges them to "hurry, so that you get there before midnight" (p. 273). The hasty departure in the middle of the night gestures toward the flight of the Israelites from Egypt in the middle of the night, a departure so precipitous that they had no time to let their dough rise. The blaring of trumpets Karl hears is the counterpart to the blast of rams' horns that was the signal for the Israelites in the wilderness to begin their march. The very stress on music—specifically trumpets and drums, indifferently played—may recall the Exodus song of triumph at the Sea of Reeds, with Miriam dancing to the beat of a timbrel. The ragtag constitution of the crowd of volunteers—"What destitute, disreputable characters were here assembled . . . !"(p. 296)—who flock to the Nature Theatre alludes to the "mixed multitude" who join the Israelites in their flight from Egypt. The image of a man and wife with a small child in a baby carriage on which Karl focuses harks back to Moses's "With our children and our old people we will go."

The Oklahoma fragment breaks off, appropriately enough, with an evocation of the crowded train rushing westward through a vast landscape teeming with variety and pulsing with energy: "narrow, dark, jagged valleys opened out and one tried to follow with a finger the direction in which they lost themselves; broad mountain streams appeared, rushing in great waves down to the hilly lower ground and driving with them a thousand foaming wavelets" (p. 298, translation modified). In terms of what I have called the spatial thematics of the novel, the Oklahoma Theatre is clearly conceived as an opening up to unlimited horizons after all the visions of claustral constriction. The wilderness, or at any rate the glimpse of it we are vouchsafed at the end of the concluding fragment, modulates into the Promised Land itself. Given the fact, moreover, that many of the recruits for the Theatre have been dressed up as angels, the Theatre also incorporates an intimation, vaguely farcical as one would expect in Kafka, of a return to paradise, a final circumvention of the sword-wielding angel whose avatar stood at the gates of Eden in the first paragraph of the novel. Although Kafka did not, after all, work out this thematic conclusion, the idea he began to sketch was that acting, playing, music, and art would provide the alternative to the world of futile, grinding labor in which the protagonist had been trapped. Another parallel from Dickens suggests itself which sheds light on Kafka's intention even if he was not actually familiar with this particular novel: in *Hard Times*, the escape from the modern realm of crushing industrial labor and the equally crushing process of education founded on the principles of utilitarianism is the circus, where fancy—that is, imagination—reigns and where work becomes play.

By now I hope it has become clear that Kafka has fashioned in his biblical novel a rather curious and ingenious amalgam of scriptural materials beginning with the banishment from Eden, conflating the story of Jacob and Joseph with the account of the enslavement in Egypt and the liberation from bondage in Exodus, and integrating all these biblical motifs into several conventional patterns of the nineteenth-century novel, from Bildungsroman to picaresque, projected onto the landscape of a fantastically transformed America. I do not necessarily presume a priority of the biblical scheme in his own creative process. He clearly had a number of models in mind, from the generic one of the Bildungsroman to the psychoautobiographical plot of expulsion from the family by a punitive father, a plot that he variously traced in stories such as "The Metamorphosis" and "The Judgment" as well as in "Letter to His Father." Nevertheless, the importance of the Bible to his imaginative project deserves far more attention than it has received. The resourcefulness and wit with which biblical materials have been deployed reflect a certain characteristically modernist exuberance in the use and transmutation of traditional materials akin, for example, to Chagall's exuberant transmogrification of motifs taken from Yiddish folklore in his great panoramic mural for the Moscow Yiddish Art Theater.[9] The imaginative freedom, however, with which Kafka alludes to the Bible does not mean that the intention or effect of his work is explicitly to subvert the authority of Scripture. A brief comparison with the use of the Joseph story in a more traditional novelist may help us place Kafka's relation to the Bible in the evolution of literary history against a background of theology. Fielding's *Joseph Andrews* (1743) also follows the fortunes of an innocent young male protagonist who is the repeated object of sexual assault by lustful older women. The novel includes two hilarious replays of Genesis 39, in which the lubricious Lady Booby assumes the role of Potiphar's wife, futilely trying to draw Joseph into bed with her. After her second failure, she has him expelled from her household, where he has been working as a servant, and he is then thrust into a picaresque series of mishaps and adventures on the road before his final triumph. As in *Amerika*, one story from Genesis is yoked with others—Joseph's pastor and comic mentor, Abraham Adams, evokes both Abraham the first father and the innocence of the first man in the Garden. Here, too, the biblical materials are conjoined with European literary conventions: the plot of mistaken identities and ultimately happy coincidence harks back to Hellenistic romance; the self-ironic narrator ostentatiously presents his narrative as a comic epic; and elements of the picaresque are evident as well.

Fielding shares, then, with Kafka, a spirit of playful inventiveness in his redeployment of biblical motifs in a contemporary setting. The chief difference is that the eighteenth-century writer confidently assumes the Bible as a timeless source of moral authority, almost a kind of practical guide for skirting the moral pitfalls of everyday life, accessible to anyone who reads it with common sense. He is bolstered in this assumption, as the eminent Fielding scholar Martin Battestin has shown, by a stockpile of set moral values attached to the figures of Joseph and Abraham in the Latitudinarian sermons of his era.[10] Kafka's use of the Bible is quirkier, less predictable. The Bible as he reads it abounds in paradoxes, which he on his part compounds by imposing an exegesis that is itself often highly paradoxical: the promised land can become the site of Egyptian bondage; the pyramids are touched by the shadow of the Tower of Babel, behind which may loom the distant outline of the Great Wall of China. The paradoxical reading of the Bible, of course, is not at all a modern invention. It flourished especially in the heavily charged climate of Jewish mysticism, and Scholem's argument for an affinity between Kafka and the Kabbalah is pertinent precisely in this regard. What must be added is that Kafka shares neither the confidence of Fielding the common-sense Protestant believer nor of the Jewish mystics in the Bible as a faithful map of the moral life. In his treatment of the Joseph story, virtue does not prevail. The young man is physically overwhelmed by the woman who pulls him into her bed; the aggressive women he subsequently encounters continue to be too much for him; incarceration is not a temporary way-station to brilliant ascent, like Joseph's Egyptian prison, but a recurrent ineluctable fate engendering in the narrative an irreparable break before the planned final episode of liberation. Fielding, encouraged by Anglican homiletic tradition, sees the biblical characters as morally exemplary figures, even if he also satirically complicates the representation of his contemporary Abraham. Kafka, projecting a protagonist out of his own richly layered sense of personal inadequacies and imagining a world more convoluted and more resistant to human agency than that of the Bible, makes his characters swerve or fall away from their biblical models, and does not hesitate to reverse the biblical plots to which he alludes.

Kafka's writing undermines any sense that the Bible is a fixed source of authority or a reliable guidebook. For him the Bible has become a fluid entity, the components of the biblical corpus imagined in restless circulation, doubling back on one another, challenging or unsettling one another, and sometimes challenged by texts beyond the canonical corpus. The effect produced by his imagining biblical patterns in a contemporary setting is whimsical, sometimes vaguely grotesque, at moments deliberately absurd. And yet, the canon continues to confront him, to address him, to demand that he make sense of his world through it. In *Amerika* he proceeds from the assumption that the Bible can provide him a resonant structure of motifs, themes, and symbols to probe the meaning of the contemporary world. If his existential doubt, his perception of a labyrinth of contradictions in both the text and the world, are modernist, his urgent engagement in Scripture is traditional. "Turn it over and over, for everything is in it" is a maxim to which at least sometimes he might well have subscribed, though always with the proviso that some of what he turned up in turning it over might subvert the Bible's own explicit affirmations, and certainly those of most readings presupposing its canonical standing.

NOTES

1. Gershom Scholem, "Ten Ahistorical Theses on the Kabbalah," in *'Od Davar* (Tel Aviv: Am Oved, 1989), 37.

2. Franz Kafka, *Parables and Paradoxes* (New York: Schocken Books, 1961), 35. All quotations from the reflections on the Tower of Babel are from this edition.

3. *The Correspondence of Walter Benjamin and Gershom Scholem, 1932–1940*, edited by Gershom Scholem, translated by Gary Smith and Andre Lefevre (New York: Schocken Books, 1989), 243.

4. Moshe Halbertal, *People of the Book: Canon, Meaning, and Authority* (Cambridge: Harvard University Press, 1997), 19.

5. Kafka criticism has not really registered the centrality of biblical allusions in *Amerika*. Symptomatically, Ralf R. Nicolai's *Kafkas Amerika-Roman "Der Verschollene"* (Würzburg: Königshausen und Neumann, 1981) includes an index of motifs and themes that runs to 177 items without incorporating a single biblical text.

6. Franz Kafka, *Amerika*, translated by Willa and Edwin Muir (New York: Schocken Books, 1962), 103–104. All citations from the novel are from this edition.

7. John Hollander, *The Gazer's Spirit* (Chicago: University of Chicago Press, 1995), 185.

8. I am indebted to Bluma Goldstein for this formulation.

9. For an illuminating exposition of these motifs in Chagall see Benjamin Harshav, "Chagall: Postmodernism and Fictional Worlds in Painting," in *Marc Chagall and the Jewish Theater* (New York: The Guggenheim Museum, 1992), 15–60.

10. Martin Battestin, *The Moral Basis of Fielding's Art* (Middletown, Conn.: Wesleyan University Press, 1959).

STANLEY CORNGOLD

Allotria and Excreta in "In the Penal Colony"

This essay has two mottoes, and both are riddles. The point of the first, from Hölderlin's drama *Empedocles*, is quickly felt: "Nichts ist schmerzlicher ... denn Leiden zu enträtseln" (Nothing is more painful ... than unriddling suffering).[1] The second, by Lionel Trilling, reads: "To comprehend unconditioned spirit is not so very hard. . . ." I am thinking of how easy readers make it for themselves when they grasp unthinkingly the moment of alleged enlightenment in the Old Commandant's penal process. "But," continues Trilling, "there is no knowledge rarer than the understanding of spirit as it exists in the inescapable conditions which the actual and the trivial make for it."[2] In writing about allotria and excreta in "In the Penal Colony," I shall be writing about certain nonsimple forms of the trivial (allotria) and the actual (excreta), two products of human activity whose ontological status is by no means evident.[3]

Put the most radically serious quest for justification side by side with foolishness and nonsense: put the strongest, most intensely-felt life side by side with inattentiveness and giddy play. Allotria troubles the consciousness of every reader of "In the Penal Colony." There is a good deal of difference between how this story has come down to us, as a systematically pure and grave conceptual meditation on the one hand; and, on the other, how it actually reads. Then we will be struck by the emphasis on such matters as blood

From *Modernism/Modernity* 8, no. 2 (April 2001): 281–93. © 2001 by Johns Hopkins University Press.

and vomit and sputum and muck and oil and the disposal system laid out to contain them; and we will be struck by the high jinks, horseplay, capers, antics (it turns out that there are a great many words for this neglected category) imbricated in this construction.

"Allotria" means what's irrelevant (*das Nicht-Sachgemäße*), what's nonsensical (*Unfug*)—clowning about, cutting up—exactly what the officer in "In the Penal Colony" calls "childish nonsense" (*den Unsinn eines Kindes*) when he is unable to convince the explorer of the value of the penal system he represents. I quote:

> It did not look as if the officer had been listening. "So you did not find the procedure convincing," he said to himself and smiled, as an old man smiles at childish nonsense and yet pursues his own meditations behind the smile.[4]

Not to find the procedure convincing—a serious matter, seriously argued—is, the officer concludes, senseless resistance. But to note this is to smile and "pursue [one's] own meditations behind the smile." Perhaps this is explicit instruction on how we are to read allotria in "In the Penal Colony," read the several pages in the story dramatizing such childish nonsense, for we are beset by them, and they are a hermeneutic puzzle. For example:

> The explorer, down below, watched the [officer's] labor uninterruptedly, his neck grew stiff and his eyes smarted from the glare of sunshine over the sky. The soldier and the condemned man were now busy together. The man's shirt and trousers, which were already lying in the pit, were fished out by the point of the soldier's bayonet. The shirt was abominably dirty, and its owner washed it in the bucket of water. When he put on the shirt and trousers both he and the soldier could not help guffawing, for the garments were of course split up behind. Perhaps the condemned man felt it incumbent on him to amuse the soldier, he turned around and around in his slashed garments before the soldier, who squatted on the ground beating his knees with mirth. All the same, they presently controlled their mirth out of respect for the gentlemen. ["IPC" 162]

Or, again:

> The soldier and the condemned man did not understand at first what was happening, at first they were not even looking on. The

condemned man was gleeful at having got the handkerchiefs back, but he was not allowed to enjoy them for long, since the soldier snatched them with a sudden, unexpected grab. Now the condemned man in turn was trying to twitch them from under the belt where the soldier had tucked them, but the soldier was on his guard. So they were wrestling, half in jest. ["IPC" 163]

"Childish nonsense," "beating his knees with mirth," "gleeful," "half in jest," what is the meaning of such things? They occur at a moment of utter crisis. After all, the officer is about to lay himself on the machine!

One or two things further to this "allotria"—this other Otherness, other to allegory (*allos*: Greek for "other" [we shall see that allotria is other to *pedantry*]): it has a past. I did not say it's named as such in Kafka (it *is* in Thomas Mann's *Doctor Faustus*: As a schoolboy, Adrian Leverkühn, the serious composer, would not be suspected of it).[5] But the thing is readily enough identified in Kafka's story—as "childish nonsense"—and the thing itself is found throughout Kafka's work: in *Metamorphosis*, for example, it is what Gregor Samsa practices en route to consolidating his identity as a vermin, playfully taking bits of food in his mouth and then spitting them out, aimlessly navigating the junk in his room. Allotria is the compulsory life content of the vermin—as long as he is not yet being tortured to death. It is also something that Kafka flashes out of the narrator's relation to his composition (the semiosis), as when Gregor is shown casting a bewildered glance upwards to the wall where the photograph hangs of Gregor Samsa, Army lieutenant, his hand on his short sword, ready to impale his dreadful Other. Or when Joseph K. stares wonderingly at the tourist who has come to arrest him in a safari suit replete with pockets, pleats, buttons, straps—the name of this captor is Franz![6] And, most famously, now again at the level of the mimesis: the antics of the twin assistants in *The Castle*. It is the sort of thing that made Kafka's audiences laugh aloud at his readings, but they did not laugh when he read "In the Penal Colony" in Munich in 1916 (a woman is said to have fainted). "In the Penal Colony" is no laughing matter.

One historical use of the term "allotria" might help to conceptualize it. None other than John Wesley writes:

We have no right to dispose of anything we have, but according to His will, seeing we are not proprietors of any of these things; they are all, as our Lord speaks, *allotria, belonging to another person*; nor is anything properly *our own*, in the land of our pilgrimage. We shall not receive *ta idia, our own things*, till we come to our own country.[7]

This allotria is the nontrivial inauthentic as such, and a good deal more significant than "time-wasting." It is lent us by God. The Wesley passage points up the odd dual nature of the thing: it is above and also below the civilized norm: it is divine and it is improper. More, if it is an essential quality of Gregor Samsa and all vermin (*Ungeziefer*) then it cannot be returned to God, as being (MHG. *ungeziber, unziver*) "unsuited for sacrifice," unacceptable to God.[8]

Why does Kafka allow, indeed encourage, such displays of allotria? The answer is overdetermined—at least. For him it is bound to the theater; one crux is the story as theater. The operation of the torture machine is *ein Spiel*—a play. "And then the performance begins" (Und nun beginnt das Spiel), says the officer [106, "IPC" 147]); later we hear of the parliamentary assembly, too, as a "Schaustellung," a mise-en-scene or "public spectacle" (115, "IPC" 158).[9] The events of "In the Penal Colony" comprise a theatrical play, with the chief spectator in a cane chair in the orchestra, the whole a kind of amphitheater, with palisades, as you recall from the outset. And—to say this directly—allotria belongs on the principle that, if this is a scene, then any amount of stage business is permissible. Indeed, you will scarcely find a longer work of Kafka's without its complement of stage business. This is the legacy of his highly developed instinct for play and performance of the demotic kind: his heroes are almost never artists but they are *artistes*—trapezists, cabaret singers (the mouse Josephine), hunger artists—circus performers, parts of the theater of alternative communication: staged, distantiated, fictional conveyances of feeling, everything opposite to the immediate conversational discourse which, as Kafka said, drained the life out of him.

Even the death-dealing machine itself clowns in a parody of the Taylor speedup system and the circus performance: it collapses as an extravagant excretion of its gears, as in the circus an endless quantity of persons are expelled from a small hidden space in a red volkswagen. Here we verge on a crossing of allotria and excreta, allotria itself being a sort of excrescence on the normal social essence.[10] But I delay discussion of this element—waste matter, dejecta—until after spelling out a further motive or two for Kafka's vaudeville. His vaudevillian practice, in principle admissible, marks his modernity as such—an impertinent mixing of genres and levels of communicated feeling, medial feeling (we may think of artistes themselves as yet odder types of medial communication). The point is that for all its impropriety and distastefulness, allotria works *distractingly*, and its plain function is the way it may work as relief from terror. I cite a sentence from *The Picture of Dorian Gray*, which may prove Wilde's usefulness to readings of Kafka. Dorian Gray, having heard a disturbing idea, listened, open-eyed and wondering. . . . He watched it [a bee] with that strange interest in trivial things that we try to develop when things of high import make us afraid, or when we are stirred by some new emotion for which we cannot find expression, or when some thought that terrifies us lays sudden siege to the brain and calls on us to yield.[11]

There is another motive. In his diary entry of 9 February 1915, Kafka complained of "In the Penal Colony." He had written the story in the late fall of 1914 in the course of writing or failing to write *The Trial* but had not sought to publish it, in good part because he thought he'd botched the ending. Further evidence of this assumption is the presence in the diary entries for August 1917 of a number of sketches of alternative endings, none of which Kafka used. In the course of this essay, however, I shall have recourse to refer to several of them.

I said he had botched the ending of "In the Penal Colony" and to his mind he had botched the whole of it too; on 4 September 1917, he wrote to Kurt Wolff: "Perhaps there is some misunderstanding concerning the 'Penal Colony.' I have never been entirely wholehearted in asking for it to be published. Two or three of the final pages are botched [*sind Machwerk*], and their presence points to some deeper flaw; there is a worm somewhere which hollows out the story [*der selbst das Volle der Geschichte hohl macht*]."[12]

If we rely on Kafka's evaluation, this worm alludes to a certain "element" which he saw—it appears—in the story he began writing in February 1915 that he calls the "dog story," which has not survived. (This is not, of course, the splendid "Investigations of a Dog," written in 1922.) This "dog story," if this is indeed the story that Kafka is thinking of when he continues his diary entry with the words, "Just now read the beginning," is "in spite of all its truth wicked, pedantic, mechanical, a fish barely breathing on a sand bank [*trotz aller Wahrheit böse, pedantisch, mechanisch, auf einer Sandbank ein noch knapp atmender Fisch*]" (11:77).[13] "Mechanical," "sand bank," and "fish" might be clues that he is also or, indeed, directly thinking of "In the Penal Colony." For the words "mechanical" and "pedantic," we substitute "allegory" and "abstraction"—this is what the scholar Ingeborg Henel has done, as representing to excess one tendency of Kafka's art—as opposed to the liveliness that Kafka saw in abundance in "The Stoker," the first chapter of his "American novel" *Der Verschollene* (He who was never again heard from).[14] It is not hard to guess what Kafka might have meant by pedantry, allegory, or abstraction in the case of "In the Penal Colony": it is the machine and the law and the scenes of political wrangling conjured by the officer, none of which has its foot in lived experience or which could be said to arise from "the translation of an idea into an image, pure construction."[15] But we are not obliged to be satisfied with his own judgment; it is much too cursory, and it leaves out too much of what in the story is not of the order of allegory but rather of allotria. Portions of this work, a constellation, dance on the border of conceptual knowledge: mimetic allotria, bodily excreta, odd signs; randomly functioning allusions; plays on words that have been expelled from the circle of communication and made thing-like; and the bag of fragmentary, unincorporated endings.

Allotria is a key term, as that being beside the point, that going off topic, that is unrecoverable as allegory. Itself an insubstantial irrelevance, allotria both is and is attracted to elements that are extruded and expunged from healthy, directed life—its excreta. Children and madmen, who are drawn to excreta, whose play is so much excreta, cannot but seem foolish—or worse—in the eyes of adults. They are at best distractions from, at worst obstacles to, the rational conduct of life. So it will not come as a surprise that Kafka is guilty because "on his own admission he is depraved and takes pleasure in filth [*Schmutz*]."[16] I now come to some excremental oddities in "In The Penal Colony" (I use the word "excremental" in its various senses of "superfluous," "non-nutritive," and "of matter to be evacuated"), and am in this way looking askance at and away from the story's great themes of just sentencing, truthful writing, canonical law, torture, and illumination. But we will be making a return.

The excremental speaks for itself—or does it? In this story—and in the history of its versions—the process of excretion functions as a species of speech . . . uncannily: it is the body's mute howl of pain, its resistance to being evacuated of its substance. It is a marker of the body, of man's embodiedness, of the all-too-tender and recalcitrant flesh that will not submit to discipline. It expresses itself as a protest. What is then disgusting about such expressions, such excreta, may be their half-living character: they are remains of the body even as they leave the body, neither at first alive nor dead, an unwonted revelation (outside) of the body (an inside). Hence, they are forbidden objects of curiosity and an inducement, to the nonsqueamish, to play—allotria.[17]

* * *

In the second half of this essay, I want to fill in a quadrilateral: the fact of allotria and excreta at the order of the mimesis; and allotria and excreta at the order of the semiosis—I mean, the relation of the author-*cum*-narrator to the act of composition or scription. There is allotria in "In the Penal Colony" at the order of the composition, at the order of the tropes, in Kafka's aberrant literalization of the metaphor "dog." This is a rhetorical play, and it connects to serious matters, belongs to an economy involving the political. Consider the metaphor of the prisoner as dog. We are, after all, here in the *Tropen*, the tropics—setting for a scene of political terror—and we are also among the tropes, *turns* of phrase. The apparent allotria of tropic play belongs to an economy of the political administration of torture.

Consider politics, further. Consider it as the decent (or indecent) application of power to persons, especially as this power is produced, stored and conveyed by institutions—viz. the "apparatus" or "machinery" of the law in "In the Penal Colony" and the apparatus or machinery of (the very story) "In the Penal Colony." This interinvolvement of the two sorts of power is plain in the first paragraph, which situates the apparatus of the torture machine and its spectators in its sandy amphitheater. The most graphically represented of the spectators and indeed participants is the prisoner, "a stupid-looking, wide-mouthed [wide-muzzled (*breitmäuliger*)] man with bewildered [abandoned by authority (*verwahrlostem*)] hair and face"—an animal-like creature, guarded ["led about" would be truer] by a soldier, "who held the heavy chain controlling the small chains locked on the prisoner's ankles, wrists, and neck, chains that were themselves attached to each other by communicating links" ("IPC" 140). Having been treated like a dog (he has even been struck on the nose by a whip), it comes as no surprise that he has become doglike. Kafka depicts this in the striking manner that is at once typical and still enigmatic, as we shall see. The text continues: "In any case [additionally (*übrigens*)—there is a world of significance in this harmless conjunctive phrase], the condemned man looked so like a submissive dog [*so hündisch ergeben*] that one might have thought he could be left to run free on the surrounding hills and would only need to be whistled for when the execution was due to begin" (ibid.). Doggishly submissive (*hündisch ergeben*) is a metaphor. But the intensifier *so* added on to *hündisch ergeben* literalizes that metaphor: the prisoner is now no different from a dog. There are two interinvolved processes here, one political and one rhetorical. The man is brutalized by a violent application of political power; and the metaphor, too, is submitted to a kind of violence in being robbed of its floating status as trope and more or less literalized.

I say "more or less" literalized, for as becomes evident after a moment's reflection on this process, every metaphor is an unsettled semantic force-field. This is a Kafkan awareness par excellence. To tamper with the relation between tenor and vehicle—thing compared and comparison—is to generate monsters (even independently of the literal meaning of the metaphor "dog"); so even more is at stake here than that a man has been turned into a dog. The aberrant literalizing of the metaphor suggests that he has been turned into a monstrous collage of dog features and man features outside of any ordinary scale of things—neither man nor dog, he is rendered more brutal than a man, more monstrous than a dog.

This literalizing moment was a crucial one for Kafka in the story. He hated, as I said, the ending of "In the Penal Colony"; and unlike the case of "The Metamorphosis," whose ending he also hated, he left behind several fragmentary versions of possible alternatives in his diaries. These are extraordinarily lurid. One reads:

> "What?" said the explorer.
> The explorer felt too tired to give [any further] commands or [indeed] to do anything. He merely took a handkerchief from his pocket, gestured as if he were dipping it in the distant bucket, pressed it to his brow and lay down beside the pit [this emphasizes the excrement-containing pit and bucket]. He was found in this position by the two men the Commandant had sent out to fetch him. He jumped up when they spoke to him as if revived. With his hand on his heart he said, "I am a cur [*Hundsfott*] if I allow that to happen." But then he took his own words literally [*wörtlich*] and began to run around on all fours. From time to time, however, he leaped erect, shook the fit off, so to speak [*riß sich förmlich los*], threw his arms around the neck of one of the men [and] tearfully exclaimed, "Why does all this happen to me!" and then hurried back to his post. [*D* 178; *G* 11:152]

This diary entry dates from 7 August 1917; he had written "In the Penal Colony" three years earlier, ca. 15 October 1914. Notice the administration of political authority and also the mad, foolish play with figurative language (allotria of the signifier). This play returns, too, to the first paragraph of the story but here, as an unincorporated fragment, remains excreted.

I want to dwell on this relation of the play with rhetoric and the seriousness of the political administration of terror. In these examples from the beginning and end of the story, the will and the ability to tamper with the metaphor goes to the artist, who obtains thereby an extraordinary rhetorical power not without marginal political power (since this metaphorical labeling lends itself to political use). This monstrous literalization is the rhetorical equivalent of the political, where the political—in this our painful modernity—has come to mean the construction of types of men and women by the application of force and the constructive destruction of men and women as persons as good as dead: vermin, outlaws, rogues.

I do not claim that Kafka *says* that the political and the rhetorical are involved in one another, duplicate one another, or cause one another. Yet he does show this complication happening. Thus I claim, simply, that it takes place. The word-play that has a great deal to do with torture-play is not merely marginal to the text and its time. But the effort to say what this connection is in truth—whether, as Cultural Studies has it, the political play contains and comprehends the rhetorical play; or whether the rhetorical play, marginally outside politics, in turn provokes political acts and a subtle knowing representation of political acts (J. M. Coetzee writes of "the freedom of textuality, however meager and marginal that freedom may be")—Kafka's story cannot *say* this.[18]

Addressing this rhetorical dimension of the story entails addressing one sort of play, one form of the marginal, that has the power to usurp center stage. We must now look at the disgusting, and then at three textual cruxes triggered once more by rhetorical details. All bear on the process of *reading* a work interrupted by allotria and excreta.

* * *

"'Read it,' said the officer. 'I can't,' said the explorer" ("IPC" 148). There is no information on how the victim's reading process is to take place; it requires a strenuous and ultimately frustrating effort of interpretation on our part. The writing is of two types—the first is called "the actual [real] script(ure) [*die wirkliche Schrift*]" and "the [authentic] script(ure) itself [*die eigentliche Schrift*]"; the second type of writing is ornamental, consisting of "embellishments [*Verzierungen*]" (107; "IPC" 149). One might be inclined to call the second type inauthentic, secondary, derivative, employing the semiotic model of the metaphor. The real, authentic meaning is borne along, as the tenor, by the trope—the metaphor as such—which then might pass away, its semantic work as vehicle having been done. But this cannot be right; this is not the function of the embellishment, since reading the ornament is *essential* to the work of justice, to "the kind of sentence we pass [the form of our judgment—*die Form unseres Urteils*]" (103, "IPC" 144). The form is not complete, the essence of the punishment does not happen until the ornament, too, has been deciphered. Nor is there any suggestion that the embellishments, rightly deciphered, amount to getting the message—the sentence as violated commandment is different from its embellishments—but not essentially different.[19] In the *Tropen*, in the tropics, all are tropes (*Tropen*): the designation of the real, the authentic sentence, is already gnawed on by this secondary and derivative function; and so we are inclined to ask, Of what are they the figures, the fictive (after all not real or authentic) script? But we are unable to say more than that they are essential. This is artistic (*kunstvoll*), beautiful but nonsimply beautiful handwriting, "no calligraphy [*keine Schönschrift*] for schoolchildren" (107, "IPC" 149). He clearly signifies something within what the officer calls "*das Gesamturteil* [the general or broad-gauged judgment]" (109, "IPC" 151), but what?

Perhaps it signifies, in the sense of mirroring—or completing a structural parallel with—the function of the ostensibly trivial (allotria) and excremental in the story as such—the curlicues and embellishments being equivalent to the plethora of "useless" details. They are marginal and excremental, suspending any possible assertion of the precedence, as essential, of issues of justice over the other issues of art and aesthetics. Here we are returned to the historical dispute among modes of criticism and modes of literary classification, within Kafka studies, in respect to "In the Penal Colony." Is it, as a story of a punishment that raises substantial questions of law and justice and just sentencing, to be classified with those other stories of Kafka (as Kafka explicitly intended), with "The Metamorphosis" and "The Judgment"; or should it be classified with, par excellence, "A Hunger Artist," as a story of art and performance for which no audience any longer exists?[20] "Nor did the colony itself betray much interest in this execution": this citation immediately resonates with the opening of "A Hunger Artist" (100, "IPC" 140). But these are structural formalities. The matter of the embellishment poses the crucial question: if the epistemological status, as we say, of the ornamental script(ure) is undecidable, if the relation of trope to diegesis is unfathomable, what then is the status of the understanding that is given to the prisoner's faculty of reason (*der Verstand*) in the sixth hour?

This question has hardly ever seemed to be stated as a problem before. In the sixth hour the culprit grasps his sentence—so runs the conventional understanding—but does he? Surely not. First, because the process requires a *twelve-hour* deciphering; second, because what Kafka (unlike his English translator) has written is, the process requires a twelve-hour "*deciphering* [*Entziffern*]" (108). This phrase immediately calls attention to the signifier (*Ziffer*), but you would not think so, reading the Muirs's translation of "*es geschieht ja nichts weiter, der Mann fängt bloß an, die Schrift zu entziffern*" as, "Nothing more happens than that the man begins to understand the inscription [the script(ure)]" ("IPC" 150). What is wrong is a tendency that this translation betrays; this "to understand" recalls the rational enlightenment provoked in the sixth hour, when enlightenment comes to the most dull-witted (*Verstand geht dem Blödesten auf*), encouraging us to conclude that the event of understanding coming alive is equivalent to the truth of an ethical commandment being grasped by reason (ibid.). And that truth is? Whatever it is, it is *not* the truth of the verdict. One *must* consult the German! *The moment of ecstasy is not that of understanding the script(ure); it is a moment of recognizing that here there is script to be deciphered.* "Script(ure) [*Die Schrift*]," as the Prison Chaplain in *The Trial* informs Joseph K., this writing made deep, "is unchanging, invariant [*ist unveränderlich*]."[21] We deal then not with combustion of the script (à la Walter Benjamin) but with the ineradicability of a fact: here there is writing; here is the task of the translator. But if the prisoner deciphers the script with his wounds, and if at the end of things the prisoner is (virtually) nothing more than his wounds, then perfection of justice consists in the wounds deciphering the wounds or, equivalently, the script deciphering the script, leaving no margin free for rational enlightenment or any other manner of interpretation. "How the inscription takes form on the body [*wie sich die Inschrift im Körper vollzieht*]" is by no means equivalent to the "happening of justice" (*daß Gerechtigkeit* [*geschieht*])," if by the latter is meant the prisoner's understanding of his sentence (106, 111). He cannot understand his sentence until he is emptied out of his substance, until he has been *excreted*.[22]

In this analysis I am associating the concepts of understanding and interpretation as they have traditionally been associated in a German hermeneutical tradition marked especially by Friedrich Schlegel and Friedrich Schleiermacher. The concept of "decoding," however, with its connotations of automaticity and of transformation only, or chiefly, along the axis of the material signifier constitutes a departure. Here, one could well think of Kafka's aphorism against interpretation, written in 1922: "It is enough that the arrows fit exactly in the wounds that they have made" (*D* 206; *G* 11:203).

We as readers of Kafka remain concerned with our access to an understanding of what genuinely, authentically, occurs within the *Gesamturteil* of the story as a whole. It is the question of whether it is possible for us to achieve any proper understanding of the prisoner's tormented reading process as such. And here I want to call attention to two minor, marginal, rather excremental cruxes at the order of scription—one parenthesis and one (following the authority of Max Brod) crossing-out. Excreted matter has an exact semiotic correlative in the parenthesis: it is excluded from the sentence while it still belongs to the economy of the sentence the way that excreta—noticed, half-organic, half-alive stuff—belongs to the economy of the body. The parenthesis is unique as a syntactical element in requiring no corresponding adjustment in the sentence as a whole in order to accommodate it, just as there is a provision in every body for excreted matter that does not disturb the economy of the whole and permits it to function as it normally and otherwise functions.

The parenthesis occurs at the close of the mutilation of the officer. The passage reads, as we carry over Kafka's *parenthesis* from the edition (and only the edition) of Paul Raabe: "And here, almost against his will, he had to look at the face of the corpse. It was as it had been in life; no sign was visible of the promised redemption; what the others had found in the machine the officer had not found; the lips were firmly pressed together, the eyes were open, with the same expression as in life, the look was calm and convinced, through the forehead went the point of the great iron spike." [121, "IPC" 166] Thereafter come the three asterisks and the unsatisfactory ending.

Who says—and on what authority—that the officer found no trace of the promised redemption? The officer remains convinced; he has not registered the shortfall in the promised redemption. But he is the only authority we have for the existence of any such redemption. I suggest that the uncertainty of the claim that "no sign was visible of the promised redemption" in the death of the officer is marked, emphasized by the parenthesis. Within it is contained the (incomplete) excremental at the order of rhetoric. This is an odd detail of a sort found to my knowledge in no other work of Kafka—a "detail" of utter importance. It is a paradoxical construction, implying, to begin with, a sort of tentativeness of utterance. For what is the meaning of the marker "parenthesis" except that of an addition, an "*übrigens*," a remainder, an only secondary reflection, whose retention in the body of an argument is a matter that cannot be allowed to disturb the writer, who has more serious, forward-looking concerns? The argument, as it is constituted without the parenthesis, takes precedence: the writer will not undertake to integrate the parenthetical matter; and yet, in this instance, regarding the question of whether the officer found meaning in his ordeal—No, not a trace of it was to be found!—is of crucial importance. It is the story's leading idea. How can one find the story's leading idea between parentheses?

It is as if what's contained in the parenthesis, a bracketing off—meaning non-pertinence, what's off the point, scarcely belonging—were itself provisory only, subject to revision, even to reversal. And yet—or, precisely—what is here at stake is nothing less than the meaning of the whole. Was there ever in truth such a procedure as the glorious operation of the machine? was there ever so worthy an alternative to the inefficient justice of liberal states? could a death ever be justified in the consciousness of the victim in this way? could the truth of one's derelict life ever be inscribed on the heart?[23] And could, incidentally, Nietzsche's account of the genealogy of morals be affirmed—was there ever a moment of dawning moral enlightenment powerful enough to irradiate and transfigure an entire people? Sane societies require a token of hope, the promise of a future. Accordingly, the punishment in the penal colony is such a token, because it promises a transfiguration of an entire community before death.

These are some of the questions taken up in a parenthesis in "In the Penal Colony" as published—overwhelming questions to which Kafka's answers are belied by his parenthesis—questions reviewed and answered differently in the three or four fragmentary endings. I shall therefore address one more

pertinent item from these diary manuscripts in the event of a moot crossing-out. The text of these endings in the latest Fischer, so-called manuscript
edition, a printed transcription by and large faithful to the manuscripts, gives
as the diary entry for 8 August 1917: "Und wenn auch alles unverändert war,
der Stachel war doch da, krumm hervorragend aus der geborstenen Stirn" (*G*
11:353). In (my) English, this reads: "And even if everything was unchanged,
the spike was still there, protruding crookedly from his shattered forehead."
But if you read the standard English translation of the diaries, you get instead:
"And even if everything remained unchanged, the spike was still there, crookedly protruding from his shattered forehead *as if it bore witness to some truth*"
(*D* 178; emphasis added). The addition of this last phrase is explained in a
footnote of Max Brod, Kafka's editor and literary executor: "The clause, 'as
if it bore witness to some truth,' was struck out by Kafka in the manuscript"
(*D* 322). So this footnotation "as if it bore witness to some truth," having,
then, precisely parenthetical status, returns to a *crossing out* (leaving in the
empirical state of affairs of the transmission of the manuscript the perplexing
uncertainty about whether Kafka's intention in having crossed out the phrase
"as if [his shattered forehead] bore witness to some truth" is to be respected).
If respected, the sum of things is left intact and pure and *no* trace of the
promised redemption was indeed to be seen. But it is equally compelling to
preserve this velleity (it is *not* preserved in the manuscript edition)—to find
in the officer's report the positive substance of justice—for it would convey a
most important indecision and nostalgia and intense imaginative yearning in
Kafka, he who had written (while still young) of his desire to write his being
into the depths of the paper and to draw up that writing into him.

The words "as if it bore witness to some truth" are remarkable ones to
cross out. Kafka's own reading confirms the reader's suspicions. This is not
a story about true sentencing but about its disappearance, its traceable disappearance in the intricacies and hollow places of fiction. Throughout, the
narration of (principally) the reception—on the part of the Explorer—of the
narration produced by a fanatic of a ceremony who can no more than imply
that a prisoner's (attempt at) deciphering the truth of his sentence is achieved
with his death. The truth of this procedure is then nullified when it is empirically enacted by the same fanatic on himself. But what we have lost as an
"acquist of true experience," we have gained as a tolerable experience of the
trivial of allotria and the excremental.[24] What is tasteless in the actual and
trivial is etiolated, bled of its loathsome horror, by this multiplication of narrative foci and foyers—a gesture which, by driving truth out of art, enlarges
its scope. In this work the tastelessness of trifling allotria and the excremental
(a kind of expressiveness) are symbols together of the distasteful that now has
a place in art and can be borne. Its "meaning" is reflexive only. It points to the

vast, unlimited—because truth-bled—order of the signifier in art. This is a conclusion perfectly consistent with Hegel's view of the end of art as the end of an art that would need to be validated by the truth it can now no longer represent.

Notes

1. Friedrich Hölderlin, *Sämtliche Werke* (Stuttgart: Kohlhammer, 1961), 4:21.

2. Lionel Trilling, "Introduction" to *Anna Karenina*, cited in Leon Wieseltier, "Get Smart: Lionel Trilling's Exhilarating Pursuit of Moral Realism," review of *The Moral Obligation to Be Intelligent*, *Los Angeles Times* Book Review, 11 June 2000, 4.

3. According to Malcolm Pasley and Klaus Wagenbach, Kafka composed "In the Penal Colony" between 4 and 18 October 1914. *Sämtliche Erzählungen*, ed. Paul Raabe (Frankfurt a.M.: Fischer Taschenbuch, 1970), 398. Citations in German from this edition of "In the Penal Colony [*In der Strafkolonie*]" will be given in the text of this essay as page numbers in parentheses.

4. Franz Kafka, "In the Penal Colony," in *Franz Kafka: The Complete Stories*, ed. Nahum N. Glatzer, trans. Willa and Edwin Muir (New York: Schocken, 1971), 160; hereafter abbreviated "IPC".

5. "Kretzschmar hatte nichts dagegen und begünstigte es sogar, daß dieser von Gescheitheit vibrierende Jüngling auch musikalisch vorauseilte und sich mit Dingen zu schaffen machte, die ein pedantischer Mentor als Allotria verpönt haben würde [would have forbidden as time-wasting]." Thomas Mann, *Doktor Faustus* (Frankfurt a.M.: Fischer Taschenbuch, 1991), 101. For an English language version, see *Doctor Faustus*, trans. H. T. Lowe-Porter (New York: Vintage, 1948), 73.

6. So much for Theodor W. Adorno's claim that Kafka's characters are all subaltern (all "*Gestalten der Subalternität*") in "Aufzeichnungen zu Kafka," in *Prismen: Kulturkritik und Gesellschaft* (Frankfurt a.M.: Suhrkamp, 1955), 324. Cf. "Notes to Kafka," in *Prisms*, trans. Samuel and Shierry Weber (London: Spearman, 1967), 259.

7. John Wesley, *The Good Steward*, Sermon 51. Available from www.ccel. org/w/wesley/sermons/sermons-html/serm-051.html; Internet.

8. Kafka studied medieval German literature at the University of Prague in 1902. Klaus Wagenbach, *Franz Kafka, Eine Biographie seiner Jugend (1883–1912)* (Bern: Francke, 1958), 100. He assiduously consulted Grimm's etymological dictionary; cf. Max Brod, *Über Franz Kafka* (Frankfurt a. M.: Fischer, 1966), 110, 213.

9. This word is, incidentally, conspicuous in the opening scene of *The Trial* describing K.'s arrest. Franz Kafka, *Der Proceß, Roman*, in der Fassung der Handschrift, ed. Malcolm Pasley (Frankfurt a.M.: S. Fischer, 1990), 15.

10. Allotria and excreta have this in common: they are distinctively nonexclusively human, being common to both human beings and animals, especially to children and childlike beings who have no natural dislike of what Kafka calls *Schmutz*—what adults term physically and morally filthy.

11. *Oscar Wilde*, ed. Isobel Murray (New York: Oxford University Press, 1989), 65.

12. Franz Kafka, *Letters to Friends, Family, and Editors*, trans. Richard and Clara Winston (New York: Schocken, 1977), 137; Franz Kafka, *Briefe 1902–1904*, ed. Max Brod (Frankfurt a.M.: Fischer, 1958), 159.

13. The English quotation comes from *The Diaries of Franz Kafka, 1914–1923*, trans. Martin Greenberg (New York: Schocken, 1949), 114–5; hereafter abbreviated *D*. The German quotation comes from Franz Kafka, *Tagebücher, Band 3, 1914–1923, Franz Kafka, Gesammelte Werke in zwölf bänden, Nach der Kritischen Ausgabe*, ed. Hans-Gerd Koch (Frankfurt a.M.: Fischer Taschenbuch Verlag, 1994), 11:77; hereafter abbreviated *G*.

14. *Kafka Handbuch in zwei Bänden*, ed. Hartmut Binder (Stuttgart: Alfred Kröner, 1979), 229.

15. Ibid.

16. Detlev Kremer, *Kafka: Die Erotik des Schreibens* (Frankfurt a.M.: Athenäum, 1989), 7.

17. This life-in-death connects to the peculiar life-in-death of the corpse of the officer at the close. The face of the corpse "was as it had been in life" ("IPC" 166). Mark Anderson has written most suggestively of this aspect of the piece, "the existential condition of being caught between death and life," in "The Ornaments of Writing: 'In the Penal Colony,'" in *Kafka's Clothes: Ornament and Aestheticism in the Habsburg Fin de Siècle* (Oxford: Clarendon Press, 1992), 187–8.

18. Coetzee writes of history as "a society's collective self-interpretation of its own coming-into-being," against which "the freedom of textuality, however meager and marginal that freedom may be," might be asserted. J. M. Coetzee, *Doubling the Point: Essays and Interviews*, ed. David Attwell (Cambridge, Mass.: Harvard University Press, 1992), 206.

19. Recall the phrase: "Jetzt geschieht Gerechtigkeit" (111). Also see Friedrich Kittler on Faust's feckless attempt to interpret the *sign* of the Earth Spirit. "For once, Faust does not just glimpse and gaze at signs. The first unperformable stage direction in European theatrical history declares that 'he seizes the book and mysteriously pronounces the sign of the spirit.' 'Mysteriously,' indeed. This event, speaking out loud, is possible for books composed of letters, but not for a collection of magic ideograms. . . ." *Discourse Networks 1800/1900* ed. David E. Wellbery, trans. Michael Metteer, with Chris Cullens (Stanford, Calif.: Stanford University Press, 1990), 6.

20. See Margot Norris, "Sadism and Masochism in Two Kafka Stories," *Modern Language Notes* 93 no. 3 (1978), 430.

21. Franz Kafka, *Der Proceß*, ed. Malcolm Pasley (Frankfurt a.M.: Fischer, 1990), 298.

22. The hunger artist nourishes himself on his own flesh; the flesh of the culprit in "In the Penal Colony" is scraped out of his body and excreted as so much useless blood and tissue.

23. "I will put my law in their inward parts, and write it in their hearts" (Jer. 31.33). Cited in Malcolm Pasley, "In the Penal Colony," in *The Kafka Debate: New Perspectives for our Time* (New York: Gordian, 1977), 302.

24. The phrase is Milton's, at the very close of *Samson Agonistes*; to Samson is attributed "new acquist / Of true experience," John Milton, *Complete Poems and Major Prose*, ed. Merritt Y. Hughes (New York: The Oydssey Press, 1957), 593.

RUSSELL A. BERMAN

Tradition and Betrayal in "Das Urteil"

Few works as brief and compact as "Das Urteil" (The Judgment) loom so large in the landscape of literary history. This short story of deceptive simplicity but replete with unresolved questions represented a breakthrough for Kafka and became a magnet for critical readers, who were drawn to its simultaneous sparseness and intensity. Kafka himself reports how he wrote out the full text in one exhausting sitting in the night of 22–23 September 1912, marking a definitive separation between his early literary attempts and his mature accomplishments: "Die Verwandlung" (The Metamorphosis) followed in November and December, even as he made extensive progress on the novel fragment that Max Brod would later dub *Amerika* (Binder 123–25). There can be no doubt that the completion of "Das Urteil" brought Kafka's creative productivity to a new level, ushering in the series of works that has become central to modernist world literature. We know that Kafka wished to have Brod destroy much of his writing; "Das Urteil" was not on the list. On the contrary, it is one of the few texts that Kafka continued to regard with satisfaction (Stern 114). Indeed it occupies a special place as a key to Kafka's major achievement and to a much broader definition of literary sensibility in the twentieth century (Sokel 34). "Das Urteil" represents a breakthrough, redefining the literary tradition of the canon; and it is a redefinition that unfolds precisely through the logic of the text.

From *A Companion to the Works of Franz Kafka*, edited by James Rolleston, pp. 85–99. © 2002 by the editor and contributors.

Why this sudden outburst of creativity and why did it take the form of "Das Urteil"? There is of course a biographical context, and much criticism has dwelled on it, endeavoring to explain the troublesome narrative with reference to data from Kafka's life. His meeting with Felice Bauer, who would become his fiancée, took place in August 1912. It is to her that he dedicated the story, she figures clearly as the model for Georg's fiancée, Frieda Brandenfeld (whose initials she shares), and in his correspondence with Felice, he refers to "Das Urteil" as her story. The prospect of marriage raised questions for Kafka regarding his own commitment to the life of a writer and the renunciation of bourgeois security, while both the conventionalism of marriage and the unconventional prospects of a literary career represented potential provocations to the troubled relationship between Kafka and his father. Hence the plausibility of referencing the prominent themes of the narrative—the father–son conflict, the relationship to the distant friend, and the imminent marriage—to Kafka's own biographical situation. Indeed critics have proposed explaining "Das Urteil," especially the altercation between Georg and his father, by mustering Kafka's letter to his father of 1919 as evidence of the strained family ties (Binder 132; Neumann 217).

Attempts to resolve the complexities of the story by drawing attention to possible literary sources are not fundamentally dissimilar to biographical connections: both attempt to explain—which is not to say, "explain away"— the phenomenon of the literary work through objective external data. In this manner, "Das Urteil" has been connected to a fairy tale from Prague, to aspects of Dostoevsky (especially *Crime and Punishment*), and to Brod's novel *Arnold Beer* (Binder 126–31). In no case is the evidence as compelling as in the estimation of the importance of Kafka's experience of Yiddish theater, which he frequently attended in the period prior to writing "Das Urteil." The family constellations, the use of unrealistic gestures, and the peripatetic reversal of fortunes all can be seen as derived from the performances that we know Kafka attended (Binder 132–34; Beck). A further, related potential source is the liturgy for the Jewish Day of Atonement, the Yom Kippur holiday, which in 1912 fell on 21–22 September, that is, the day before the night in which Kafka wrote the text. We know that he attended the synagogue that year, so the associated liturgical tropes were presumably on his mind, including most importantly the imminence of a divine judgment about to be rendered, pending atonement.

As important as these biographical and intertextual references may be in illuminating single aspects of the text, they necessarily fall short of a penetrating account of the work itself. Kafka's personal relationship to his fiancée or to his father, or for that matter, his reading habits or religious belief are ultimately private matters. Interpretations of the story that tie it too firmly to such personal information fail to account for the fascination that this text in particular has exercised on both professional critics and the larger reading public. Thus Ronald Gray comments:

> Has Kafka done more than cater for himself; is there anything here for the reader, in so far as he is a "common reader," someone who reads for pleasure and enlightenment rather than research? The quantity of biographical information needed for understanding the story suggests that it is essentially esoteric, that it has value for its position in Kafka's work, as a gateway, rather than as an accomplished achievement in itself. (72)

Treating the text as an expression of primarily private matters in effect suggests that the text has little merit as literature on its own, that Kafka's own estimation of the text was wrong, and that it should only be read symptomatically or at best merely as a study toward the mature work, beginning with "Die Verwandlung." This approach, ultimately, leaves Georg alone in the private room where the story commences: Kafka's personal vehicle, perhaps, toward a career as a writer, but not a significant imaginative accomplishment on its own terms. We should not underestimate the attraction of such a critical strategy, for it minimizes the challenge that the text poses to the reader, who must grapple with its perplexing account of human relationships: the paralogical character of the dispute between father and son, the undecided standing of the friend, the glaring discrepancy between everything we know about Georg and the severity of the verdict, and, perhaps most of all, the unquestioned obedience with which the capital sentence is carried out.

Yet we should also be very wary of adopting the underlying assumption that these apparently irresolvable tensions within "Das Urteil" undercut its literary standing. On the contrary, it is precisely this nearly impenetrable network, layer upon layer of distinct meanings, that makes up the substance of the achievement. "Das Urteil" became a breakthrough for Kafka's own career, just as it represents a crucial elaboration of his thinking on justice and guilt, the grand theme of his later writing. Moreover the very intricacy and seemingly problematic nature of the text set a new standard for the possibilities of literary writing, redefining the nature of literary achievement and therefore of literary judgment and canonicity. The topic of the text is a judgment passed on the son—and we will see how perplexing the possibility of that judgment turns out to be—but it is even more a judgment on literature, its institutionalization, and its potential. "Das Urteil" calls for a rejudgment of literary life.

The fascination of "Das Urteil" derives initially from the breathtaking discrepancy between the commencement of the story and its conclusion, a fall from complacent security to suicide, magnified by the brevity and rapid pace of the narration. All seems right in the world of Georg Bendemann, until suddenly, and without a fully compelling explanation, all seems wrong, and this reversal draws the reader into an infinite loop of rethinking, the unceasing search for the explanation of the verdict and its execution. Yet on closer examination neither the initial stability nor the concluding leap simply carries a single, fixed meaning, for the narrative is more complex than it first appears. It is of course true that the narrative commences with a seemingly familiar and conventional rhetoric of literary realism, introducing a standard figure, a young businessman, who is moreover the carrier of an unproblematic and firmly centered perspective. We find him in his own private room, seated at his desk, or more precisely, a "Schreibtisch" (writing table, *L* 39, *CS* 77) where he has just concluded a letter; meanwhile he can gaze out the window, surveying a bridge, a river, and the hills beyond. This sort of hero, and the associated epistemological integration of private and public knowledge—the personal letter and the external view—had constituted the standard requisites of poetic realism in Germany at least since 1848, with their harmonious balance of subjective and objective components (Hohendahl 376–419). Indeed long before 1912, the structures of realistic writing had been appropriated by a commercialized entertainment literature and to this day, and not only in Germany, they remain the standard fare of popular fiction. Yet Kafka flaunts the signs of realism at the outset of "Das Urteil" in a way that overstates them and thereby undermines them. The announced temporality, a Sunday morning in the height of spring, conveys a fairy tale atmosphere compounded by the "It was" with which the text begins. The generic tension between the tropes of realism and the markers of the fairy tale should set the reader on guard. Georg's smug confidence at his desk is not fully warranted, for, in broader terms, the epistemological closure promised by conventional realism, particularly in its commercial and popularized variation, is about to be called into question through a redefinition of expectations for literary authenticity.

Literary realism, strictly speaking, was about the prominence of sensuous details, the realia of life, in the literary text, and their arrangement in a presumably reasonable order. It is therefore noteworthy, as John Ellis has pointed out, that the descriptions in the first paragraph are slightly out of focus. Georg is in one of a row of houses, characterized as distinguishable only in terms of their color and height: yet surely color and height, the importance of which is casually minimized by the narrator, are precisely the most prominent sorts of qualities that realism might address. In addition, the qualification of the green of the landscape across the river as "schwach" (weak) is an odd usage in German, where an alternative adverb might have been chosen (Ellis 76–77). The very substance of the realist project of objective description seems to be breaking down, and this is corroborated by the role that Georg plays as the presumed agent of the observational perspective. He would seem to be well suited to stand in as an allegory for the writer at his desk, surveying the world before him. Yet we find him distracted and inattentive, playfully sealing the letter (as if it were of no particular importance) and surely taking little notice of the world beyond the window. There is a hint of an explanation in the professional identification of Georg as a businessman, as if the alienation from the world, his inattention, as well as the guilt that will be imputed to him in the course of the narration, were consequences of capitalist culture and the regime of private property in which he is located. At least this is a possible point of departure for a Marxist approach to "Das Urteil." Yet those class indicators are also standard markers for nineteenth-century realism, and it is that literary culture that is being prepared for scrutiny through the remarkable subtlety of the first paragraph. Realistic expectations are being raised and undermined at the same time. As J. P. Stern has noted, "In Kafka's story, the sensational is avoided because the transition from the realistic to the surrealistic or fantastic is gradual" (119). The collapse of realistic epistemology, which will be carried out in the father's judgment and Georg's death, is in effect already announced between the lines of the superficial order of the placid beginning.

In addition to this subversion of realistic description, the text, from the outset, introduces an irritation with regard to narrative perspective. From the "It was a Sunday morning" of the beginning, the reader is led to expect an omniscient narrator discussing the object of the story, Georg, his subjectivity, and his objective standing in the world. The first paragraph shifts quickly from the narrator's view of the row of houses to Georg's perspective, the landscape across the river. This perspectival disruption is continued, alternating between objectifying description and subjective point of view, when the narrator and the reader appear to be aligned with Georg's subjectivity itself, particularly through the use of indexical terms. Thus the suggestion is made that the friend in St. Petersburg move his business "here"; later, it is reported that Georg's business has "now" grown: as if the narrator and the reader were assumed to share Georg's here and now. The realistic convention of distinguishing neatly between the omniscience of the narrator and the limited subjectivity of a character has disappeared for Georg, although it is also maintained, insofar as the other figures, in particular the father, continue to be treated as objects of reportage. The father's thinking is nowhere as exposed as is Georg's, and consequently the reader is asked to accept a story about Georg, from the outside so to speak, while also participating directly in Georg's thought. The separation between the subjective interiority of the private room and the objective external view, which turns out to be unsustainable in any case, is similarly undermined through the formal structure of the narrative itself. The individual, or bourgeois, autonomy enfigured by Georg at his desk is losing its underpinnings.

The conclusion of the story is equally complex. At first, Georg's demise would appear to signify the absolute reversal of the celebration of his autonomy in the opening scene, the transition from comfortable privacy to his public execution. The complacent worldview of the outset has been demolished. Yet just as that beginning is far from one-dimensional, already signaling problems about to erupt, the conclusion cannot be read simply as the abnegation of the hero. The father is reported to collapse in the wake of the judgment, indicating a more variegated relationship to his son than the simplistic model of a stereotypical father–son conflict would permit. The encounter with the maid in the stairway, including her call to Jesus and her covering her face, is intimated to be a missed opportunity, placed in a curiously opposite relationship to Georg—"aber er war schon davon" (L 52; "but he was already gone," CS 87)—although the significance of the conjunction "but" is nowhere explicated. Even more perplexing is the role of the retarding moment, when Georg has jumped over the railing but is still holding onto the bridge. The execution has been delayed for an instant, allowing Georg to profess his love for his parents and to wait until a bus passes, presumably in order to drown out the sound of his fall and to allow for his death in a paradoxically public anonymity.

If the insistence on the security of privacy at the outset of "Das Urteil" is subverted through the unraveling of a realist epistemology, the corollary at the conclusion is that the irrevocably terminal character of Georg's plunge, the carrying out of the execution, is qualified in several different ways. It is as if the conclusion were less conclusive than the plot itself would suggest. As noted, the father collapses, and with him, the easy binary opposition of father and son, judge and criminal, is at least called into question. The two are not opposites but, on the contrary, participants in a shared regime, characterized possibly by some guilt (if such can be determined). In that case, however, it is a collective responsibility and not an individual culpability. That "Das Urteil" is not a narrative of Georg's fate alone is indicated furthermore by the complex of imagery of love: the maid's "Jesus," Georg's call to his parents, and the approach of the "Autoomnibus," a term which etymologically announces the problem of the autonomous individual in relation to the comprehensive collective (L 52). (To this network of signs, one should also add the references to St. Petersburg, the Russian cleric, and the father's claim to be the representative of the friend: all indications of a Christian semiotics of representation.) If the fall into the river suggests a baptismal possibility of rebirth, so too does the redemptive invocation of "unendlicher Verkehr," the last words of the story: never ceasing traffic, that is, the ongoing life of the human community, but also endless intercourse in a specifically sexual sense. Stanley Corngold writes of the "joy and sheer force of the 'Verkehr,' the erotic upsurge and infinite traffic of the concluding sentence" (40). The initial impression that the story concludes with Georg's death in the wake of the father's pronouncement turns out to be not quite right, given the father's fate, the invocations of community, and the intimation of the possibility of love and rebirth. In this light, it is especially important to note that while we read that Georg lets himself fall from the bridge, the text does not in fact report his death. On the contrary, in the place of death, we learn of the infinite traffic, with its multiple connotations, surely quite distinct from a definitive and fully terminal conclusion. Whether Georg's death is muffled beneath the passing of the bus, or the infinite traffic somehow redeems him, is left undecided by the text itself.

Thus the most basic frame of the story leads into an interpretive vortex. The reader's first approximation of the plot cannot fail to trace an arc from the protective environment of Georg's room on a Sunday morning in spring to the presumption of absolute destruction through the plunge from the bridge. The discrepancy between beginning and end necessarily elicits efforts to make sense out of the report: what could possibly justify the execution of the nice young man who had been writing a letter to his friend one fine Sunday morning? Yet the enigma of "Das Urteil" is that the beginning and end stand in a closer and less exclusive relationship than the veneer of the plot suggests. If there is an alternative path into "Das Urteil," it has to begin with the recognition that the tension between Georg at his desk and Georg on the bridge is less stringent than appears initially. In that case, the narration turns out to be not at all about a reversal of fortune, certainly not an individual's misfortune, but rather about the nature of judgment in general and its relation to fortune and the way of the world. To explore this option requires a closer look at the fabric of the story and the character of the discourse in between the opening and the end, which have turned out to be less polar in their opposition than the reader might have initially estimated.

If the beginning and the end of "Das Urteil" are linked, it is due to a stated problem, a discursive discrepancy between a normative expectation of deliberative speech and the constantly elusive, hermetic substance of individual topics. On the one hand, both Georg and the father (in different ways, to be sure) engage in processes approximating rational argument, either directly in their exchange or, in Georg's case, indirectly in his reported thought process. These deliberations invite the reader to accept rational debate as a proper standard, that is, a certain logical, nearly jurisprudential modality of argument is established as a background measure for evaluating various decisions, such as Georg's choosing to inform his friend of the engagement, or the father's verdict itself. Kafka's repeated deployment of deliberative speech frames the material and suggests that judgment is, in the end, supposed to make sense. Yet repeatedly the text demonstrates a disjunction between these deliberations and their topic. Pursuing this line of inquiry is tantamount to the recognition that what may be at stake here is a judgment not so much on Georg but on the possibility of judgment altogether.

The critique of judgment is most salient in the treatment accorded to evidence in the text. Deliberative speech presumes evidence, which is the topic of the deliberation, just as it assumes the possibility of interpreting that evidence. It insists that, in order to render judgment, reference be made to facts and to the significance that those facts are imputed to entail. These are expectations that Kafka insinuates through the justificational claims made by Georg and by his father. Yet these are hardly outlandish or unfamiliar to the reader, for they form the basis of modern understandings of legal process: proper judgment is presumed not to be arbitrary, but must instead be based on adequate evidence and its proper evaluation, according to established rules of argument.

In "Das Urteil," however, while the expectations regarding the quality of deliberation are announced, most evidence is indicated, in one way or another, to be corrupt and inconclusive, open to such a range of interpretation that it turns out to be useless for the cases at hand. Among the more salient examples of this subversion of evidentiary argumentation, one can point to the explanations for Georg's rise in the family business. The comments are part of a passage that is surely ascribed to the narrator, and therefore one might expect to find an exercise of narrative omniscience. Instead, one faces a series of three distinct accounts, each prefaced with a "perhaps," and the last of which is, in effect, no rational explanation at all, but rather an invocation of fortunate accidents (Swales 360). Thus, in the context of presumably rational deliberation on the nature of the correspondence between Georg and his friend and, more specifically, on the nature of Georg's business success, the very basis of the argument, the evidentiary underpinning, is declared to be merely conjecture. This is a crucial point, since the father will later accuse his son of conspiring against him in the business.

This disjunction between a formally rational argument and inadequate or incompatible supporting evidence occurs repeatedly. The pertinent facts are either inconclusive or inappropriate to the claims made. To prove Georg's affection for his father, the narrator references their taking lunch in the same restaurant, but the passage leaves open whether they actually eat together. Indeed the image of their evenings, each with his own newspaper, suggests more separation than comity. Similarly, it is reported that Georg's Russian friend failed to express adequate sympathy at the news of the death of

Georg's mother, and this is taken to be symptomatic of the worrisome social alienation imputed to the friend alone in a distant land. Yet we also learn that the friend did in fact urge Georg to join him in Russia, an expression of affection that stands in marked contrast to Georg's own vacillation on whether to invite the friend to his wedding. Hence the very premise of Georg's judgment of his friend, the friend's social isolation, is not at all corroborated by this particular point; indeed the facts could be taken to prove the opposite, not the friend's disaffection, but Georg's.

The disjunction between argumentative claim and asserted fact even characterizes moments of seemingly uncontroversial discourse. Georg's noticing that the father has kept his window closed leads the father to indicate that this is his preference. Georg then replies that it is warm outside, "wie in Anhang zu dem Früheren" (*L* 44; "as if continuing his previous remark," *CS* 81). It is by no means clear what the innocuous comment about the weather is intended to mean: an extension of the implied criticism that the window is not open or a confirmation of the father's preference for keeping it closed. It is as if rational exchange were being simulated, but its lack of substance becomes clear at each point, even in a discussion about the weather. The text signals this slide toward a decomposition of argument, that is, the absence of a compelling logic, by indicating that the subsequent remark is only "as if continuing" what had preceded.

Finally, it should be noted that it is not only Georg but his father as well for whom deliberative pronouncements are subverted by the slipperiness of the facts. His opening attack on Georg is characterized by a series of statements that retract aspects of the implied accusations. At first he complains that Georg may not be telling him the whole truth, but then proceeds to limit his own discourse by promising to avoid matters not relevant, that is, presumably not pertinent to the discussion of the friend. Having attacked Georg for not being fully forthcoming, he is effectively announcing that he too will exclude certain topics from discussion. Yet he immediately reverses himself by invoking reportedly unfortunate events, otherwise unspecified, that have taken place since his wife's death. He emphasizes twice that "maybe" (vielleicht) the time will come for their deliberation (*CS* 82; *L* 45). Thus the accusation is suggested but nearly voided in the same instant. Similarly, he proceeds to suggest that he may be missing aspects of the business, implying that Georg could be deceiving him, while explicitly refraining from making such a claim. These several interlinear accusations become even less accessible to any potential rational defense by Georg, because the father also concedes that his own memory is fading. The consequence of the passage is therefore to suggest a wide range of misdeeds on Georg's part, within a rhetoric of rational judgment, while at the same time keeping any specific facts at arm's length and, indeed, most specific accusations as well. Any effort to explain the accusation in a manner that would allow for a properly deliberative rejoinder would be constrained by the irreducible gap between rational norm and an ultimately unreachable experience, beyond precise specification.

Deliberation in "Das Urteil" is therefore robbed of the sustenance that relatively secure factual evidence might be expected to provide. In addition, deliberation fails in a second sense with regard to summative judgments as well; that is, just as the evaluation of (elusive) particular points has been seen to be inadequate, the comprehensive verdicts turn out to be untenable. Neither Georg's judgment of the friend (the first verdict we encounter) nor the father's judgment on Georg (the second verdict) turns out, on close scrutiny, to display a compelling logic. On the contrary, argument and experience appear to be at odds in both cases, although the contradictory character of judgment functions differently in each. The text foregrounds Georg's ostentatious displays of concern for his friend. These in turn are belied however by his deep-seated reluctance to invite him to the wedding. Indeed his repeatedly professed concerns for the friend's well-being appear to be little more than excuses to keep him away. Thus Georg's judgment of the friend and his situation in Russia are a function of a complex psychological motivation, which have been explored by many critics. Hidden concerns, buried beneath the surface, force Georg to rationalize his unwillingness to issue the invitation. It is here that Kafka's interest in Freud and Nietzsche comes to the fore, the recognition of ulterior and unconscious motives. As Gerhard Kurz has written, "The archaeological impulse, the search for the 'city beneath the cities,' unites Nietzsche, Freud, and Kafka in a single configuration as modern excavators of the human psyche" (128). Georg's insistence to his father that his initial hesitation to inform his friend of the wedding was driven only by his consideration for the friend's well-being—"aus keinem anderen Grunde sonst" (*L* 45; "that was the only reason," *CS* 82)—is stated so emphatically that a critical reader must surely see through the pretextuous nature of the claim.

While Georg's judgment of his friend is patently fraudulent, the dubiousness of deliberative speech holds all the more for the father's estimation of Georg. In this second case, the tenuous nature of judgment is demonstrated emphatically by the interpolation of multiple self-contradictions into the discourse of the father. His bitter attacks on his son are undermined repeatedly by the self-negating character of his own speech. Thus he first calls into question the very existence of the friend in St. Petersburg only in order to reverse himself by insisting that he has maintained a clandestine connection to that self-same friend and indeed represents him legally in his homeland. In a second example, he appears to accuse Georg of delaying his marriage for too long and, simultaneously, to criticize his aspiration to marry at all.

Georg ends in a double bind: his engagement to Frieda is both too early and too late. Finally, the father's judgment on Georg's character is equally oxymoronic. Georg stands accused of aspiring to independence and maturity too ambitiously (in the business and in the engagement), while he is also attacked for still being childish: a "Spassmacher" (joker) and his father's "Früchtchen" (offspring, literally: little fruit). Clearly the accusations hurled at Georg are mutually exclusive. It is impossible to identify a clear logic in the father's condemnation that might encompass the various and mutually incompatible elements of the tirade. In other words, judgment is certainly rendered, and quite harshly, but the judgment does not meet the standard of normativity established earlier by the deliberative discourse. In the case of Georg's evaluation of his friend, the text suggests ulterior motives that color the judgment: hence the incompatibility of argument and conclusion. In the case of the father's verdict on his son, we simply face the blatant untenability of the several assertions. In both instances, "Das Urteil" points to the structural weakness inherent in judgments, no matter how inescapable the act of judging may be.

The weakness of judgment has at least two sources. The first involves the use of language: for all of Kafka's own linguistic precision, Georg is frequently unable to control his speech. Language gets the better of him, or remains beyond his grasp, sometimes erratic, sometimes recalcitrant, but never fully under his control. Without an effective command of language, he is hardly in a position to argue his own case. Evidently, the logic of argumentative judgment cannot count on the linguistic capacity that it would require to be successful. Consequently, language can have unintended consequences, as in the correspondence with the friend: attempting to make vacuous small talk, Georg elicits a curiosity by reporting a stranger's marriage, which he had mentioned merely as a way to avoid more substantive topics. Alternatively, his several interjections during the father's outburst, all intended to ward off the attack, turn out to be pitifully inadequate. He lacks the rhetorical prowess to mount a compelling counter-argument. In addition, judgment is further destabilized by a second deficiency, the progressive decomposition of Georg's subjectivity. Facing his father, he is described as increasingly forgetful, losing the coherence of consciousness that would be necessary to mount a defense. This stands in marked contrast to the staging of a self-assured autonomy in the opening scene, although there too Georg's slide into distraction was already quite pronounced. The loss of memory in the exchange with the father can be taken to corroborate the father's implicit accusation that the son has forgotten his deceased mother. Georg's presentism entails a gradual repression of the past; if there is a judgmental moral to be drawn from his execution, it is that the loss of a past implies the loss of a future as well.

The particular genius of the work is that, demonstrating the faults that adhere to any process of judgment, it still draws the reader inexorably into an obligation to judge. Yet any judgment on "Das Urteil" is unlikely to escape the fate of judgment that the narrative itself has displayed. One possible critical response, confirmation of the verdict, must ascribe a logical coherence to the father's accusation that is absent in the text itself. Alternatively, efforts to retract the judgment and to defend Georg derive primarily from a modernist or tendentially feminist bias against the patriarchal authority of the father and would, taken consistently, argue to reverse any conviction (Neumann 220–21). Finally, to judge the text a demonstration of the impossibility of judgment altogether involves the critic in the performative contradictions of postmodern sensibility: insisting that judgment is impossible, in an imagined world of absolute indeterminacy, but nonetheless partaking willingly in the prerogatives and privileges of a judge (Corngold 40).

It is however impossible to take sides with either the accuser or the defendant, since both of their arguments are marred by major flaws. Nor can a close reader of "Das Urteil" declare the impossibility of judgment altogether— a claim obviously contradicted both by the central event of the narrative and the critic's own reading process. On the contrary, the story simultaneously demonstrates a necessity of judgment and a universal complicity in guilt. Both Georg and his father judge, and both share in a guilt (which is why the father collapses as his son runs—presumably—to his death). Moreover, in the course of his conversation with Frieda, Georg implicates his friend in the guilt, while it is after all Frieda's insistence on Georg writing the letter to the friend that precipitates the crisis. If "Das Urteil" appears on first reading to be Georg's story (an effect heightened by the interior monologues), on reflection it grows increasingly expansive. From the single, private room, it turns into a father–son conflict, which is broadened by the roles of Frieda, the friend, and the mother, and on the margins, the Russian monk and the masses, until the arrival of the "Autoomnibus" and the infinite traffic.

This widening in the course of the narrative lends extra weight to the father's accusation that Georg has only thought of himself. Guilt is inherent in the process of individuation and self-enclosure; the alternative is the embrace of the multiple relations of a community. Georg's initial self-absorption has hardly led to a genuine independence. On the contrary, the isolated autonomy of the beginning is nothing more than the beginning of the end for the weak individual, complicitous in a condition of universal alienation. Hence not only his incapacity to defend himself with argument but his obedient acceptance of the verdict. The ultimate problem of "Das Urteil" is not the dubious quality of the father's pronouncement—we know that any judgment will necessarily be tenuous—but rather Georg's acqui-

escence. What sort of culture produces a personality so willing
even to the point of self-destruction?

It is a culture of self-absorbed isolation, a culture of narcissism, in wh.
the individual is so self-centered that he becomes self-blind (Lasch). It is a
culture in which self-interest has become congruent with betrayal: Georg's
betrayal of his friend and the memory of his mother, as well as his disregard
for his father. It is however above all a culture characterized by a degraded
mode of writing, for the text in which Kafka achieved his own breakthrough
to literary maturity is very much about writing. It is the author Georg,
the type of the isolated, reflective, and distracted writer, whom we meet at
the outset. We learn that he is quite satisfied to generate texts intention-
ally devoid of substance and that he attempts to use language strategically
in order to manipulate the reader. It is a writing furthermore that appears
to require no particular effort, as he closes the letter with playful slowness.
Yet the most trenchant characterization of this literary world is the verb:
Georg has just completed, "beendet," the text, and it is this term that recurs
in an inverted variation in the conclusion, "unendlicher Verkehr," "unending" traffic (L 52; CS 88). The implicit criticism inherent in "Das Urteil" and
directed against established literary life entails its complacent capacity of closure, closed forms and closed minds, associated with an isolated and therefore
weakened subjectivity. Georg's text stands alone, and it is for that reason facile
and mendacious, an epistolary corollary to the degraded realism of the culture
industry implicitly invoked in the stereotypical images of the first sentence.
"Das Urteil" presents an alternative: a literature that is open to the community, its traditions, and its past, a canonic literature that has the capacity to
achieve a public and collective life. The vision of the Russian priest who has
cut a cross in his hand suggests an authentic writing, presaging the corporeal
script of "In der Strafkolonie" (In the Penal Colony). The liberal individual
at his writing desk, for all of his professed sincerity and enlightenment, turns
out to be willing to acquiesce in his own self-destruction and is incapable of
an independent judgment of substance; in contrast, the religious masses can
carry out a revolution. Kafka's appeal to a literature that resonates with the
profundity of tradition, that is an "Angelegenheit des Volkes" (a matter of the
people), as he wrote in the famous diary entry of 25 December 1911, represents one of the most severe verdicts on the culture of modernity, with its loss
of memory, its atomism, and its perpetual flight from the difficult complexity
inherent in any judgment.

WORKS CITED

Beck, Evelyn Torton. *Kafka and the Yiddish Theater: Its Impact on His Work.* Madison: U of
     Wisconsin P, 1971.

may have the form of a third-person narrative with an omniscient narrator, but its perspective is normally limited to the point of view of a single character (see, for example, Cohn). It is clear that, for Kafka at least, the boundary between the two was not very strong, as is evident from the manuscript of *Das Schloß* (*The Castle*). The opening of the novel was originally composed in the first-person, but Kafka changed his mind. He crossed out the first-person pronouns and inserted the familiar and personally resonant letter K. in their place, thus converting his novel to the *erlebte Rede* style with a few strokes of the pen.

In *Das Schloß*, Kafka evidently did not wish to foreground the first-person perspective, though he wanted on the whole to maintain it. In the last stories, on the other hand, he clearly did wish to draw attention to the involvement of the narrators in the narratives. These stories are personal. That they were intensely personal for Kafka himself is evidenced by the fact that "Josefine die Sängerin" and "Der Bau" present as their central characters artists who are animals with a human consciousness. This amalgam of the animal and human is one of Kafka's most frequent themes, and it is also one of his most personal concerns. The very idea of the animal–human combination arises from the circumstances of Kafka's personal life, the linguistic accident that made the name of an avian animal (the crow or jackdaw—Czech *kavka*) the name of his family. On top of this was the peculiar fact that his parents had given him the Hebrew name Amschel, a word commonly associated among Central European Jews with another black bird, the *Amsel* ("blackbird"). Franz/Amschel Kafka, a person highly sensitive to language, could not avoid noticing that language had dubbed him an animal, and this not once but twice. It was an essential element of his being, and it is hardly surprising that it ends up a leading motif in his fiction (see Koelb 18–20).

Nor is it surprising that this motif comes into particular prominence at the end of Kafka's career. While contemplating what it meant to be who he was, he could hardly have come up with a more fitting fictional image than the insecure animal-artist living on the edge of oblivion, a description that fits both Josephine, the mouse-singer, and the builder of the burrow. Well aware that he was himself near the edge of the abyss, Kafka felt the need to consider what it was about his work that kept him so immersed in it even under such grim circumstances.

The story Max Brod published as "Der Bau" (The Burrow) appears as a long untitled fragment in Kafka's notebooks. In its original context it follows a paragraph featuring a protagonist called K.—probably a different K. from the figures we are familiar with from the *Proceß* and *Schloß* manuscripts, but possibly not—which begins "Dann lag die Ebene vor K. . . ." (*EP* 165; Then the plain lay before K. . . .). The use of the letter K. to signify an important fictional character is a noteworthy feature of Kafka's rhetorical strategy. While on the one hand it clearly refers back to the author's own surname, on the other it conveys a sense of mystery and openness, as the missing letters tantalizingly call on the reader to fill them in. This deliberate omission of important or even crucial information is one of the most typical and most effective of Kafka's rhetorical strategies. It engages the reader in a potentially endless act of trying to complete the text, to supply the missing context, and to find a significance appropriate to the clues that the text actually offers.

The paragraph that precedes the "Der Bau" fragment may in fact bear an interesting relation to the quite different material that follows. It concerns K.'s arrival at a house that he assumes to be his. The house is very dilapidated, and at first it seems to have been long uninhabited. But, as he enters, two distressing things happen: first, he disturbs a cat, which in response makes a distinctly un-catlike noise—"so schreien Katzen sonst nicht"; and second, he hears from upstairs "eine zitternde fast röchelnde Stimme" (a quavering, almost wheezing voice) asking who's there (*EP* 165). We cannot know for sure just how quickly Kafka moved from this K.-related material to the "Der Bau" fragment that follows, but there does seem to be at least one noteworthy connection: the "K." fragment, like the other, is concerned with a dwelling that is supposed to belong to the central character but which turns out to contain a mysterious other, known only by the unpleasant noise it makes. This idea may have set Kafka to thinking about elaborating the idea of such a dwelling in other terms. In any case, he did in fact stop working on the "K." fragment and turned to the much more substantial project beginning "Ich habe den Bau eingerichtet" (I have completed the construction of my burrow).

Although Kafka never finished the work and never gave it a title, one has to think that Kafka's literary executor Max Brod was following a basically sound instinct in his edition of Kafka's manuscript, not only because he decided to go ahead and publish the piece, fragment though it was, but also because he supplied the very appropriate title "Der Bau." (For reasons that will be explained shortly, the English title "The Burrow" is not quite so appropriate.) Perhaps Brod had noticed that the German word "Bau," along with related words, has a special importance in the notebooks from this period in Kafka's life. An especially telling entry expressing Kafka's frustration—almost despair—over his difficulties with writing occurs earlier in the same larger set of documents containing "Der Bau." He speaks of a plan to move away from fiction to a kind of biographical writing:

> Daraus will ich mich dann aufbauen so wie einer, dessen Haus unsicher ist, daneben ein sicheres aufbauen will, womöglich aus dem Material des alten. Schlimm ist es allerdings wenn mitten im

Bau seine Kraft aufhört und er jetzt statt eines zwar unsicheren aber doch vollständigen Hauses, ein halbzerstörtes und ein halbfertiges hat, also nichts. (*EP* 10)

[I plan to develop ["aufbauen"] myself out of this material, rather like someone with an unsteady dwelling who wants to build ["aufbauen"] a more secure one nearby, if possible out of the materials of the old one. Of course things could go badly if his strength gives out in the midst of construction ["Bau"], and now instead of an insecure but nonetheless complete house he has one half destroyed and one half completed—in other words, nothing (trans. mine).]

The German word "bauen" brings together a set of senses combined in no single English word, for it means both "to dig or delve in the earth" (a farmer is called a *Bauer* in German) and, more generally, "to build, construct," with the extended metaphorical sense of "develop." Beyond these conventional senses, the word had an additional, very personal significance for Kafka, since the surname of his longtime friend and sometime fiancée Felice Bauer contained the very same root. Just as the paragraph quoted above links the issue of autobiographical material with the notion of "bauen," so does Kafka's life experience link the possibility of personal development, in particular the founding of a family, with an alliance to a Bauer. The name Bauer thus has nearly the same depth of resonance for Kafka as his own; and just as we find numerous crows, jackdaws, and all sorts of human-like animals in his stories, so do we find here a protagonist who is precisely a "Bauer" (builder, burrower) in the most fundamental, literal sense. Of course he is also an animal–human amalgam, so that there is an element of the "kavka" in him as well. The narrator of "Der Bau" is thus, in literature, a sort of offspring of a marriage between a Kafka and a Bauer that almost, but never quite, took place in real life.

We can also see in the house-building fragment a link between the construction ("aufbauen") of a text and the development ("aufbauen") of a human self. This is once again a very common Kafkan theme, one that is investigated in the fragment in an atmosphere of the direst anxiety. The burrow-builder, in spite of the self-satisfaction he expresses in his opening statement, is filled with nagging fears that at times reach the level of pure dread (e.g. "bleibt nur die Annahme der Existenz des großen Tieres" [*EP* 201; "it only remains for me to assume the existence of a great beast," *CS* 353]). What is at stake is the very existence of the builder, not only because the strange noises he hears might signal the presence of a dangerous predator, but because, if the integrity of the construction is compromised, the meaning of its constructor's existence is put into question. There is, after all, little more to the life of this creature than its building activity. The story is exclusively concerned with the burrow, its construction, and its properties. We know nothing about the narrator apart from stray hints that come in the course of his discussion of the structure.

This is quite in keeping with Kafka's sense of himself as having practically no existence apart from literature. What Kafka was making when he wrote was nothing less than himself, a self that was for him a kind of house that was constantly under construction and reconstruction. It is quite logical, even inevitable, under such circumstances that in the story the burrow-builder's anxiety about his building should escalate almost immediately to a terror of physical violence. The burrow is in effect an extension of his body, and harm to it is indistinguishable from a wound. The narrator is quite explicit: "die Empfindlichkeit des Baues hat mich empfindlich gemacht, seine Verletzungen schmerzen mich als wären es die meinen" (*EP* 203; "the vulnerability of the burrow has made me vulnerable; any wound to it hurts me as if I myself were hit," *CS* 355). And paradoxically, the more he extends and refines this burrow-body, the more vulnerable he becomes, because "Eben als Besitzer dieses großen empfindlichen Werkes bin ich wohlverstanden gegenüber jedem ernsteren Angriff wehrlos" (*EP* 203; "simply by virtue of being owner of this great vulnerable edifice I am obviously defenseless against any serious attack," *CS* 355).

The exact nature of the threat to the builder's vulnerable structure is not known to him; he can only make anxious guesses. He is by nature trepidatious, and he believes in the existence of enemies: "es gibt auch solche [Feinde] im Innern der Erde, ich habe sie noch nie gesehen, aber die Sagen erzählen von ihnen und ich glaube fest an sie" (*EP* 167; "enemies in the bowels of the earth. I have never seen them, but legend tells of them and I firmly believe in them," *CS* 326). Such enemies cannot be seen, and even "selbst wer ihr Opfer ist hat sie kaum gesehen, sie kommen, man hört das Kratzen ihrer Krallen knapp unter sich in der Erde, die ihr Element ist, und schon ist man verloren" (*EP* 167; "their very victims can scarcely have seen them; they come, you hear the scratching of their claws just under you in the ground, which is their element, and already you are lost," *CS* 326). Thus only a noise indicates the presence of such a terrifying danger. No wonder, then, that any unidentified noise causes the burrower to worry, and no wonder, too, that the most wonderful experience he knows is the total silence of his burrow. When that silence is broken, even if only by a barely perceptible whistling noise ("Zischen oder Pfeifen," *EP* 200), there can be no peace for the burrower.

The noise that bothers him at first seems to be the work of the little creatures he calls "Kleinzeug" ("small fry," *EP* 193 *et passim*), very possibly the mice he mentions early in the narrative and allows to share his dwelling because they serve as a ready source of food (*CS* 327). But this reassuring explanation doesn't satisfy, for the noise—if indeed there really is a noise— can be heard all over the burrow, even in its innermost core. The very ubiquity of the frightening sound occasionally affords a temporary reassurance: perhaps it means that the great beast is still very far away. But the narrator's imagination will not be satisfied with such explanations, and he continues to fear the worst.

Indeed the narrator's power of imagination ("Einbildungskraft"), specifically mentioned as the source of his notion of a great beast (*EP* 201), is surely as much the source of his problem as is the noise itself. The alien whistler with its terrible claws and jaws is just as much a construction of the narrator as is his beloved burrow. He has built the one by zealous digging, the other by obsessive acts of imagination. Both are aspects of the narrator's self, perhaps equally valid expressions of that self. We can see how deeply the burrower identifies himself with the burrow in his apostrophe to it:

> Euretwegen Ihr Gänge und Plätze, und Du vor allem Burgplatz, bin ich ja gekommen, habe mein Leben für nichts geachtet nachdem ich lange Zeit die Dummheit hatte seinetwegen zu zittern und die Rückkehr zu Euch zu verzögern. Was kümmert mich die Gefahr jetzt, da ich bei Euch bin. Ihr gehört zu mir, ich zu Euch, verbunden sind wir, was kann uns geschehen." (*EP* 187).

> [It is for your sake, ye passages and rooms, and you Castle Keep, above all, that I have come back, counting my life as nothing in the balance, after stupidly trembling for so long, and postponing my return to you. What do I care for danger now that I am with you? You belong to me, and I to you, we are united; what can harm us? (*CS* 342)]

Here is rhetoric of a very specific sort, in the form of a series of "rhetorical" questions. Such questions are called rhetorical because they appear not to seek an answer but rather to deny the existence of the thing put into question. "What do I care?" means "I don't care," and "what can harm us?" means "nothing can harm us." The possibility that these particular questions are rhetorical seems even stronger in Kafka's manuscript, where there are no question marks.

But of course one cannot be certain that the questions really are "rhetorical" in this way. Kafka writes in such a way as to prevent us from being absolutely sure that his questions do not expect an answer. As the narrative continues, it becomes clear that the burrower does indeed care and that he believes he can be harmed. So these could be genuine questions, and they could have very unpleasant answers. "What can harm us?" "What do I care?" In fact, the narrative goes into a great deal of detail about what could harm the burrower, and how he could be harmed, and why he should care. Even if the danger exists only in his imagination, it remains a powerful force in a world that is entirely constructed by the narrator. Since so much of the burrower's world is the product of his imagination to begin with, that world is particularly vulnerable to enemies that exist inside that same imaginative space.

The imagined enemy communicates its presence by a discourse of piping or whistling that may itself be another product of the imagination. He admits that the noise that bothers him is almost inaudible and that nobody but himself would hear it. But in effect it makes no difference whether the noise comes from the external world of the "earth" or the internal world of the burrower's psyche, since it is not so much the noise itself as what is made of it that matters. The sound becomes important only in the construction of the narrator, where we understand "construction" both as a thing built and a thing interpreted (construed). Even if the noise is trivial, faint, hardly perceptible, perhaps not really there at all, its significance is at least potentially profound. This little tiny noise might be the most important thing in the burrower's universe, and within the space of the story it indeed becomes so, no matter what uncertainties remain about its exact nature. Indeed, shortly before the fragment breaks off, the burrower confesses: "Ich bin so weft, daß ich Gewißheit gar nicht haben will" (*EP* 206; "I have reached the stage where I no longer wish to have certainty," *CS* 358).

Certainty of any kind also eludes the narrator of Kafka's very last story, "Josefine die Sängerin, oder Das Volk der Mäuse" (Josephine the Singer, or the Mouse Folk). He, too, urgently wants to know the meaning of a piping or whistling sound ("Pfeifen") made by an enigmatic and possibly dangerous creature, and ultimately he, too, must be content with guesses.

Of course there are a number of significant differences between the "Der Bau" fragment and "Josefine." For one thing, Kafka completed the latter text and published it during his lifetime, so we have what we can consider an "authorized" text to work with. For another, the narrator of "Josefine" is not also the central figure in the tale but rather an observer with only limited direct participation in the events narrated. This distance between the teller of the story and its leading characters complicates the tale's rhetorical structure, for there is an additional layer of language that lies between the reader and the voice of the protagonist. When we hear the voice of the burrower, we hear it directly; but when we hear Josephine, we hear her as she is heard and understood by someone else. We can be very sure that Kafka made a deliberate decision to insert this interpreting other between us and the heroine, for it is precisely the problem of what to make of her singing—if it is indeed "singing" that she does—that stands at the heart of the fiction.

Still, despite these and other differences, it is difficult indeed not to see a strong resemblance between these two stories so urgently concerned with a noise described by the German word *Pfeifen* ("whistling" or "piping"). One is tempted to believe that Kafka has moved from one part of the burrower's world to another, one only hinted at near the beginning of the burrower's narrative when he mentions the field mice who dig certain holes he finds useful. Perhaps the piping "Mouse Folk" of this last story are not-so-distant relatives of these little burrowers. And it is difficult, too, not to see the work of the burrow-builder, an activity that lies somewhere between inborn instinct and highly conscious art, reflected in the activity of a mouse-singer whose song is hardly distinguishable from the natural piping sounds made by all mice.

Readers of Kafka have long since noticed that many of his later fictions deal either explicitly or implicitly with art, artists, artworks, and audiences, and that he is particularly concerned with forms of art that border on or curiously merge with ordinary, non-artistic pursuits. In addition to "Der Bau" and "Josefine" there is the famous and much interpreted tale of "Ein Hungerkünstler" (A Hunger Artist), in which the art practiced—abstention from food and drink—is presented as the sole possible lifestyle for an artist who has never found any food he could stomach. Is this art? Should we admire it and reward it? Should we pay any attention to it at all? Very similar questions arise in the case of Josephine's singing, and it is quite clear that Kafka wanted his readers to share his urgent interest in them.

"Ich habe oft darüber nachgedacht, wie es sich eigentlich mit dieser Musik verhält," says the narrator early on in his exposition (*D* 350; "I have often thought about what this music of hers really means," *CS* 360). In a more literal translation, the narrator is wondering "how matters really stand with this music." In other words, he is not so much concerned with how to interpret any particular performance of hers as with the question of what place her singing has in the larger scheme of things. The question comes up because no one, including the narrator, is exactly sure what Josephine does, if anything, that deserves any special notice:

> Ist es denn überhaupt Gesang? Ist es vielleicht doch nur ein Pfeifen? Und Pfeifen allerdings kennen wir alle, es ist die eigentliche Kunstfertigkeit unseres Volkes, oder vielmehr gar keine Fertigkeit, sondern eine charakeristische Lebensäußerung. Alle pfeifen wir, aber freilich denkt niemand daran, das als Kunst auszugeben, wir pfeifen, ohne darauf zu achten. . . . (*D* 351–52)

[So is it singing at all? Is it not perhaps just a piping? And piping is something we all know about, it is the real artistic accomplishment of our people, or rather no mere accomplishment but a characteristic expression of our life. We all pipe, but of course no one dreams of making out that our piping is an art, we pipe without thinking of it.... (*CS* 361)]

The problem becomes complicated by two curious facts: first, Josephine's piping, ordinary though it may be, draws eager, receptive, and enthusiastic audiences; and second, Josephine, ordinary though she may be, demands for herself special privileges on account of the status she claims as a unique artist.

One thing, at least, about Josephine's piping appears clear: it has a profound effect on those who listen to it. The narrator confesses that, no matter how ordinary her vocalizing may be, "dringt doch—das ist nicht zu leugnen—etwas von ihrem Pfeifen unweigerlich auch zu uns" (*D* 362; "there is yet something—it cannot be denied—that irresistibly makes its way into us from Josephine's piping," *CS* 367). For a moment her singing becomes the most important thing in the world, a kind of "Botschaft des Volkes zu dem Einzelnen" (*D* 362; "message from the whole people to each individual," *CS* 367). In this way the otherwise unremarkable little singer becomes the voice of the entire community and thus, in some sense, as valuable as the whole community. That, at least, is the claim she wants to press.

Josephine's ability to hold and affect her audience may serve as evidence that her piping is really a form of art; but not everyone believes it, particularly because this very ability is also a significant problem for the community. From time to time "such large gatherings have been unexpectedly flushed by the enemy, and many of our people left lying for dead" very possibly because Josephine "attracted the enemy by her piping" (*CS* 371; "solche Versammlungen unerwartet vom Feind gesprengt wurden, und mancher der unsrigen dabei sein Leben lassen mußte ... durch ihr Pfeifen den Feind vielleicht angelockt hatte," *D* 367). The consequences of this "art" can be nothing short of disastrous for its adherents, and yet the audiences continue to assemble. Is this evidence that Josephine's singing is remarkable, or does it only prove that her audience is courageous, foolhardy, or perhaps some bizarre combination of both?

In fact the narrator pays nearly as much attention to the nature of Josephine's audience as he does to Josephine herself. Kafka clearly meant to keep both artist and public firmly in focus when he gave his story a double title, the first half naming the singer and the second specifying the community that forms her audience. And he connected the two with the rhetorically complex little word "or." The complexity arises from the fact that "or" can be used in either an exclusive or inclusive way. "Give me liberty or give me death!" is a forceful use of the exclusive "or," since the speaker clearly considers the two possibilities mutually incompatible. But one can also use "or" in circumstances where one thing can readily substitute for another. "In this recipe you may use butter or margarine": the implication is that it doesn't much matter which. You could presumably even use a combination of both butter and margarine if you didn't have quite enough of either to do the whole job. The German word "oder" behaves in exactly the same way. In the case of Kafka's title, though, it is impossible to say whether the reader is supposed to understand the "oder" as an inclusive or exclusive "or." Are we supposed to make a choice between Josephine and the Mouse Folk, or are we to believe that one can take the place of the other?

The issue is far from trivial. It is a frequent claim of the artist—an artist such as Thomas Mann, to name one prominent example that Kafka knew well—that the artist can indeed "take the place" of the group by serving as its collective voice. The individual represents the whole people. At times, so the narrator reports, just such a thing seems to happen when Josephine sings. But at other times, as in the passage quoted above in which Josephine's singing puts the group in deadly danger, it appears that artist and community are at odds, that the welfare of one is harmful to the other. Kafka's story does not attempt to resolve this question; rather it seeks to pose it in the most forceful way possible.

Josephine herself makes the whole matter more difficult by drawing herself apart from the group that nurtures and protects her. She even scoffs at the very idea of obtaining protection from the community: "Ich pfeife auf euren Schutz," she says (*D* 359), which literally means "I whistle (or pipe) on your protection." The desperate translator grasps at straws and comes up with "Your protection isn't worth an old song" (*CS* 365–66). The locution that Josephine employs turns the word used for her artistic activity, piping ("Pfeifen"), into a vulgar gesture of rejection. It also forces the reader to reconsider the whole question of what it is that Josephine does when she sings: *sie pfeift auf das Volk*, to express it in the terms the story presents. The German pun tacitly proposes that when Josephine pipes for the people, she also "pipes on" (that is, rejects) the people. The people, however, placidly disregard this rejection and continue to listen to her piping in rapt silence, "mäuschenstill" ("quiet as a mouse"). Now perhaps this is no great feat for people who really are mice, but still it bespeaks respect—a respect that Josephine, for her part, does not reciprocate.

She separates herself even further from the people by demanding special treatment:

Schon seit langer Zeit, vielleicht schon seit Beginn ihrer Künstlerlaufbahn, kämpft Josefine darum, daß sie mit Rücksicht auf ihren Gesang von jeder Arbeit befreit werde; man solle ihr also die Sorge um das tägliche Brot und alles, was sonst mit unserem Existenzkampf verbunden ist, abnehmen und es—wahrscheinlich—auf das Volk als Ganzes überwälzen. (*D* 368–69)

[For a long time, perhaps since the very beginning of her artistic career, Josephine has been fighting for exemption from all daily work on account of her singing; she should be relieved of all responsibility for earning her daily bread and being involved in the general struggle for existence, which—apparently—should be transferred on her behalf to the people as a whole. (*CS* 371)]

Kafka had a very personal stake in this claim for exemption from daily work. He had in fact actually achieved something like the dispensation Josephine desires, though not because of his art. He had been pensioned off from his job at the Workers' Accident Insurance Company because of his illness, and this respite from the need to earn a living allowed him—for a short time—to devote himself entirely to his writing. Josephine, however, has no success in persuading the community to approve her request. In marked contrast to her singing, her rhetoric falls on deaf ears: "Das Volk hört sie an und geht darüber hinweg. Dieses so leicht zu rührende Volk ist manchmal gar nicht zu rühren" (*D* 369; "The people listen to her arguments and pay no attention. Our people, so easily moved, sometimes cannot be moved at all" (*CS* 372).

But Josephine persists: "hat sie ihn [den Kampf] bisher nur durch Worte geführt, fängt sie jetzt an, andere Mittel auszuwenden" (*D* 372; "hitherto she has used only words as her weapons but now she is beginning to have recourse to other means," *CS* 373). These other means include a claim of injury, a threat to alter her performance by cutting the embellishments ("Koloraturen"—the translation has "grace notes"), and a protestation that she is too exhausted to perform. None is effective. Finally Josephine plays what she must believe is her trump card: she disappears. Surely her complete absence, the utter loss of her song, will persuade the Mouse Folk of her unique value.

Of course even this ultimate gesture is futile. The community finds that the absence of her singing is not detectably different from its presence. With a gentle, excruciatingly candid simplicity, the narrator asks a set of devastating rhetorical questions:

War ihr wirkliches Pfeifen nennenswert lauter und lebendiger, als die Erinnerung daran sein wird? War es denn noch bei ihren Lebzeiten mehr als eine bloße Erinnerung? Hat nicht vielleicht vielmehr das Volk in seiner Weisheit Josefinens Gesang, eben deshalb, weil er in dieser Art unverlierbar war, so hochgestellt? (*D* 376–77)

[Was her actual piping notably louder and more alive than the memory of it will be? Was it even in her lifetime more than a simple memory? Was it not rather because Josephine's singing was already past losing in this way that our people in their wisdom prized it so highly? (*CS* 376)]

The power of Josephine's art is by no means denied; what is denied is only that Josephine is needed for that power to find expression. The memory of her singing might actually be even more powerful than its physical presence, since the process of imagination that makes memory possible need not be constrained by the rough contingencies of the real world. It can let the imagined song soar higher, farther, and purer than any real-life song ever could.

The lines that close "Josefine die Sängerin" were the last Kafka ever wrote. When he speaks of the little mouse singer in the final words of the text as being "vergessen ... wie alle ihre Brüder" (*D* 377; "forgotten like all her brothers," *CS* 376), he was certainly thinking of his own future. We would be mistaken, though, to assume that Kafka saw his story's end, or the end of its heroine, as a melancholy one. The forgetting that is to befall the singer is placed in sharp contrast to the remembering of the song. Indeed, the community's forgetting of Josephine is possible and even likely precisely because the memory of her song is so secure. The artist may disappear forever, but the art remains intact and alive in the imagination of the audience.

Kafka believed in, and wanted us to believe in, the power of imagined discourse. This power could be corrosive and even lethal, as it seems to be in the "Der Bau" fragment, or it could be healing and revivifying, as it is in "Josefine." In either case, the locus of that power is not in its producer, whether the terrifying piping beast or the fragile piping mouse, but in those who hear the piping and make something of it. Kafka believed that those who imagine might make something of his often tentative, often incomplete, sometimes barely comprehensible art and turn it into a force far more powerful than his failing presence could ever be. In that way he, like Josephine, could attain the "gesteigerte Erlösung" (*D* 377; "heights of redemption," *CS* 376) and join the vast and peaceful community of the forgotten.

WORKS CITED

Cohn, Dorrit. "Erlebte Rede im Ich-Roman," *Germanisch-Romanische Monatsschrift* 19 (1969): 305–13.

Kafka, Franz. *The Complete Stories.* Ed. Nahum Glatzer. New York: Schocken Books, 1971. (*CS*)

———. "Der Bau." *Das Ehepaar und andere Schriften aus dem Nachlaß.* Ed. Hans-Gerd Koch. Frankfurt am Main: S. Fischer Verlag, 1994. (*EP*)

———. *Drucke zu Lebzeiten.* Ed. Wolf Kittler, Hans-Gerd Koch, Gerhard Neumann. Frankfurt am Main: S. Fischer Verlag, 1994. (*D*)

Koelb, Clayton. *Kafka's Rhetoric: The Passion of Reading.* Ithaca and London: Cornell UP, 1989.

MARTIN PUCHNER

Kafka's Antitheatrical Gestures

N̲o writer seems less made for the theater than Franz Kafka, withdrawn in his study, as we picture him, obsessively writing to keep everything safely away. This image of Kafka may be the artificial product of modernist myth-making, but enough of it rings true to question seriously whether Kafka's scripture has anything to do with the theater at all. And yet Kafka's austere writerliness does not proceed without constant reference to the theater. Kafka experimented with dramatic fragments; he was infatuated with a traveling group of Yiddish theater players for which he became the quasi-manager; and he recorded his keen interest in such canonical authors of modern drama as Strindberg, Kleist, Grillparzer, Hauptmann, Offenbach, and Hofmannsthal. His diaries and notebooks are full of vignettes about specific productions as well as brief reflections on the theater. On 9 November 1911, Kafka records, "Vorgestern geträumt: Lauter Theater" [Dreamt yesterday: everything theater], and this theatrical dream can be taken as a point of departure for investigating the significance of the theater for Kafka's oeuvre.[1]

Insisting on the centrality of the theater for Kafka also implies rethinking the way we understand modernist literature; it means putting pressure on terms such as écriture, writerliness, and literariness that have become all-too-familiar instruments for institutionalizing and canonizing literary

From *Germanic Review* 78, no. 3 (Summer 2003): 177–93. © 2003 by Heldref Publications.

modernism from Mallarmé and Joyce to Stein and Kafka. No matter how much these and many other authors celebrate self-referentially the act of writing as the required ritual of high modernism, this writing is firmly, if not always visibly, connected to the theater. This does not mean that we should be content with noting that writers such as these are in some vague sense "theatrical"; rather, what is needed is a reflection on the manner in which they are engaged with the theater, if often in a conflictual or even adversarial manner. Mallarmé, Stein, and Joyce wrote extensively about the theater just as they often chose the dramatic form. Their dramas, however, are either repelled by or in competition with the theater. It is in a comparable manner that the theater acts on Kafka's oeuvre, namely as a frame against which much of his writing struggles and to which it therefore remains calibrated.

As in the case of Mallarmé, James, Stein, Joyce, Hofmannsthal, Yeats, and Beckett, Kafka's engagement with the theater determines his writing even and especially when it is no longer explicitly about or for the actual stage. Therefore, one might measure Kafka's texts through a triangle formed by modernism, theater, and writing. These three terms create an area of congruence: a modernist antitheatricalism, a field determined by a struggle with and against the theater that is the motor of much modernist writing. When Mallarmé writes closet dramas that shun the stage as vulgar and celebrate writing as privileged medium; when Joyce in the "Circe" chapter of *Ulysses* turns to the dramatic form without desire for a stage production; when James rewrites his plays as novels; when Stein creates texts that resemble plays but have no *dramatis personae*—all these are moments when the most central writers of modernism develop their style by using aspects of the theater to keep it at a distance, by turning the dramatic form against the theater. These writers are far from indifferent to the theater. On the contrary, they testify to the centrality of the theater for modernism, but as something that must be resisted. Likewise, I will argue, Kafka's prose is not so much theatrical as it is antitheatrical, presenting dramatic and theatrical scenes and characters only to decompose and recompose them according to a specifically literary poetics. Kafka relates to the stage through a resistance to the theater, and it is against this resistance that directors have sought to turn his texts into theatrical performance.

More surprising, perhaps, than this literary and dramatic rebellion against theatrical presentation is the fact that modernist antitheatricalism influenced theatrical practice itself. Directors who made it their business to bring modernist closet dramas on the stage also imported their antitheatricalism and then had to confront this antitheatricalism in the theater. Far from paralyzing the theater, antitheatricalism became one of the engines for innovation on the stage, prompting directors such as Lugné-Poe and E. G. Craig to rethink and question their understanding of actors, mise-en-scène, and the dramatic text. Kafka adaptations to the stage, both in their successes and failures, are part of this tradition of antitheatrical theater. These productions do not reveal that Kafka's work was always somehow theatrical and therefore secretly made for the stage, but rather they indicate that the theater was drawn to Kafka, as to other antitheatrical modernists, precisely because of his resistance to the theater.

I. Antitheatrical Drama

The claim that modernist writing derives from a contentious relation to the theater finds in Kafka a particularly satisfying example, for we can examine directly the struggle between literature and theater in his early experiments with the dramatic form. What is so central about these short dramatic scenes is not their intrinsic value nor their theatrical imagination but the very unease with which they relate to the theater. The earliest such dramatic fragment, jotted down in a diary in 1911, presents three dialogues between two characters. The author's discomfort with the theater emerges not so much in the dialogue itself but rather in the use of the stage direction, that part of the dramatic form most directly calibrated to the actual theater. Kafka's stage directions, however, do little by way of indicating motivation, of sketching scenes, or of outlining the basic stage business of entrances and exits. In the third dialogue, for example, one stage direction laconically arrests the text with a sudden, enigmatic gesture, indicating that Karl, while complaining, "Weil du keine Rücksicht nimmst" [Because you never care for my feelings, *T* 126], is rubbing his fingers, "reibt sich die Finger." The connection between speech and gesture remains opaque. The stage direction is entirely descriptive, stubbornly refusing its traditional role of providing a frame for theatrical adaptation and interpretation. All this stage direction does is to zoom in on a single gesture, or even a part of a gesture, and detaches it from its immediate corporeal and theatrical context.

Similarly isolated and extracted gestures are prominent in Kafka's other dramatic texts. A second fragment, written in 1913, presents a dialogue between a man and a woman that soon turns into a physical fight before it ends abruptly in a tableau of frozen gestures. Further fragments, all less than a page long, indicate the same obsessive attention to details of gestures, such as a "ungelenk ziehende Bewegungen" [clumsy, dragging movements], a compulsive "[he] nagt an den Lippen" [is biting his lips], or "[she] zieht die Tragbänder der Schürze in die Höhe" [is pulling up the ends of the apron, *T* 232]. In none of these excessive details can we hope to find additional information about motivation, character, or stage action. It is not, however, that Kafka wrote all these dramas without considering the theater at all. On the contrary, his stage directions strategically mislead the reader by pretending that a theatrical performance is indeed the purpose of these dialogues, but then frustrate this expectation by undermining the traditional function of the stage direction. It is by turning the stage direction against the stage that Kafka develops his first antitheatrical strategy.

How this use of the stage direction would end up influencing Kafka's later writings can be fathomed from his longest dramatic piece, *Der Gruftwächter* [*The Crypt Guard*] (1916–1917), which was found by Max Brod among Kafka's octavo notebooks and published in 1936 together with other texts from the literary bequest under the title *Beschreibung eines Kampfes*.[2] Again, we have excessive details and arrested gestures, but now something of an acting style emerges out of the more-developed movements and interactions: These figures engage in an extreme form of melodramatic acting that will remain a persistent feature of Kafka's later work. At one point, a guard "wirft sich weinend hin" [throws himself to the ground, crying, *B* 225], while other characters do such things as show their trembling fists, cry, and raise their index fingers threateningly. The center piece of *Der Gruftwächter*, however, is a narration, as the guard describes his nightly battle against family ghosts who are trying to escape from the crypt. From the ghostly knocking on the window with "inhuman" fingers, "Das sind nicht menschliche Fingerknöchel" [these are not human knuckles, *B* 227], we are introduced to a scenario in which the guard is actually lifted up from the ground as he pushes the ghosts back in a manner that resembles more a dance than a fight: "schon schaukeln wir im Kampf" [already we are swinging (rocking) in the battle, *B* 230]. Here, the choreography of gestures and the interaction of characters are entirely detached from the requirements of the stage. The guard's story thus takes over and continues the decomposition of the theatrical scene Kafka had begun in his antitheatrical stage directions.

With this piece, Kafka moves from stage direction to descriptive narration. After the *Gruftwächter*, Kafka never returned to drama. Not that Kafka simply realized that he was made for narrative rather than for drama; rather, the origin of his narrative style in the stage direction indicates how much his later narrative prose continued to be tied to the theater, if by way of decomposing it. One might say that Kafka's prose originates not so much in drama but in a combination of the antitheatrical stage direction and staged storytelling.

The formal transition from drama to narrative can be observed live, as it were, in a piece that Kafka wrote first as drama only to rewrite it immediately as a (very) short story. At an unusually early hour, a maid announces an unexpected visitor, Kleipe, to her master, a student. Trying to justify his calling on the student at such an untimely hour, the visitor stutters that he and the student both come from the same small city of Wulfshausen. Again, the dialogue is secondary; what really matters are the gestures that postpone and supplement the visitor's verbal explanation:[3] "Kleipe: *geht langsam zum Bett und sucht auf dem Weg durch Handbewegungen etwas zu erklären. Beim Reden hilft er sich durch Strecken des Halses und durch Hoch- und Tiefziehen der Augenbrauen*: Ich bin nämlich auch aus Wulfenshausen" [Kleipe: *goes slowly toward the bed and on the way tries to explain something with his hand-gestures. He stretches his neck and raises and lowers his eyebrows to assist his speech*: You know, I too am from Wulfenshausen, *T* 270]. The hand gestures precede the verbal explanation, and even when he finally gets the sentence out, he still has to revert to gestures—this time the movements of the neck and eyebrows—to explain his early visit. All this is described in a stage direction that well exceeds the speech it is putatively "assisting"; additional stage directions single out other peculiar aspects such as the visitor's unusually long arms, "lange Arme." The stage direction indeed dominates this dramatic text, and it must have been this fact that compelled Kafka to rewrite the entire text as a narrative story.

The narrative version is much shorter, condensing over half a page of dramatic text into two sentences, benefiting from a medium that does not have to worry about actors' continual presence and interaction on a stage. The first sentence introduces the story in a most conventional narrative style: "Gegen fünf Uhr früh, einmal im Winter, würde dem Studenten durch das halbbekleidete Dienstmädchen ein Gast gemeldet" [Around five o'clock on a winter morning, a half-dressed maid announced a visitor to the student, *T* 270]. The next sentence renders what is left of the theatrical scene itself:

"Was denn? Wie denn?" fragte der Student noch schlaftrunken, da trat schon mit einer von dem Dienstmädchen geliehenen brennenden Kerze ein junger Mann ein, hob in der einen Hand die Kerze, um den Studenten besser zu sehen, und senkte in der anderen Hand den Hut fast bis zur Erde, so lange war sein Arm.

["What now," asked the student, who was still sleepy, as a young man was already entering the room with a candle, which he had borrowed from the maid, raised with the one hand the candle to see the student better, and lowered the hat with the other hand almost touching the floor, so long was his arm. *T* 270]

This narrative version proceeds by isolating a gesture, pushing it to its limit (the arm touching the floor, the candle abruptly raised to the face), and freezing it in a tableau so that its aesthetic component—the symmetry of the one hand raised and the other lowered—exaggerates and exceeds the function of greeting. This isolated gesture not only freezes the imaginary theatrical space but decomposes the very elements—the integrity of characters, the continuity of theatrical action—on which theatrical space and the continual presence of actors depend. Refusing to connect gesture and dialogue, Kafka demotivates his characters, and by isolating specific gestures, he decomposes what would otherwise be their continued existence as acting bodies on a stage.

This decomposition characterizes the relationship of Kafka's later ouvre to the theater, motivated by a struggle against the theater. This struggle begins with stage directions, continues with staged narratives, and is fully developed once Kafka rewrites these stage directions and staged stories in the narrative form.

At times, the theater and the performing arts enter his texts thematically, as in the hunger artist and the display of his gradually disappearing body; the ape's mimetic adaptation of human speech and gesture; the questionable talents of Josefine, a singer and performer within a society of mice; and the audience's embarrassment caused by the performing dogs. In these texts, Kafka also reflects on the audience, on its participation and constitutive role in the creation of a performance. It does not matter so much, for example, how well Josefine sings as long as the audience takes pleasure in what she is doing. In fact, the audience's voyeurism becomes intrusive; it bothers, for example, the hunger artist and the singing dogs, plagued as they are by an acute case of stage fright. But it is not necessary for Kafka to embed his figures in actual theatrical scenes. Theatrical posing and the audience's eager gazes can happen anywhere. *The Trial* exposes the voyeurs witnessing the arrest of Josef K., and the grisly execution in *The Penal Colony* is justified through its cathartic effects on both the victim and the audience: "alles Theater."

More important than the actual theater and its audience is the manner in which Kafka takes apart the performing body, analyzing it as isolated gestures and poses, entirely disconnected from one another. From this perspective, I would like to reconsider what many critics have referred to as Kafka's "dramatic" style, in particular Joseph Vogl's account of "enacted scenes," and also analyze the manner in which Kafka estranges movements and gestures from their context.[4] I want to pursue the concept of estrangement further, for the Brechtian term "estrangement" itself derives from an antitheatrical impulse, what Brecht called his deep "distrust of the theater."[5] Kafka's prose arises from a similar distrust and a similar desire to play off the narrative—or epic—against the theater, a form of writerly antitheatricalism that nevertheless keeps the theater close at hand.

II. Critique of the Theater

Inspired by Max Brod's essay "Axiome über das Drama" ["Axioms on Drama"] published in the journal *Schaubühne* [*The Stage*], Kafka began writing down reflections on drama and theater from which we can deduce a critique of theatrical representation, the belated theory to match his antitheatrical practice. Brod theorizes that the theater alone is capable of a full and continuous representation of characters and scenes, whereas the novel has to pick and choose, contenting itself with highlights of a few essential moments. The abundance of an actual theatrical performance is thus set in contrast to the necessary restraint of the novel. Kafka agrees with this distinction but reverses the values: The necessary ellipses and economy are the novel's strength and the continuous presence of scenes, the theater's curse.

What most bothers Kafka and many modernist, antitheatrical writers is the physical, unmediated, and continuous presence of human actors in the theater. In a passage that is as metaphorical as it is intricate, Kafka describes the process of personification, "Vermenschlichung," that occurs once a text is turned into theatrical performance:

> Dadurch gerät das Drama in seiner höchsten Entwicklung in eine unerträgliche Vermenschlichung, die herabzuziehen, erträglich zu machen, Aufgabe des Schauspielers ist, der die ihm vorgeschriebene Rolle gelockert, zerfasert, wehend um sich trägt. Das Drama schwebt also in der Luft, aber nicht als ein vom Sturm getragenes Dach, sondern als ein ganzes Gebäude, dessen Grundmauern mit einer heute noch dem Irrsinn sehr nahen Kraft aus der Erde hinauf gerissen worden sind.

> [The drama, in its highest development, brings about an insufferable humanization (re-anthropomorphization), and it is the task of the actor to pull it down, to make it bearable by wearing the prescribed role loose, fraying it apart so that it blows about around himself. The drama is hovering in the air, but not as a roof that is carried by a storm, but as a whole building, the foundation of which is ripped out of the earth with a force that still today comes close to madness. *T* 92]

Like Mallarmé, Maeterlinck, and other turn-of-the-century theater reformers, Kafka is both intrigued and appalled by the anthropomorphization or personification that is the inevitable consequence of the presence of human actors on a stage. For Kafka, this personification is so strange that he resorts

to a far-fetched metaphor, which, however, is itself borrowed from the theater, namely that of an ill-fitting costume. The actor does not impersonate
the role mimetically, but rather "wears" it like a dress so that the role "blows
about him" like a piece of cloth. Moreover, this humanization is not a completed process—a well-fitting dress—but an incomplete and ill-fitting one.
The actor must "loosen" the role that is constantly in the process of breaking
down, of "fraying out." To this first metaphor Kafka adds a second one that
takes the drama to be "flying in the air" with the actor's awkward humanization "pulling it down." The actor is somehow caught in a double-edged
struggle, a struggle against a role he must both impersonate and keep at
bay—wear like a dress and fray—and against a drama that he both uproots
and pulls down again.[6]

A different entry combines these two metaphors, the dress and of the
struggle with drama:

> Manchmal scheint es, daß das Stück oben in den Soffitten ruht, die
> Schauspieler Streifen davon abgezogen haben, deren Enden sie zum
> Spielen in den Händen halten oder um den Körper gewickelt haben,
> und daß nur hie und da ein schwerabzulösender Streifen einen
> Schauspieler zum Schrecken des Publikums in die Höhe nimmt.

> [Sometimes it seems as if the play were resting up there in the
> decoration of the ceiling, that the actors have torn strips from it,
> holding the ends playfully in their hands or having wrapped it
> around their bodies, and that only here and there a stripe that is
> hard to tear is pulling up the actor in the air, which is scaring the
> audience. *T* 92]

The drama is somewhere in the air, and if the actors tear pieces from it,
the unbearable humanitization of the drama is made bearable, presumably,
because the play appears only in strips and pieces, at no point fitting the
actor fully and neatly, thus resisting a tight mimesis of a human character.
The actors are struggling with the play, tearing it apart, but the play strikes
back by pulling them up in the air, carrying them away and thus subjecting
them to its own will. Role, play, and the acting body are thus never in congruence; the play and the actor are like a curtain, a piece of cloth, or a dress
that is torn apart and appears only in pieces.[7]

In a letter to Max Brod, Kafka describes the marionette-like aesthetics of mach theater, "etwas tief Marionettenhaftes" [something deeply marionette-like, *Briefe* 214], and in yet another entry, Kafka explicitly contrasts his
own passion for details with the craft exercised by actors on a stage:

Mein Nachahmungstrieb hat nichts Schauspielerisches, es fehlt ihm vor allem die Einheitlichkeit. Das Grobe, auffallend Characteristische in seinem ganzen Umfange kann ich gar nicht nachahmen, ähnliche Versuche sind mir immer mißlungen, sie sind gegen meine Natur. Zur Nachahmung von Details des Groben habe ich dagegen einen entscheidenden Trieb, die Manipulationen gewisser Menschen mit Spazierstöcken, ihre Haltung der Hände, ihre Bewegung der Finger nachzuahmen drängt es mich und ich kann es ohne Mühe.

[My desire to imitate has nothing to do with the actor, in particular it is lacking unity and continuity. I cannot imitate that which is crude and that which draws attention and is characteristic; similar attempts have always failed, they are against my nature. However, I have the urge to imitate the way in which certain people handle their walking stick, the way they are holding their hands, and the movements of their fingers, and I manage to do it without difficulty. *Briefe* [61]

Acting and actors are foreign to him precisely because of the continually personifying nature of theatrical representation. Kafka himself fails in the task of presenting a "unified" [*einheitlich*] character; all he can do is mimic details. It is in this critique of the actor that Kafka participates in the modernist, antitheatrical tradition, ranging from Mallarmé and Yeats to Craig and Beckett. What these writers and directors object to is the physical presence of human bodies on the stage that impress onto the theater an irreducible and seemingly unmediated form of continuous and character-driven mimesis, resistant to abstraction, dislocation, and estrangement.[8] Some directors, such as Craig, respond to this problem by demanding that actors be replaced with marionettes, and others, such as Yeats and Beckett, by arresting actors in urns and ash bins. Like them, Kafka fantasizes about a drama that arrests actors and keeps them from acting altogether: "das beste Drama [wäre] ein ganz anregungsloses zum Beispiel philosophisches Drama, das von sitzenden Schauspielern in einer beliebigen Zimmerdekoration vorgelesen würde" [The best drama would be one without stimulation or movement, for example a philosophical drama, read by actors sitting surrounded by an irrelevant decoration. *T* 91]. Not only are the actors sitting; Kafka describes this drama as "anregungslos" which describes the absence of stimulation and also includes the meaning of "regungslos"—without movement. The suggestion that such a drama would be philosophical points in the direction of Plato and the fact that the long antitheatrical tradition originates not in Aristotle but in Plato's dialogues; Kafka imagines what could be called a Platonist theater.[9]

This reading or closet theater is just a speculation on Kafka's part, but what he actually does in his own writings has the same effect, namely the undoing of theater. Instead of writing philosophical closet dramas or arresting actors, Kafka takes apart these human bodies in the act of writing down their gestures. In this, his use of the literary against the theatrical is akin to the modernist closet drama, including the closet dramas of Mallarmé, Hofmannsthal, and Joyce, which likewise fragment the stage through the medium of literature.

III. Writing Down Actors

In emphasizing Kafka's decomposition of actors, I do not mean to suggest that actors were for him just theoretical or hypothetical figures. On the contrary, Kafka's dramatic experiments and emerging theory of the theater coincide with his acquaintance with several actors through his engagement with the Yiddish theater. Since Evelyn Torton Beck's magisterial study *Kafka and the Yiddish Theater* (1971), it has become impossible to consider Kafka's relation to the theater without an account of his particular relation to the Yiddish theater, and so it is necessary to apply my argument to this, Kafka's most well-known theatrical episode.[10]

Beginning in May 1910, Kafka and Max Brod adopted the habit of frequenting the Café-Restaurant Savoy where a Hassidic theater group from Lemberg gave regular performances that lasted, with interruptions, until January 1912.[11] Kafka recorded more than one hundred pages of visits to the theater, to the *varieté*, and to other types of theatrical performances in his diaries, but his visits to the Yiddish theater left the most lasting impression. Not only did he become a regular in the Café Savoy, he also befriended the actor Jizchak Löwy, organized guest performances for this theater troupe in other cities, and tried to raise money and recognition for the Yiddish theater among the *blasé* Prague Jewish middle class that regarded the Hassidic actors and their language as primitive, foreign, and improper.[12] And, of course, he fell in love with the actor Mania Tschissik. There can be no doubt, then, that this encounter with the Yiddish theater constitutes Kafka's most intimate and sustained engagement with the theater.

He engaged the Yiddish theater primarily through the mode of literary decomposition. This is exemplified in Kafka's love for Mania Tschissik, which he noted in his diary could only be satisfied "durch Literatur oder Beischlaf" [through literature or intercourse, *T* 107]. Kafka, it may come as no surprise, chose literature. The kind of literature, however, through which Kafka "satisfied" his love for Tschissik, is not just the writing of literature in general but a particular type of writing against the theater. This literature does not take the form of the dramatic fragments but of extensive notes, descriptions, and transcriptions of theatrical scenes and episodes, many of them centered on Tschissik's performances, which Kafka jotted down in his diaries. In them, Kafka experiments with different types of writing on the theater, the plot of the performance, the quality of the singing, and the significance of the play. In particular, however, Kafka is intrigued by the actor's gestures, postures, and mannerisms.[13] One day, for example, be notes triumphantly: "Neu an ihr erkannte Bewegungen: Drücken der Hand in die Tiefe des nicht sehr guten Mieders, kurzes Zucken der Schultern und Hüften beim Hohn, besonders wenn sie dem Verhöhnten den Rücken zukehrt" [I recognized some new movements: the hand pressed at the depth of the shabby bodice, short jerks of the shoulders and hips when expressing scorn, especially when she turns her back toward the scorned, *T* 107]. Anything that can enlarge his inventory of gestures is noted in the diary, which becomes his storage space for gestures to be used in his later literary oeuvre.

To wrest gestures from the theater and to store them in his diary, Kafka needed to develop strategies for representing these gestures in writing. The diary not only supplies the gestures Kafka will use in his fictional texts but also imposes on them a particular mode of representation that appears in his stage directions. In his diaries, Kafka perfects his technique of representing theatrical gestures by radically isolating them, taking them out of their original context, and depersonifying or dehumanizing them. Kafka here continues a genre of writing against the theater and the actor's body developed in Mallarmé's *Crayonné au théâtre*. It is a tradition characterized by a singular form of attention to details of gestures and specifically one that detaches them from their theatrical context. At the heart of this project stands a poetics of the moving body, the question of how exactly one can capture actors' or dancers' movements through words: "Notwendigkeit, über Tänzerinnen mit Rufzeichen zu reden" [Necessity of writing with exclamation marks about dancers, *T* 198]. Competing with the theater, the text must create its own technique of writing movement, for which the use of question marks is perhaps not a particularly sophisticated but telling proposal.

Beside punctuation, Kafka also develops a rhetoric, a figurative mode of representing gestures. In one of the numerous pieces on Tschissik, he writes:

21. Oct. 1911: Ihr Gang bekommt leicht etwas Feierliches, da sie die Gewohnheit hat, ihre langen Arme zu heben, zu strecken und langsam zu bewegen. Besonders als sie das jüdische Nationallied sang, in den großen Hüften schwach schaukelte und die parallel

den Hüften gebogenen Arme auf und ab bewegte, mit ausgehöhlten
Händen, als spiele sie mit einem langsam fliegenden Ball.

[Her way of walking is somewhat ceremonious since she has
the habit of slowly lifting, extending, and moving her long arms.
Especially when she was singing the Jewish national anthem,
moving her hips with her arms, bent in concordance to the hips,
moving up and down with hands curved as if she were playing with
a ball that was flying slowly. *T* 82]

Kafka wants to create a poetics of movement with which to capture theatrical acting in descriptive prose. After characterizing Tschissik's mode of
gesturing as "ceremonious" he goes on to encode the specific kind of ceremony within the language of his text. Tschissik's hands, slowly moving up
and down, certainly do evoke the impression of ceremony; but when Kafka
notes how her arms describe the same curve as her hips do, the characteristic
of ceremony is replaced by the image of a slow dance, which gives way to a
hypothetical game, "als spiele sie mit einem langsam fliegenden Ball" [as if
she were playing with a ball that was flying slowly]. The final image of the
ball is added onto the moving body; it is not itself tied firmly to the test of
the sentence, but adjoined by "as if" that keeps the actually executed gestures
and the hypothetical game apart, an impression reinforced by the fact that
the ball is flying impossibly slowly. In fact, the entire ball game is nothing
but a comparison; it does not fit and needs to be adjusted retrospectively.
All of these elements do not quite work. It is as if Kafka wanted to make
trouble for the machinery of theatrical presentation by inserting ill-fitting
comparisons, hypotheses, and projections, a writing that takes apart the
stage through series of "as ifs" and figurative pantomimes.

Gestures in the Yiddish theater, however, are not only ceremonious,
they are also melodramatic. Because of the often loud audience, gathered
in bars and cafés around provisional stages, the Yiddish actors must take
recourse in gestures, because their words, polyglot words, are in danger of
being misunderstood if they are heard at all.[14] Max Brod noted the often
unintentionally comical presentations in the Café Savoy and the tendency
toward kitsch and wild exaggerations (139). Similarly, Kafka observes that
the main fault of these actors is simply that they make too much of an
effort, "so ist doch auch dieser auf der Bühne herabgeschneite Schauspieler
nur deshalb schlecht, weil er zu stark nachahmt" [this actor who has suddenly appeared on the stage is so bad only because he imitates too much, *T*
161]. Peter Brooks has identified this type of exaggerated gesturing as the
basic feature of melodramatic acting, characterized by the insufficiency of

speech.[15] Melodramatic gesturing signals this insufficiency and the resulting struggle for expressing in gesture what cannot be adequately expressed in language. These gestures do not succeed in taking over the work of articulation and must content themselves with announcing their own failure. In a similar manner, Kafka highlights the way in which gestures replace insufficient words without forming a fully articulated second language. Kafka does not seek to translate gestures back into language but contents himself with registering their effects and also their limits:

> Aus der Menge ihres wahren Spiels kommen hie und da Vorstöße der Faust, Drehungen des Armes, der unsichtbare Schleppen in den Falten um den Körper zieht, Anlegen der gespreitzten Finger an die Brust, weil der kunstlose Schrei nicht genügt. Ihr Spiel ist nicht mannigfaltig; [...] das Sichaufrichten beim Widerstand, das den Zuschauer zwingt, sich um ihren ganzen Körper zu kümmern.

> [From the multitude of her true play, here and there we see sudden jerks of the fist, turns of the arm, which is dragging invisible trains around the body in the folds of the dress, and how she puts her outspread fingers to her breast, since her artless scream does not suffice. Her playing is not much varied (...) the way she stands up when posing resistance forces the audience to pay attention to her whole body. *T* 83]

The moments Kafka singles out—the violently gesturing arms, clenched fists and outspread fingers pressed to the breast in emotional turmoil—are melodramatic gestures, because the emotions expressed are too overpowering to be conveyed in language; even screams fail. The center of expression is thus dislocated from the mouth to the body as a whole, "das den Zuschauer zwingt, sich um ihren ganzen Körper zu kümmern" [forcing the audience to pay attention to her whole body]. Kafka does not worry about whether this gesturing body succeeds in giving expression to emotions and passions. Nor does he show any interest in evaluating this acting as acting. Instead, he takes melodrama as the material that allows him to exercise his own project of analyzing melodramatic gestures by decomposing them.[16]

The Yiddish theater uses another mode of gesturing, akin to the melodramatic project of encoding emotions and passions in gestures and poses where language fails: pantomime. Here too, however, Kafka does not simply seek to represent pantomime in his texts but to detach it from its original theatrical context. He characterized Tschissik's ceremonious gesturing "as if playing with a ball"; the pantomime here lies not in the gesture of the actor but in the eye of the beholder or, rather, in Kafka's text. The same act of what might be called projected pantomime—of figuring gestures in terms of pantomime—returns when Tschissik's gesturing arm is said to be "pulling invisible trains around the body in the folds of the dress." The dancer's gestures are described as acts of pantomime, gesturing "as if" the actor were in a certain situation and "as if" a specific stage prop were at hand. Although melodrama signals the limits of speech, pantomime is premised on its absence but also on the ability of gestures to take its place. In pantomime, however, speech is not the only thing that is absent. Almost as important is the absence of central stage props and other contextual elements: a ball game is enacted without a ball; a boxing match executed without ever hitting the opponent. Purposeful movement is arrested halfway or otherwise deprived of its goal; what has been a means to an end—throwing a ball; hitting an opponent—becomes an end in itself. It is the elimination of purpose that turns pantomimic gestures into signs, signaling the suggestion of a ball game or a boxing match without it really occurring onstage.

In another example of projected and therefore figurative theatricality, we can see Kafka's view of theater as a space where causality and motivation can be not only feigned but inverted:

> Schönes: wie Frau Tschissik unter den Händen der römischen Soldaten (die sie allerdings erst zu sich reißen mußte, denn sie fürchteten sich offenbar, sie anzurühren) sich wand, während die Bewegungen der drei Menschen durch ihre Sorge und Kunst fast, nur fast, dem Rhythmus des Gesanges folgten. Das Lied, in dem sie die Erscheinung des Messias ankündigte und, ohne zu stören, nur infolge ihrer Macht, Harfenspiel durch Bewegungen der Violin-Bogenführung dastellt.

> [Beauty: the way Mrs. Tschissik twists and turns in the hands of the Roman soldiers (whom she first had to pull towards her, since they apparently were afraid to touch her) while the movements of the three men, due to her anxiety and manner, almost exclusively followed the rhythm of the song. The song, in which she announced the appearance of the Messiah and, without interruption, through only her power, represented harp playing by the movements of the violin-bow. *T* 107]

What Kafka creates is a scene of projected, figurative pantomimes: the actor evokes the image of harp-playing even though there is no such instrument at hand, and the way she does so is by imitating another type of movement:

the movements of the violin bow. It remains unclear whether she is actually holding a violin bow in her hands, using it as a prop for the harp-imitation, or whether she is miming—at least for the observer Kafka—the harp by miming the gesture of violin bowing. This double pantomime follows another curious twist on stage gestures: although the actor is supposed to be roughly handled by the Roman soldiers, Kafka notes that in fact it is the other way around; it is she who has to pull the soldiers, who are too shy to play rough, so that she and not the soldiers is performing the active part. Again Kafka's text intervenes in the theater, separating action, stage prop, and effects on the audience. No gesture remains itself but instead refers to something else so that nothing on stage can be taken at face value—at one point, he observes that actors embracing one another on stage are in fact holding each other's wigs: "Wenn die Schauspieler einander umarmen, halten sie einander gegenseitig die Perücken fest" (*T* 172). This is not an interpretation of a performance; it is an analysis that separates its components, disconnecting them from one another, undoing the coherent space of the theater and the continuous action that unfolds there. Undoing the theater, however, does not create chaos; on the contrary, it is that which leads to the aesthetic itself, what Kafka simply calls beauty, "Schönes!"

IV. Antitheatrical and Minor Gestures

Since Walter Benjamin's early essays on Kafka, the term often attributed to the theatrical traces in Kafka's writing is that of gesture or of a gestural language.[17] Here too, a discussion of Kafka's antitheatricalism, the way in which his texts decompose actors, can provide a way of understanding the gestural in a new light. At first sight, gestures seem to belong simply to the theatrical, and the notion of a gestural language thus points toward a theatrical quality in Kafka's writing. In light of the preceding analysis, however, I will argue that Kafka's so-called gestural style, too, must be understood in terms of his larger antitheatricalism.

Kafka's technique of decomposing Tschissik and her fellow actors of the Yiddish theater provides the best point of departure for this argument, for the term "gesture" in Kafka's mind, was firmly connected to Yiddish. Kafka experienced Yiddish, a language considered uncouth among Prague's upper-middle-class Jews, primarily in the Yiddish theater. In his lecture on Yiddish, therefore, Kafka defines this language entirely in terms of the Yiddish-speaking, Eastern European actor: "Jargon ist alles, Wort, chassidische Melodie und das Wesen dieses ostjüdischen Schauspielers selbst" [Yiddish is everything, word, Hassidic melody, and the essence of this east-Jewish actor himself, *H* 309]. Yiddish, in Kafka's eyes, is essentially musical and theatrical language, a language of actors.[18]

There is only a small but a significant step from the theatrical to the gestural, from a theatrical language to a gestural one. In a letter to Max Brod, Kafka describes Yiddish as "eine organische Verbindung von Papierdeutsch und Gebärdensprache" [a combination of Paper-German and a language of gestures, *Briefe* 336]. *Paper-German* refers to an administrative language imposed on Prague by Vienna. This bureaucratic German is now confronted with a particular kind of corporeal language, *Gebärdensprache*. When Kafka talks about this dialect as a body language, he means this literally, physically, and gesturally, continuing the type of transcription that was so characteristic for his writings on actors and the theater. The passage continues: "wie plastisch ist dieses [. . .] den Oberarm ausrenkende und das Kinn hinaufreißende: Glauben *Sie*! oder dieses die Knie aneinander zerreibende: 'er schreibt. Über wem?'" [How plastic it is, this (. . .) "You believe this!" that dislocates the arm and pulls up one's chin, or this "he writes. About who? (sic)," that grinds down the knees on one another, *Briefe* 336]. Specific expressions and idioms seem to be intrinsically tied to certain gestures and movements, such as pulling up the chin, throwing the arms about, and grinding knees. It is almost as if Kafka's machine of decomposing gestures is now being applied to gestural language or the gestural effects of language itself. The gestures inscribed in or evoked by Yiddish are not continuous theatrical actions, but isolated, decomposed, and enigmatic gestures like the ones isolated by Kafka's antitheatrical stage directions.

In addition, Yiddish is not simply a gestural language but a combination of a hypothetical and unspecified gestural language and Paper-German. This combination of Paper-German and a language of gestures is a heterogeneous mix of body and bureaucracy, and one that leads to a contested interaction between them: Gestures introduce an element of instability, an ungovernable movement, into proper or Paper-German, which comes to life only when "Judenhände sie [die Sprache] dürchwühlen" [Jewish hands rake (it) up (the German language), *Briefe* 337]. What Kafka describes here is a process of undoing and redoing German that makes it both familiar and strange. On the one hand, Yiddish consists exclusively of foreign words, "Fremdwörter"; on the other hand, however, Kafka assures his audience, "wie viel mehr Jargon Sie verstehen als Sie glauben" [You will understand much more Yiddish than you think], arguing that Yiddish is a mixture of chaos and order: "In diesem Treiben herrschen aber wieder Bruchstücke bekannter Sprachgesetze" [one can find fragments of well-known linguistic laws, *H* 306, 307]. It is this combination of familiarity and estrangement that Deleuze and Guattari took as the definition of a minor literature.[19] We can take it also as a description of the peculiar relation between literariness and theater that marks Kafka's prose, between a paper language and a gestural one, and thus define Kafka's decomposed, antitheatrical gestures as "minor" gestures.

The earliest critic who applied a notion of gesture to Kafka's oeuvre was Walter Benjamin, and it is therefore in response to his reading that an antitheatrical reading of the gestural in Kafka must be developed. Benjamin writes: "Kafkas ganzes Werk [stellt] einen Kodex von Gesten [dar]" [Kafka's whole work presents a codex of gestures].[20] And in notes for an essay on Kafka, we can find a further specification: "Gesten [. . .] die immer wieder neu vom Verfasser inszeniert und beschriftet werden, ohne ihren symbolischen Gehalt einer bestimmten Stelle auszuliefern" [gestures that are ever staged anew and inscribed by the author without delivering their symbolic substance at a particular place, 173].[21] Gesture here becomes a special case of Benjamin's master-trope: allegory. Gestures are "staged" [inszeniert], but they are also "inscribed," "subscribed," or better yet, "labeled" [beschriftet] in the manner of the allegorical *imago* whose meaning is assured by a controlling *subscriptio*.[22] What is specific about the allegorical gesturality of Kafka, however, is that the gestures Kafka represents are often opaque and therefore tender the act of reading difficult. Although the language referring to gestures can be read immediately, the signifying gestures to which it refers cannot. The language of gesture works by suggestion, not by explicit reference; it remains opaque or, as Benjamin terms it, "cloudy." In a comment on *Vor dem Gesetz*, he writes, "Etwas war immer nur im Gestus für Kafka faßbar. Und dieser Gestus, den er nicht verstand, bildet die wolkige Stelle der Parabeln. Aus ihr geht Kafka's Dichtung hervor" [Kafka could grasp some things always only in gesture. And this gesture, which he did not understand, forms the cloudy (nebulous) spot of the parables. From this gesture, arises Kafka's fiction. *Benjamin über Kafka* 27]. In the middle of the parable, instead of a *tertium comparationis*, instead of an element that would allow for a transposition of the parable and hence for its comprehension, we are left with a gesture that remains vague no matter how much we may try to label it with meaning.

Gesture thus escapes rigid labeling and fixed meaning, and it is for this reason that the category of gesture has surfaced with such frequency in the several "crises of language," especially the one that is most closely associated with Kafka, namely the turn-of-the-century crisis of language whose spiritual center was Vienna.[23] Drawing on older debates about the origin of language from Vico to Warburton and from Condillac and Rousseau to Herder, this crisis of language took the form of a widespread obsession with finding a more expressive alternative to conventional and therefore dead—should we say "paper"?—language. This is the way in which Werner Hamacher reads Benjamin's figure of the "cloudy spot," arguing that in Kafka gesture is "what remains of language after meaning is withdrawn from it and it is gesture that withdraws from meaning" (329).[24] In this line of argument, gestures are the expressive substrata of a language without meaning, and the projected theater in Kafka would be the technique with which Kafka stages this expressive or expressionist language of gestures.

What is less often mentioned in discussions of the crisis of language is its relation to the theater. The best example is Hugo von Hofmannsthal, one of the most prominent representatives of this crisis, who decided to stop writing narrative prose and to write drama and opera instead, for only on the stage is language truly aided and taken over by gesture. In Kafka, as always, there is not such a direct solution. On the contrary, gesture for him not only implies a critique of language but also, and more importantly, a critique of the theater. This is true not only for Kafka but also for his first "gestural" commentator, Benjamin, whose writing and thinking was itself deeply engaged in a conflicted relation to the theater, a relation that is nowhere as clear as in his *The Origin of the German Trauerspiel*. Its object of study is a form of drama that hovers on the edge of the closet drama, because the *Trauerspiel* was never a major performance genre. Even when it was performed, it appeared only as private, closed stagings, semi-stagings, or dramatic readings. Thus, Benjamin develops a theory of an allegory that is never far from writing and scripture, an attempt to theorize a theater that encompasses writing.[25] Benjamin is engaged in a form of modernist antitheatricalism that compulsively rewrites the theater as text. This antitheatrical understanding of Benjamin can be extended to Kafka as well. Kafka's so-called gestural style should not be understood simply as a name for some vaguely theatrical quality but for the contest between text and theater or, more specifically, between the Yiddish of actors and Paper-German. Kafka does not so much borrow from the Yiddish theater as write against it; he does not simply transport gestures from the stage to the page but decomposes and recomposes them according to the antitheatrical logic of his writing.

Benjamin's and Kafka's antitheatricalism, like most antitheatricalism, always comes back to the live human actor on a stage, and it is in relation to the actor that the antitheatrical impulse can be detected most clearly. Benjamin compares Kafka's characters to actors, but the only actors he identifies are the foreign, non-naturalistic, and stylized actors of the Chinese theater. It is not necessary to venture quite so far, even though Chinese and Japanese theater did have an influence on the modernist theater, for the foreignness of Kafka's gestures stems not from their being Chinese, but from Kafka's technique of decomposition, which functions whether or not the actors thus decomposed were originally Chinese, Yiddish, or Habsburg-Austrian. Decomposing actors is one of the primary activities of modernist and avant-garde theater, and so it is in this decomposition that the tradition of modernist antitheatrical theater and Kafka's antitheatrical literature meet. It is perhaps in light of this qualification that we can understand Adorno's attempt to critique Benjamin's "theatrical" reading of Kafka by claiming that Kafka should be understood in relation to film.[26] What Adorno had noticed was precisely Kafka's antitheatrical impulse, which indeed means that Kafka's scenes and characters are no longer simply of the theater. However, this does not necessarily turn them into cinematic exercises unless one remembers, as Benjamin himself did in his most well-known text of the artwork in the age of mechanical reproducibility, that film can be understood in an antitheatrical sense: it does away with live actors, decomposing them through cuts, close-ups, and framing. Modernist literature as represented by Kafka undertakes a similar feat through techniques of writing, which therefore should be called antitheatrical if it is understood that the prefix "anti" does not signify a simple negation of the theater. Rather, it signifies a struggle against the theater in which the theater leaves its mark on literature. It is this struggle from which Kafka's writing derives.

Notes

1. *Franz Kafka Gesammelte Werke, Tagebücher*, ed. Max Brod (Frankfurt a.M.: Fischer, 1989) 112. All references to Kafka are to this edition. The English translations are my own.

2. Jörg W. Gronius presented a study on Kafka's dramatic writings, the theatricality of his narrative texts, and their dramatic adaptations. *Kafka im Theater: Über Adaptionen des "Prozeß" und Menschen im Hotel* (Berlin: Copy-Center in Dahlem, 1983). Date established by Jost Schillemeit in *Kafka-Handbuch in zwei Bänden*, ed. Hartmut Binder (Stuttgart: Kroner, 1979) 497.

3. Julia Kristeva considers gesture as that which belongs to the process of articulation, the means of production of language. The end product of this corporeal and gestural process would be the conventional sign. *Semiotike: Recherches pour une sémanalyse* (Paris: Éditions du Seuil, 1969).

4. Joseph Vogl, *Der Ort der Gewalt: Kafkas literarische Ethik* (München: Fink, 1990) 5ff. Also see Wolfgang Jahn, "Kafka und die Anfange des Kinos," *DGS* 6 (1962): 353–68.

5. Bertolt Brecht, *Gesammelte Werke in 20 Bänden*, vol. 17 (Frankfurt a.M.: Suhrkamp, 1967) 991. For a more comprehensive version of this argument, see my *Stage Fright: Modernism, Anti-Theatricality, and Drama* (Baltimore: Johns Hopkins UP, 2002).

6. This metaphor, derived from the sphere of dress and clothes, is part of a larger pattern, a fascination with dress and ornament as analyzed by Mark M. Anderson in his *Kafka's Clothes: Ornament and Aestheticism in the Habsburg Fin de Siècle* (Oxford: Clarendon, 1992).

7. Mallarmé uses the same set of images—weaving a role like a dress with a loosened train—to characterize the transformation of the human dancer into a depersonalized figure on the stage.

8. Compare Joseph Roach, *The Player's Passion: Studies in the Science of Acting* (Newark: U of Delaware P, 1985).

9. For a more comprehensive argument about Platonist theater see Puchner, *Stage Fright*, and Elinor Fuchs, "Clown Shows: Anti-Theatrical Theatricalism in

Four Twentieth-Century Plays," *Modernism and Anti-Theatricality*, ed. Alan Ackerman and Martin Puchner, spec. issue of *Modern Drama* 44.3 (2001): 337–54.

10. Evelyn Torton Beck, *Kafka and the Yiddish Theater: Its Impact on His Work* (Madison: U of Wisconsin P, 1971).

11. Historical material taken from Hartmut Binder et al., ed., *Kafka Handbuch* (1979).

12. When Kafka brought home his new friend Löwy, his father remarked in front of the friend about "foreigners" being brought to the house and about "useless" acquaintances (*T* 234).

13. Georg Guntermann notes Kafka's interest in faces and gestures but sees in the focus on details always the implication of a *pars pro toto*, a promise of the whole (44–47). Guntermann, *Vom Fremdwerden der Dinge beim Schreiben: Kafka's Tagebücher als literarische Physiognomie des Autors* (Tübingen: Niemeyer, 1991).

14. Description based on Beck (1971).

15. Peter Brooks, *The Melodramatic Imagination* (New York: Columbia UP, 1985) 11.

16. In this, he oddly parallels the history of modern theater and drama from Eugene O'Neill to Heiner Müller, which can be seen as so many decompositions and recompositions of melodrama.

17. In his study, *Kafka in neuer Sicht: Mimik, Gestik und Personengefüge als Darstel-lungsformen des Autobiographischen* (Stuttgart: Metzler, 1976), Hartmut Binder considers Kafka's represented gestures primarily as expressions of the character's interiority (117–63), as does Guntermann (50). Although it is limited by the paradigm of psychologically expressive gestures, Binder's study nevertheless constitutes a useful and detailed analysis of Kafka's fascination with gestures in his novels as well as in his diary.

18. In this sense, Kafka both participates in and works against the history of abjecting Yiddish and of portraying it as a hidden and mysterious language. Sander Gilman, *Jewish Self-Hatred: Anti-Semitism and The Hidden Language of the Jews* (Baltimore: Johns Hopkins UP, 1986). One may wonder to what extent Kafka here participates in the old anti-Semitic topos of identifying actors and Jews, analyzed famously by Max Horkheimer and Theodor Adorno in *Dialektik der Aufklärung: Philosophische Fragmente* (Frankfurt a.M.: Fischer, 1969) 177ff.

19. Gilles Deleuze and Felix Guattari, *Kafka: Towards a Minor Literature*, trans. Dana Polan (Minneapolis: U of Minneapolis P, 1986).

20. *Benjamin über Kafka: Texte, Briefzeugnisse, Aufzeichnungen*, ed. Hermann Schweppenhäuser (Frankfurt a.M.: Suhrkamp, 1981) 18.

21. Compare Rainer Nägele, *Theater, Theory, Speculation: Walter Benjamin and the Scenes of Modernity* (Baltimore: Johns Hopkins UP, 1991) 159.

22. Bettine Menke points out the significance of allegory for Benjamin's understanding of Kafka in "Das Schweigen der Sirenen: Die Rhetorik des Schweigens," *Vortäge des Augsburger Germanistentags 1991; III, Methodenkonkurrenz in der germanistischen Praxis*, ed. Johannes Janota (Tübingen: Niemeyer, 1993).

23. See Allan Janik and Stephen Toulmin, *Wittgenstein's Vienna* (New York: Simon, 1973).

24. Werner Hamacher, *Premises: Essays on Philosophy and Literature from Kant to Celan*, trans. Peter Fenves (Cambridge: Harvard UP, 1996) 329.

25. One of the few critics to have devoted attention to Benjamin's peculiar relation to the theater is Rainer Nägele, in his fascinating *Theater, Theory, Speculation*
(Baltimore: Johns Hopkins UP, 1991).

26. Adorno articulates his reservation in a letter to Benjamin, collected in
Benjamin über Kafka 106. Also see Hans Zischler, *Kafka geht ins Kino* (Hamburg:
Rowohlt, 1996).

PATRICK REILLY

Kafka

Vanni Fucci uses words to wound—they are his only weapon—and his heirs take up language as an instrument of chastisement and retribution. Dostoyevsky's narrator breaks off his story just as it becomes a verbal equivalent of the knout. In O'Connor's 'Revelation,' the messenger from God knocks unconscious with a heavy book the insufferable pharisee in the waiting room. Waugh's Tony Last must read Dickens aloud till he dies. Miss Lonelyhearts' agony stems directly from the harrowing letters he can neither answer nor ignore. In all of these texts, words have become instruments for inflicting pain upon those compelled to read, speak, hear or feel them. But the most startling example in all literature of the word as punishment, of the letter that literally kills, is, without doubt, Kafka's short story, 'In the Penal Settlement': here Vanni Fucci's punitive word is carried to unmatchable perfection.

As with every other Kafka text, a critical debate has accreted round this strangely fascinating tale, but my present purpose is to focus upon the two elements already identified in the *Inferno*: the wounding power of words and the harsh but justified punishment of the guilty. The story was originally included in a volume to which Kafka gave the general title *Strafen* (Punishments) and it could be used to support his assertion that de Sade is the true patron of our age.[1] The 'great change of fortune' referred to in the text

From *The Dark Landscape of Modern Fiction*, pp. 91–111, 202–05. © 2003 by Patrick Reilly.

is not simply the substitution of one victim for another, the defeated Officer setting the condemned man free and voluntarily taking his place under the harrow.[2] It is a parable about the transition from one moral system to another, from torture to liberalism, from an ethos of vengeful retribution to one of compassion. Obvious in the larger structural sense, this is also reinforced in the many detailed allusions to religion. The Officer reveres the Old Commandant's writings as sacred scriptures, washes his hands before unfolding them, and will not allow them to pass into the profane possession, however temporary, of the Explorer. The two fine handkerchiefs, given to the condemned man by the New Commandant's ladies, recall Veronica's gift of her veil to Christ on his road to Calvary. The machine is equipped with jets of water to wash away the blood so that the message being imprinted is not blurred; this linking of blood and water evokes once again the Crucifixion. The Officer speaks of the dying man's transfiguration and of the radiance of the justice. The inscription on the Old Commandant's grave—the Explorer, significantly, must kneel to read it—exhorts his followers to 'Have faith and wait!' for the promised resurrection.[3]

Although not published until 1919, it was written in 1914, just as Europe was about to set in motion a war that, once begun, seemed to operate with a machine-like autonomy, regardless of the wills of those who began as its masters and soon found themselves its servants. Kafka's seems an anti-historical tale, describing the opposite of what actually occurred. In his attempt to recruit the Explorer as an ally against the reforms of the New Commandant, the Officer uses the term 'European' as a synonym for humane—the New Commandant will (he warns) try to enlist him as an eminent European, that is, an opponent of torture (long since abolished in Europe) in his campaign against the old, expiring regime.[4] Today this strikes us as being either ironic or laughably incorrect; far from moving toward greater liberalism, Europe was about to descend into a time of savage irrationalism. But Kafka's story ends with a prophecy of the resurrection and return of the Old Commandant, the repossession of the colony by his followers, and, presumably, the creation of new and even more abominable torture machines. No one with any knowledge of Kafka will accuse him of being too optimistic and some readers find in his story a prophecy of the catastrophe about to befall Europe. Others go further by arguing that Kafka's imagination is itself catastrophic, more attuned to the discords of hell than to the music of heaven, and caution against too easily assuming that he is necessarily on the side of the humane Explorer against the fanatical Officer. Nothing but harbour works, complains the latter at what he sees as the facile technological optimism of the new dispensation and it is far from certain that Kafka disagrees.[5] The failure of secular hopes is precisely the major theme of his writing. 'Earthly hope must be killed; only then can one be saved by true hope.'[6] Kafka obeys Kierkegaard's imperative to kill hope; but he does not follow him in his leap of Faith, that act of philosophical suicide denounced by Camus. Kafka's critical response to the social programme of the Prague Zionists shows his deep distrust of all earthly schemes of renovation and there seems no reason to think he would have made an exception in favour of the New Commandant's harbour works.[7] However hideous the machinery of salvation—*Heilsmaschinerie* is Nietzsche's term for what he saw as the religious exploitation of suffering, the age-old nexus between pain and religion—one suspects that Kafka would have preferred it to a society bereft of religious values and obsessed with technology. Nothing but harbour works! The exasperation is surely not confined to the Officer and the worthlessness of works in contributing to salvation is a recurring theme in Kafka's writing. His major indictment of modern European society is that it has no place for the Jews, but can only demand from them conformity and assimilation—it is, preeminently, a religious conception of life that Europe so disastrously lacks.

'This morning, once again after a long time, I took pleasure in imagining that a knife was being turned in my heart.'[8] This quotation from Kafka's diary, recalling Joseph's execution at the end of *The Trial*, should make us pause before too easily assuming that Kafka sympathizes with the Explorer rather than the Officer. 'In the Penal Settlement' can plausibly be presented as an attack upon the purely hedonistic conception of man found deeply embedded in the liberal, secularistic tradition of our Western world, a conception that Kierkegaard claimed was true only of what he called the aesthetic stage of human development. For Nietzsche, too, the defeat of the ascetic ideals by the Enlightenment qualities of humanitarianism, utility, welfare, sentimentality was a decadence—only through the rehabilitation of suffering and the purification it brings could Europe recover its soul. Kafka can be seen as an important member of a tradition that includes Kierkegaard, Dostoyevsky and Nietzsche, all of them thinkers who repudiate what they see as the shallow optimism that controls the conception of human destiny at the retarded aesthetic stage. Kafka's works have been mistakenly read through the spectacles of that same superficial humanism criticized in the New Commandant and his sentimental ladies, when the truth is that the Explorer, Joseph K and the superfluous land surveyor of *The Castle* are not at all the unqualified heroes they are often assumed to be.

It has been argued that 'In the Penal Settlement' is disguised autobiography, an allegory of the author's own sufferings in the penitentiary of his family, and the 'Letter to His Father' could be cited in support.[9] But the family setting is too restrictive, for the Earth itself is the penal settlement, as Schopenhauer (whom Kafka read) informs us: 'As a reliable compass for orientating yourself in life, nothing is more useful than to accustom yourself to regard this world as a place of atonement, a sort of penal colony.'[10] We know how fascinated Camus was by Kafka and, if Schopenhauer supplies the key to 'In the Penal Settlement,' we can see how Camus may have found there the hint for his own early masterpiece, *The Outsider*, with its revelation that the world is a death cell where all await, condemned, their turn for execution.

More pertinent to the present argument is the reading of the story as a parable of the sufferings of the artist. Writing is shown as both revelation and torture, an ecstatic agony in which the discoveries achieved are in proportion to the pangs experienced. As so often in Kafka, guilt and writing are insepa-rably related. The Officer is paradoxically forced to defend his own procedures even as he denies the right of self-defence to the accused man: 'I have been appointed judge in this penal settlement ... My guiding principle is this: Guilt is never to be doubted.'[11] Such a system is a prosecutor's paradise—as Joseph remarks in *The Trial*, all that is needed is an executioner, and, indeed, the Officer is simultaneously judge and executioner. When the Explorer expresses his surprise, first, that the condemned man has not been told the sentence, and, second, that he has not been allowed to defend himself against the charge, the Officer calmly justifies the system. There's 'no point in telling him. He'll learn it corporally, on his person'[12]—he'll get the point, literally. And if, as Schopenhauer says, in the penal colony of Earth existence itself is the crime, what possible defence could there be? Our state (says Kafka) is sinful, irrespective of guilt: *il n'y a pas d'innocents.*[13]

What alone saves this from being simply abhorrent is the heroic con-sistency of the Officer in upholding it. Having so inexorably judged oth-ers, he appoints the Explorer as *his* judge, committing himself in advance to whatever verdict is pronounced—if the Explorer rejects the old ways, then 'I and the Old Commandant will be done for.'[14] When the judgment does go against him, he unhesitatingly does to himself what he is so ready to do to others in a perverted variant of the familiar gospel exhortation.

The machine that dominates this story of nameless men, of men as func-tions (officer, explorer, soldier, condemned man), is a writing machine—both an instrument of torture and an image of the artist's sufferings. The machine tortures by writing its sentence (the pun is not available in German) upon and finally through the body of the guilty man. At the end, just before its final disintegration, the machine is no longer writing but simply jabbing—litera-ture has become sheer sadism, butchery, with no words being written and no sentence, no meaning, being communicated. The self-immolating zealot is simply being shredded by the machine he has so devotedly served. The nar-rator of *Notes from Underground* refers to penal correction, but this is a figure of speech. In Kafka, the metaphor becomes literal fact: the Officer is literally flayed, minced. This actualization of the figurative is not unusual in Kafka: St Augustine writes that his soul has become a spider; Gregor Samsa in 'Metamorphosis' is literally transformed into an insect as he awakens not out of but into a nightmare. 'I will give my law in their bowels and I will write it in their hearts.' What is trope in Jeremiah becomes appallingly factual truth in 'In the Penal Settlement.' He who refuses to hear must feel: the familiar German adage is hideously embodied as Kafka transposes proverb into fact. An idiom is literalized: the condemned man will get the point in the flesh.

'I have no literary interests, but am made of literature. I am nothing else and cannot be anything else.'[15] The words are Kafka's about himself, but they might easily have been spoken by the condemned man under the harrow, as he is processed from a living body into a piece of writing (from which the blood is continually washed to keep it legible) before being thrown into the grave. That Kafka saw writing as linked to guilt and punishment is indisputable: 'God does not want me to write, but I must.'[16] A pen takes the place of the forbidden fruit. He pursues this idea in words that anticipate Adrian Leverkühn's diabolic commitment to music in Thomas Mann's *Doctor Faustus*: 'Writing is a delicious reward. For what? . . . for services rendered to the devil.'[17] He excuses his failure to marry by saying that he would prove a faithless husband, nightly deserting the marriage bed in adulterous intercourse with his writing. Writing, in yet another metaphor, becomes a hunt during which prey and predator can bewilderingly exchange identities. In the 'Letter to His Father,' the latter accuses the son of having long tormented him and declares: 'If I am not very much mistaken, you are preying upon me even now with this letter as such.'[18] Kafka's denunciation of his father so easily turns into self-denunciation. Who is the tormentor, who the victim? The executioner of 'In the Penal Settlement' becomes, in the most natural of transitions, the condemned man.

'I am Literature.'[19] Kafka's self-description is the condition to which the condemned man will be reduced when he becomes an imprinted corpse, a dead letter. The machine writes after it has been programmed by the Officer who inserts the message and sets the needles to produce the prescribed result. The message to be inscribed upon the body of the disobedient soldier is 'Honour Thy Superiors,' an imperative delivered too late to be acted upon since he will die without the opportunity to obey it. The victim's body is a blank sheet to be written on and the machine has been fitted with a glass reflector, so that the sentence can be read and meditated upon while it is being inscribed. The condemned man is simultaneously text and reader—the assertion 'I am Literature' vividly exemplified, he himself the page that he struggles to the death to comprehend: understanding and death coincide, arrive together. The sinner is punished not for but by his sin, in a *contrapasso* of which Dante himself would have been proud.

When the Officer fails to win the Explorer's support for the future of the machine and the whole fading system of bloodshed and discipline—at one time, the Officer nostalgically recalls, acid was used to wash away the blood, but the old ways are being irresistibly eroded by the conquering sentimentalists[20]—he decides that the honourable course is to set the condemned man free and take his place under the harrow. Silently, significantly, the Explorer agrees and so the Officer reprogrammes the machine with a new imperative, 'Be Just,' and goes under its needles to suffer the fate that every violator of the law deserves. It echoes the sinner's demand for death in Arnold's poem, 'The Sick King in Bokhara,' but Kafka characteristically takes the principle to a macabre extreme. In the Christian mystery of redemption the Word is made flesh to be crucified for the forgiveness of sins. In Kafka, the flesh is to be made words in a sacrifice that turns out to be without meaning or redemption, in flat rebuttal of the zealot's promise. The whole purpose and justification of the punishment—the promised enlightenment through pain—is apparently withheld from the fervent believer. The Officer had earlier described with excited reverence this moment of illumination for the dying criminal: 'how quiet he grows at just about the sixth hour! Enlightenment comes to the most dull-witted . . . A moment that might tempt one to get under the Harrow with him . . . the man only begins to understand the inscription, he purses his mouth as if he were listening. You have seen how difficult it is to decipher the script with one's eyes; but our man deciphers it with his wounds. To be sure, that is a hard task; he needs six hours to accomplish it.'[21]

It is literally a case of someone dying to understand, an exegesis rather than an execution: who other than Kafka would describe the process of dying as a slow, agonizingly terminal hermeneutics? Ironically, even as the Officer exhorts the Explorer to concentrate and understand—'Can you follow it? The Harrow is beginning to write'—he himself signally fails to understand that the Explorer has decided against him: 'Had it dawned on the officer at last? No, he still did not Understand.'[22] 'In the Penal Settlement' is a text about incomprehension, despite its promise that radiant understanding comes to every condemned man at the sixth hour of his death struggle. With such an expectation, the Officer, the verdict having gone against him, confidently strips himself naked to go under the harrow for his own illumination: 'Then the time has come.'[23] It seems the more cruel that so zealous a believer is apparently cheated. Despite his aversion to the machine, the Explorer is sufficiently intrigued to search the face of the corpse for any hint of the promised enlightenment, but 'it was as it had been in life; no sign was visible of the promised redemption; what the others had found in the machine the officer had not found.'[24] The sacrifice has been offered but not, it seems, accepted.

This failure of the irrational Enlightenment is no ground for assuming that Kafka endorses the rational one, the good works programme espoused by the New Commandant. Only those implacably hostile to the Officer will withhold all sympathy; mere revulsion is checked by the way he accepts the logic of his own fierce justice in condemning himself to death. His faith in the illuminative power of the machine is total and there is pathos, if not tragedy, when it proves, at least in his case, a cheat. For he possesses the virtues as well as the vices of the zealot and he does not exempt himself from the law he implements and the Moloch he serves. The new mild doctrines he genuinely regards as a decadence. He displays a dignity that sets him above the boors he deals with, and the coarse antics of the latter, the vulgarities connected with the torn trousers, serve to highlight the austere severity of his own conduct, the tragic hero made more conspicuous by the buffoonery of the clowns.[25] The reprieved man is a vengeful, uncomprehending brute—delighted to exchange fates with the Officer, he rushes superfluously to strap him in, unable to grasp that the Officer, like Christ at Gethsemane, is choosing his crucifixion. The soldier is not against the machine, so long as someone else is in it. Neither is the Explorer, his humane aversion to the machine notwithstanding, shown as unarguably superior to the man whose fate he decides. He comes close to fleeing the scene in a far from heroic, near-ignominious fashion; our last sight is of him threatening to scourge his pursuers.

It is not a question of presenting the Officer as the story's unqualified hero, rather to show how the story resists any simple, straightforward explication. It is as much about the difficulty of deciphering texts as about the clash between different regimes and moralities. In a text itself taxing to understand, the problem of understanding written words is repeatedly emphasized. The condemned man would not understand his sentence were it not written upon his body—even then it needs six hours of agonizing scrutiny before enlightenment comes. The Officer invites the Explorer to read the sacred scriptures of the old dispensation; despite his wish to say something appreciative, all the Explorer sees is a labyrinth of criss-cross lines. Where the believer finds meaning, the outsider sees only chaos. The Officer puts the papers away, conceding that 'it's no calligraphy for school children. It needs to be studied closely.'[26] How *can* it be a simple script when it's not supposed to kill a man until he has struggled for many hours to understand it? Dying under the harrow is the reverse of euthanasia: the intention is to prolong the agony. But, in the end, we understand; even the Explorer himself (so the Officer assures him) would make the breakthrough if he concentrated hard enough under the enlightening needles. No text is finally irresistible, however costly to unlock. For the moment, however, the Explorer remains uncomprehending, unable to read the new imperative, 'Be Just,' but diplomatically prepared to take the Officer's word for it as the self-styled infallible custodian of the text.

Only the initiate can read and understand. What seems to the Explorer a mere mess of squiggles and curlicues is really, like the detailed commentaries of the Talmudists, the key to ultimate truth. That the labyrinth of lines also resembles Kafka's own manuscripts reinforces the argument of those who would persuade us to accept 'In the Penal Settlement' as autobiographical and confessional. Kafka certainly felt that his writing was at once a torture to himself and a mystification to others, no calligraphy for school children. The story ends with yet more writing to be deciphered and understood, as the Explorer kneels to read the inscription on the Old Commandant's grave: God is dead, but his word survives. Perhaps this promise of a return and a repossession is simply to be smiled at, as the patrons of the tea house smile while the Explorer kneels and reads. But the Explorer does not smile: this is no calligraphy for school children. A law supported by illegible, incomprehensible writings; an illiterate prisoner who can read only through his wounds; an outsider to whom these scriptures are simply meaningless scrawls—only the believer can access them and we either take his word or reject the whole thing as idiot sadism: all this may be absurd, but it is no laughing matter. True, the Officer warns us that these texts are difficult and 'need to be studied closely'[27]—in *The Trial*, the commercial traveller Block labours for a day over a single page[28]—and only the most slothful of wooers demands surrender at the first asking. Here, however, is the key problem for the reader of Kafka. Increasingly, dismayingly, he comes to suspect that, however long and devoted his courtship, however patiently he curbs his desire for speedy gratification, he will, in the end, like the man from the country in his lifelong wait outside the door of the Law, be left frustrated, denied and unassuaged.

The text, despite the Officer's fideist assurance, is, in the end, impenetrable, unsolvable, invincibly resistant—it has many questions but no answers and we leave it more baffled, not less. Yet to attack Kafka for not providing answers is like attacking a fireman for not starting fires. The whole purpose of his art is to leave us stranded and perplexed outside the door of the Law. No more than the Officer under the harrow will Kafka's reader find redemptive enlightenment after his struggle with the text, simply an even deeper darkness than that in which he set out. Reading Kafka is, and is meant to be, a humiliation—we do not, as in Dante, emerge to see the stars.

'In the Penal Settlement' shows the reader as victim in the most vividly horrific way, but this simply carries to a macabre extreme a readerly punishment prevalent through all his work. The reader resembles Sisyphus, with one significant difference. Sisyphus knows from the outset that he labours to no end, that the boulder will forever slip from his grasp and roll back down the hill. Camus converts this fate into an image of stoic fortitude: it is the conscious acceptance of pain without remedy and toil without end that makes Sisyphus the existentialist hero. Any hint of optimism would sabotage this: 'Where would his torture be, indeed, it at every step the hope of succeeding upheld him?'[29] Sisyphus courageously sticks with his unaccomplishable task.

Something of this is inherent in Kafka's recurrent theme of non-arrival, of failure to reach the goal. All of his stories are anti-*Märchen*, recording the hero's inability to conclude the quest: Joseph vainly seeking his day in court, the land surveyor's repeated failure to contact the castle, the man from the country derelict outside the door of the Law, the gangs of labourers toiling over an unbuildable wall, the truth-seeking dog pursuing investigations that cannot succeed—all modern recreations of Sisyphus, experiencing the same agony of inconclusion, the same frustration of never having done. But, unlike Sisyphus, they all set out with high hopes, always confident, sometimes arrogant; only after repeated failure do they come to know the futility of their labours and the unattainability of their goals. The plebeian builders of the great wall never, indeed, recognize the hopelessness of the task—it's the narrator who comes to realize this—but they work to the death accepting the official fraud that they will bring the work to completion. The others, through bitter experience, grow into Sisyphus, but this is not their initial expectation.

The reader, too, sets out confident that all that is puzzling and obscure will be made clear. From darkness to light, from Dante's dark wood to the serene, shining stars: this is the time-honoured passage in traditional fiction. Just as Joseph is confident that he can find the court and clear his name, just as K is confident that the muddle over his appointment will soon be put to rights, so the reader waits patiently for all to be resolved. Why Joseph has been arrested, what really has happened to Gregor Samsa, who is in the right in the penal settlement dispute—secure in his implicit contractual agreement with the author, the reader trustingly reads on, convinced that he will know all. Every text, however difficult, must finally give up its meaning; it is the faith of the Officer in the penal settlement—Sisyphus will push his rock to the summit.

With Kafka we encounter something startlingly unique and unnerving: a writer whose purpose is *not* to be understood, who seeks to leave the reader not less but more perplexed.[30] As in the cathedral where Joseph meets the prison chaplain, darkness grows as the text proceeds.[31] Yet there is no mystification in the language. The reader cannot console himself with the thought that it is dark because he has failed to see, that if only he tries harder, is more attentive, all will be revealed. The humiliation is in the very lucidity of his incomprehension—he understands that he will never understand. Some texts need to be read twice—*Tom Jones*, 'Benito Cereno'—before they can be seen true. But we can re-read *The Trial* and *The Castle* from now to the world's end and be no closer to a cognitive breakthrough: these boulders were never meant to reach the summit. Yet no more than Sisyphus can the reader walk away. *Wovon man nicht reden kann darüber muss man schweigen*: be silent about what is not discussable.[32] It is the ostensibly sensible advice of Wittgenstein and his false heirs, the logical positivists. Applying it to Kafka, we might say give up trying to understand the incomprehensible. It is a seductive recommendation since, not the interpretation, but the immediacy of the work is what matters. 'The scriptures are unalterable and the comments often enough merely express the commentator's bewilderment.'[33] What the priest says about the parable of the man from the country is pertinent to Kafka's work as a whole. 'The reflections they give rise to are endless and chance determines where one stops reflecting.'[34] Thus Olga crushes K's hopes of wresting from the letters sent by the castle authorities a final, unchallengeable meaning: there is none. So why not have done with futile, unending exegesis, why not forsake interpretation and simply read on without trying to elicit meaning? Stick with the boulder but forget about reaching the summit.

It is excellent advice but for one flaw: Kafka won't allow it. Nothing is more important than the work that cannot be concluded: recognizing this is what makes Camus's Sisyphus a hero. Kafka's reader can no more leave the unmasterable text than Sisyphus the unmasterable rock: walking away is not an option. 'The whole art of Kafka consists in forcing the reader to re-read'—the link with the condemned man in the penal settlement is obvious. Camus continues with reference to *The Castle*: 'Each chapter is a new frustration.'[35] The hero runs in circles, going nowhere as he desperately seeks to break the impasse. But the reader is equally frustrated, condemned to re-read without hope of release or illumination, as trapped in the text as the character in the story.

If the reader is Sisyphus, the author is Vanni Fucci, a sufferer communicating his own suffering. Canetti identifies humiliation as Kafka's chief theme: humiliated himself, he humiliates the reader. Here is where modern literature so decisively parts from the *Inferno*: there is no final return to see the stars and Kafka is the most remorseless promoter of darkness. When Auden called the twentieth century the century of Kafka, he was calling attention to this power to darken and perplex, an art to gladden the heart of Vanni Fucci. There is a path out of hell and the Pilgrim, with Virgil's help, will find it. But the only guides in Kafka (Titorelli in *The Trial*, the Superintendent in *The Castle*) are there to prevent escape. Dante knows that art alone, however exalted, cannot bring the Pilgrim to his final destination—Virgil takes him only so far before handing him over to Beatrice, to Grace. Kafka's characters have no Beatrice to point the way; grace is absent and art has defected to the darkness.

It is all the more difficult if the reader regards Kafka as a great writer who, once read, cannot be forgotten. 'He over whom Kafka's wheels have passed has lost forever any peace with the world.'[36] Many readers will endorse Adorno's tribute—for it is a tribute, since Adorno clearly regards this as a peace well lost—and Kafka's fascination for many is his unique gift for creating situations replete with potential meaning, construable in many different ways, each interpretation carrying its own conviction. This *Vieldeutigkeit*, multivalency, requires a reader as prepared as Kafka himself to make friends with his ignorance, to stand uncommitted before a number of possible readings, rather than impatiently seizing upon one while dismissing the rest. What Coleridge says is good advice for the fit reader of Kafka: 'I warn all Inquirers into this hard point to *wait*—not only not to plunge forward before the Word is *given* to them, but not even to paw the ground with impatience.'[37] In Kafka's case, the warning is even more severe, because the wait is forever, with meaning as tardy as Godot.

Not every reader has the patience. From the rich harvest of competing exegeses, it is tempting to pick one and bid relieved farewell to the rest. And the explanations—political, psychological, autobiographical, metaphysical, religious—crowd obligingly forward. The lure of a single, exclusive exegesis is that it solves Kafka, puts him in a convenient box, and liberates us from fretting interminably over his meaning. There are some who think that this boulder is really an inconsequential pebble, not worth pushing at all. Kafka is a writer of no account who simply caters to the emotions of helplessness and self-contempt characteristic of the fainéant intellectuals of his time. His stories are about weaklings for weaklings: those who admire him as artist or guide merely condemn themselves.[38]

In calling Kafka the voice of his age, Auden meant something very different. Auden's Kafka is spokesman for humanity, not the pet author of a clique of faint-hearted intellectuals. Kafka himself (despite asserting that his work embodied the negative spirit of the time) denied that it was tied to any one historical period: 'This Fear (*Angst*) is after all not my private fear although it is in fact all that and terrible—but it is as much the Fear of all faith since the beginning of time.'[39] Kafka is claiming, in effect, that every age is an age of Kafka if only it knew it—it is simply that in our own time this realization has forced its way to the forefront of consciousness. The world as Kafka depicts it has always existed; it is just that previous ages were more happily deluded.[40]

Hence the link with Kierkegaard before and Camus after. All three claim to be making statements applicable to life everywhere and in all times, but the truth of which has only been revealed as a result of the spiritual crisis of the modern era. All men, says Kierkegaard, are in despair without knowing it. All men, says Camus, are condemned without knowing it. All men, so Kafka seems to say, are guilty without knowing it. That we have to qualify in Kafka's case is characteristic of the provisionality that attaches itself to almost any statement concerning him, but no one will dispute the centrality of guilt in Kafka's work. He agrees, too, with Kierkegaard that anguish is the essential human condition; what separates them is Kafka's lack of faith—Kafka's Officer is not transfigured. Kafka accompanies Kierkegaard beyond the aesthetic stage of human development, but stops short of the ethico-religious stage. He splits from Camus by not assuming with him that men are the wronged victims of an absurd universe. Camus's presumption in favour of human innocence puts him on the side of Meursault, even of Caligula and Martha: humanity has had a raw deal. The one place Camus will not sit is with the prosecutor—the late, startling example of *The Fall* apart, Camus always appears for the defence. This cannot be said of Kafka. Despite certain misreadings of his work it is far from clear that Kafka is on the side of George Bendemann or Gregor Samsa or the Explorer of the penal settlement or Joseph K or the would-be land surveyor—he is not even consistently on his own side in the 'Letter to My Father.' The demon of ambivalence that presides over these writings forbids the adoption of any single exclusive reading—Kafka criticism is cluttered with the bodies of those who have fallen into the trap of interpretative exclusivity. There is always another word: exegesis is never-ending. If all we had was 'Before the Law,' the parable near the close of *The Trial*, the key passage and mythic core of the book, this alone would be proof of Kafka's refusal to come to an end, his resolved inconclusiveness. Joseph starts off convinced that the meaning is crystal clear and ends up baffled and unsure: 'The simple story had lost its clear outline.'[41] But his blunder was to believe that there is such a thing as a simple story. It is the error that the investigating dog condemns in his incurious companions: 'their belief that it is simple prevents further enquiry.'[42] It is the mistake about life that we all make and Kafka's mission is to expose it.

Further enquiry forever: this is his goal. He bars our route to the haven of illusory certitude, he will not let us rest easy in mistaken knowledge. This explains the paradoxical nature of the praise lavished upon him by his admirers. They celebrate him for destroying our peace of mind. Adorno's tribute tells us that it is better to be grieved by Kafka's truth than comforted by a lie. Malcolm Bradbury salutes his ability to 'raise life to the level of high anxiety,' and the verb implies an advance upon the life we lazily experienced before Kafka alerted us to our predicament.[43] Erich Heller refers to his 'power to perplex,' and the phrase opens a window upon the peculiar nature of the modern situation.[44] Other ages hailed the light-bringers, those who solved problems and answered questions—Pope's lines on Newton record this gratitude for illumination.[45] Our age, in striking contrast, exalts the one who bewilders and disconcerts; it is the destabilizer who receives our homage. We have grown suspicious of answers and dread being deceived. The light that Kafka brings is that darkness visible identified by Milton as the property of hell: it enables us to see all too clearly that we cannot, and never shall, see. 'Despair is my business.'[46] To which one can only respond that no one ever knew it better.

Others whose business was despair invariably have an antidote: St Paul's grace, Schopenhauer's detachment. What they take away with one hand, they lavishly restore with the other. Kafka's uniqueness is that he gives nothing back. 'Never before has absolute darkness been represented with so much clarity and the very madness of desperation with so much composure and sobriety.'[47] Other writers plunge us into darkness so that they may lead us to the light. Not so Kafka. This is why, in reference to Kafka, Martin Buber speaks of a Paulinism of the unredeemed, of grace eliminated in a demonic world.[48] No other writer is so remorseless. Joseph K dies 'like a dog,' the Officer dies untransfigured with the iron spike piercing his forehead, Gregor Samsa is swept away with the rubbish, George Bendemann drops defeated from the bridge into the river, K begins all over his futile round of trying to establish his identity and cure his homeliness. The message will never reach you and the one who sent it is long since dead: never was the cruel absurdity of life so calmly presented as in the single paragraph of 'A Message From the Emperor.'[49]

Torture and malice are at the heart of things for Kafka, leading some to impute to him an almost gnostic loathing for life—he is a 'religious' writer, but it is a forbidding religion, a bleakly negative theology. For Judaism, says Buber, God is hidden and this is our hope and consolation: 'Truly thou art a God who hides himself, O God of Israel, Saviour!' For to be hidden is to be there. But in Kafka God is not hidden but totally absent: the result is the Law without the law-giver, sin without God, an unredeemable world. The messianic theme is present in Kafka, but in a bleakly negative way in a succession of inadequate or perverse saviour figures. Schopenhauer denied the need for a Last Judgement in a world that is already one and Kafka seems to agree: 'There is nothing more diabolical than what exists.'[50] The prison chaplain is untroubled when Joseph objects that one of his interpretations entails an opposition between truth and reality: 'It is not necessary to accept everything as true, one must only accept it as necessary.' Joseph is understandably dismayed: 'A melancholy conclusion ... it turns lying into a universal principle.'[51] There is a hidden God in Kafka's world, who is the deceiving demon of Descartes' nightmare: no other writer has been so successful in terrestrializing hell.

We see now the blunder of identifying Kafka with his protagonists and why readers were so prone to make it after 1945. It was tempting to read *The Trial* as the work of a Jewish writer prophesying the advent of the evil regime that the Allies had just defeated. Read thus, the text is about the persecution of an everyday hero who resists to the end the tyranny of an arbitrary, inscrutable court, even though he cannot overcome its total power of life and death. Those who had just overcome Hitler hailed Kafka as a forerunner in his commitment to individual freedom against despotic power and celebrated his book as a prophecy of the fight against Nazism. Yet this is surely a reading imported into the text rather than found there. To read *The Trial* as a prophecy of political terror is both simplistic and wrong. What has Joseph's strange arrest got to do with politics at all? Compare it to what happens to the heroes of *Darkness at Noon* or *Nineteen Eighty-Four*. Kafka's protagonist is neither imprisoned nor detained. He rings a bell to summon his warders and they offer to fetch him breakfast from a nearby restaurant. He is *invited* to attend the first court meeting on a given Sunday but only if it suits him. Hitler's or Stalin's secret police were never so deferentially obliging. The court proceedings are conducted in the attics of old tenements; Joseph has to negotiate slum houses and lines of washing to find the court. His complaint about his treatment by the warders leads to *their* being punished—this is no prophecy of the world of death camps and gulags. The Whipper ('I am here to whip people, and whip them I shall') is sometimes taken as a proto-Eichmann, type of the amoral bureaucrat, ready to perform any act, however cruel, when ordered to do so because he has no life apart from his bureaucratic function.[52] But Joseph is, in fact, the character closest to Eichmann, especially to the Eichmann of the Jerusalem trial, genuinely perplexed as to how anyone could regard him as guilty. To the end he denied guilt, protesting that he was an innocent man unjustly abducted by enemy agents for judicial murder in Israel. Believing you are innocent and being so are not the same thing, as we must never forget when reading Kafka.

Not the Whipper's but Joseph's behaviour is what is so strange and singular. Why doesn't he summon help in a public building instead of testily ordering his subordinates to clean out the room? Whatever is going on, it is not political; either no 'real' beating has taken place or he is an accomplice after the fact. Is the trial actually occurring in a court within his skull? *Gerichtshof* (law court) was Kafka's word to describe the events in the hotel room when he listened in silence to the evidence against him in relation to his treatment of his fiancée. In the 'Letter to His Father' he refers to 'this terrible trial pending between us and you,' and speaks of himself as a sinner irrespective of guilt: 'one was so to speak already punished before one even knew that one had done something bad.'[53]

The Trial takes place in a private, not a political, world. It can only be presented as the heroically doomed resistance of a helpless individual against an unjust world by ignoring important elements in the text. Camus's Sisyphus resists, knowing that it's hopeless—that's why he's a hero. But Kafka's characters do hope. Joseph seeks a *Freibesprechung* (complete acquittal), although such a verdict has never been handed down. Titorelli and the priest both rebuke him for what they regard as his irresponsible optimism.[54] We take leave of the aspiring land surveyor at the end of the text still hoping, all the rebuffs notwithstanding, to penetrate the castle. Joseph admittedly collaborates at the close with his killers when he suddenly apprehends 'the futility of resistance' and decides that 'there would be nothing heroic in it were he to resist.'[55] But, whether culpably confident or fatalistically submissive, he is not to be turned into a hero victim of totalitarian tyranny without a considerable frogmarching of the text. Straight after the bizarre incident of the Whipper, he stands looking through the window, trying 'to pierce the darkness of the courtyard,' but the metaphysical darkness of the text presents a far greater problem; the reader, too, is in the dark.[56]

Not pleasant, of course, but if Kafka wants the darkness, it is not for us to insist upon introducing an inappropriate light. We must respect the text (as the priest cautions Joseph), even if it means suppressing our instinctive feeling that there can be no guilt without awareness, no sin without prior knowledge and consent. How can Joseph be guilty without knowing his crime? To ask this question, however reasonable, guarantees a misreading of the text. We end up regarding him either as the innocent victim of a corrupt court or as a sick soul with whom normal, well-adjusted people have nothing to do other than, possibly, to pity his condition. *The Trial* becomes a modern reprise of what some readers still imagine *Gulliver's Travels* to be: a case study of a neurotic individual. The pity we may feel for Gulliver and Joseph K is predicated upon our own sense of superiority: why else should it concern us if these blunderers make such a mess of things?

After 1945 it was, predictably, the first interpretation that found favour—so many innocent millions had been persecuted and killed in Europe between 1933 and 1945. 'Someone must have been telling lies about Joseph K, for without having done anything wrong he was arrested one fine morning.'[57] What else, in those years, could this be taken for but a prophecy of the political terror to come? The problem is that this is disguised first person being mistakenly read as omniscient narrator: this is *not* the magisterial author speaking—it's how Joseph thinks and feels when the arrest so inexplicably occurs. We have no grounds whatsoever for assuming that Kafka agrees. Joseph is executed at the close still ignorant of the charge against him and in our rational world of light this, in itself, is enough to prove his innocence; in

Kafka's dark world we cannot be so sure. Bunyan's Mr Badman dies the tranquil death of the just man, unaware of the damnation in store, but his creator knows he is guilty; and if bewildered indignation is proof of innocence, Eichmann should have been acquitted.[58] Nescience is a synonym for innocence only for those who insist that there can be no sin without foreknowledge. We cannot be certain that Kafka held this view. "'I don't know this law," said K.' The warder is unimpressed: "'So much the worse for you.'"[59] Even in the liberal West, ignorance of the law has never been an acceptable defence. Certainly, there is a difference between Mr Badman and Eichmann, on the one hand, and Joseph on the other, in that we know that the former are guilty and are being justly punished, whereas we are as bemused as Joseph with regard to his alleged, unspecified offence. Accordingly, so runs the argument, we must support his protestations of innocence and side with him against a crazy or sadistic court. This assumes, however, that what we know determines guilt and innocence, and precludes the possibility of our *learning* our guilt, as Oedipus and the man under the harrow do, each proceeding from a false conviction of innocence to a realization of sin. We instinctively tend to dismiss as absurd what we do not understand. 'All knowledge, the totality of all questions and all answers, is contained in the dog.'[60] We easily note the arrogance of the canine claim, but contrive to overlook it when man replaces dog. Because we and Joseph do not understand the court does not necessarily mean, at least as far as Kafka is concerned, that the court is meaningless. True, this conclusion leaves us in the same bewildering darkness as Kafka's character, but perhaps that's where Kafka wants us to be.

It is impossible to read Kafka and miss this intention to humiliate, for Kafka is Swift's greatest inheritor in continuing this tradition of humiliated man. Swift specializes in physical humiliation—man as Yahoo, noisome pest—but Kafka's is an intellectual humiliation: man as dunce, almost comically divorced from reality. Swift mortifies us in the body, Kafka in the mind—man's folly in regarding himself as the land surveyor, the measurer of all things.

Uniquely outrageous is his insistence that truth and explanation are incompatible, that to explain is to mislead: this is what we must understand if we are not to misunderstand. Kierkegaard defines maturity as understanding that you cannot understand and Kafka agrees. But where Kierkegaard introduces his Knight of Faith into the cognitive desert, Kafka demands no *sacrificium intellectus*, no submission to authority; he simply leaves us stranded in our incomprehension. In 'Investigations of a Dog' he presents the predicament of the modern mind as it attempts unilaterally, from its own unaided resources, to make sense of its condition. It is an impossible project. The investigating dog sees the scattered food and the little dogs floating in air, but cannot see the human hands that scatter and hold.[61] To seek truth in a fragmented world with fragmentary means is a doomed enterprise—it is impossible to distinguish between what is 'out there' and our consciousness of it; the only reality we can know is within our skulls. The conservative narrator of 'The Great Wall of China' refrains from asking the questions that would destabilize everything, so preserving for his less perceptive fellow citizens the tradition that he has seen through. But although the gangs of labourers continue enthusiastically at their unachievable task, the reader has been taken into the narrator's bleak confidence: the wall cannot be completed.[62] We labour in vain and for those who know this the choice is simple: be a good leper and preserve others from contagion or communicate the disease to all and sundry. Kafka chooses through his writings to expose this intellectual disinheritance, to reveal man as no longer being cognitively at home in the world: between reason and reality there is irreparable slippage.

It follows that Kafka does not provide an interpretation of the world and that, in turn, criticism cannot provide an interpretation of his work: how can you interpret a non-interpretation? What he does disconcertingly provide is an image of how experience looks when *all* interpretations are called into doubt. This underlies the virtuoso parody of rabbinical and patristic exegesis in the parable 'Before the Law,' the obvious delight in the stunning exhibition of interpretative ingenuity, the play of the mind in negating itself, as each new interpretation, like the priests of some primitive rite, emerges to slay its predecessor. Too many meanings can be even more subversive of meaning than none at all; like plants competing for the same space they end up choking each other. Logic, Nietzsche tells us, is 'the conceptual understanding of existence . . . logic calms and gives confidence.'[63] We should not look for this logic in Kafka—calm and confidence are not the commodities he deals in.

The reader who finally concedes the impossibility of understanding the text shows, in that very surrender, that he truly understands Kafka—the paradox is unavoidable. For Kafka the world is essentially turmoil, something nonrational: only the gratuitousness of the event, of the *contingit*, can reveal the essential absurdity of things—whatever is rational is wrong. The message is that there is no message. This devastating news is imparted in the most impassive way; the contrast is between the cool discipline of the writing and the latent anguish of the content, the clarity of the questions posed and the breathtaking refusal to provide answers. It is the lucidity of our incomprehension that is so chastening, for there is no obscurity in the language. Sentence by sentence everything that is happening seems perfectly clear; it is the whole that defies understanding. The narrative is intelligible; the world to which it refers is crazy.

In *The Trial* all the materials requisite for a tragic or pathetic view of existence are to hand—Camus's suffering hero, Hardy's pitiable victim. Joseph instinctively sees the man from the country as the dupe of a capriciously cruel door-keeper, understandably enough since Joseph regards himself as the victim of a parallel persecution. But the priest can account for the facts in an altogether different, equally coherent way: the man from the country may not be blameless, the doorkeeper may not be a sadistic tormentor, Joseph may not be the innocent victim of his own imagining. The principle of being innocent till proven guilty may be the cornerstone of our legal system, but that does not make it a reliable guide to Kafka's fiction. There is an entry in Kafka's diary that implies that Joseph is guilty, but it does not say of what. Bachelorhood, says Philip Rahv, for Joseph is simply Kafka in disguise.[64] Others propose selfishness, isolation, careerism, bureaucratization: the charges fall over themselves in their eagerness to secure assent. But all of this is wasted endeavour, precisely the mistake of over-precision that fails to grasp what makes Kafka so uniquely himself, for it is exactly here that the adjective Kafkaesque comes into its own. In *Crime and Punishment*, Raskolnikov, knowing his guilt, seeks his deserved retribution: the offence seeks the punishment. In *The Trial* it is the other way around. Joseph behaves as if he were guilty without knowing why—an innocent man would have ignored the 'arrest' and carried on uninterrupted with his everyday life. Instead, he pursues his persecutors, protesting his innocence, but, in reality, searching for the offence that will make sense of the punishment: the punishment seeks the offence. There is no evidence to suggest that Kafka regards his protagonists as suffering heroes or blameless victims. More plausibly, they can be seen as comic dupes, prey to their own conceits and presumptions, fabricating their worlds and then ridiculously aggrieved that the world 'out there' does not conform to their expectations. This is certainly wounding to our dearest humanist prejudices, but we have no right to assume that Kafka shares them.

Man, for Kafka, is neither tragic nor pathetic: he is comic, a joke. If Kafka's ancestor is Swift, the heir is Beckett. When he finished reading the first chapter of *The Trial* to a group of friends, everyone burst out laughing, with Kafka joining in. In his cinema version, Orson Welles emphasized the comedy of the story. It comes as no surprise to learn that in Philip Roth's imagined filmscript of *The Castle*, Groucho Marx is cast as the land surveyor, with Chico and Harpo his two assistants. Kundera tells us that 'the comic is inseparable from the essence of the Kafkan,' that 'in the world of the Kafkan, the comic is not a counterpart to the tragic . . . as in Shakespeare; it's not there to make the tragic more bearable by lightening the tone; it doesn't accompany the tragic, not at all, *it destroys it in the egg* and thus deprives the victims of the only consolation they could hope for; the consolation to be found in the (real or supposed) grandeur of tragedy.'[65] That Joseph K and the self-styled land surveyor regard themselves as the piteous victims of a heartless conspiracy proves nothing—so, too, does Malvolio, but Shakespeare thinks otherwise. Naturally, they do not enjoy their predicaments. K is a janitor in a school that has neither need nor accommodation for one. He is a superfluous, totally unnecessary man, wanted for nothing, and, however personally mortifying, this is an essentially comic situation. Vainly seeking official confirmation of his appointment as land surveyor, he receives a letter from a Castle dignitary commending him for work he hasn't done.[66] It highlights the ironic humour of his position, but it would be too much to expect *him* to laugh. Yet it's funny for all that.

The basic pattern in Kafka is comic: a crisis leads either to a sense of guilt or a condition of alienation expressing itself in the arrogant demands made by the hero. Although he gradually trims these demands, he never completely abandons them and this greater modesty results from his gradual discovery of an overarching system he can neither control nor understand. Man is not the measure of things. K assumes he is the land surveyor, but the Castle will not confirm it; initially assured of his place in the world, he finds himself houseless in existence. The mind's futile attempt to transcend its own condition—the claim to be the land surveyor—is as futile as the efforts of the investigating dog to comprehend its incomprehensible world. The dilemma is that the evidence of experience points to dimensions of experience which transcend experience. Kafka subverts the rational assumption that there is reciprocity and congruity between the world as intelligible entity and the inquiring mind; on the contrary, there is mismatch, slippage, discordance—reason is not the instrument with which to engage an irrational world. In *The Trial*, Titorelli tells Joseph that the court is completely impenetrable (*unzugänglich*) by argument, and the Castle proves equally resistant.[67]

In another's hands, it might be tragic; in Kafka's, it is high comedy, a prolonged *boutade*. A world in which nothing can be said that cannot be immediately contradicted is an essentially comic world. 'The right perception of any matter and a misunderstanding of the same matter do not exclude each other.'[68] Who, reading this for the first time, is not taken aback by the effrontery of the proposition? The instinctive reaction is to think that Kafka is joking, followed by puzzled indignation when we realize he is completely serious. Joseph, for whom it literally is a matter of life and death, is not to be blamed for missing the comedy in the priest's Wittgenstein-like dictum that 'it is not necessary to accept everything as true, one must only accept it as necessary.'[69] The victims of this comic outrage cannot be expected to see the comedy (Shylock, Malvolio, Alceste, etc.), but neither are they to be taken at their own valuation. Kundera speaks of the Kafka hero as 'trapped in the joke of his own life like a fish in a bowl; he doesn't find it fanny . . . a joke is a joke only if you're outside the bowl; by contrast, the Kafkan takes us inside, into the guts of a joke, into the *horror of the comic*.'[70] We cannot avoid the oxymoron in speaking of the experience of reading Kafka.

The reader begins to worry that he, too, is inside the bowl, that the joke's on him and that he shares in the character's humiliation. The commercial traveller, Block, suffers the most graphic humiliation in *The Trial*. Exasperated at the hold-up in his case, Joseph decides to dismiss his advocate and act for himself. At the advocate's house he meets and has a long, instructive talk with the much more experienced commercial traveller. Joseph's case is a mere infant of six months, whereas Block, in his own phrase, has been carrying his burden for five years.[71] Joseph's initial contempt for his new acquaintance gives way to a desire to learn all he can from this highly experienced man. And he learns much: that when the men in the court offices stood up in what he thought was respect to him, it was really for the Attendant. They had instantly recognized Joseph, not merely as an accused, but as a guilty man—the look on his face made this clear. (The chapter anticipates Winston Smith in the Ministry of Love, with the link between Kafka's facial guilt and Orwell's facecrime so obvious as to scarce need remarking.) Joseph learns, too, that any combined action against the court is impossible: there can be no solidarity of the accused. As with death in Pascal, so with accusation in Kafka: it is a solitary fate, despite the number of the accused. He learns about hedge advocates, those lowest of lawyers to whom some accused, desperate for a judgment, turn in betrayal of their official representatives. He hears, significantly, for the first time of the possible existence of an elite of great advocates, guarantors of acquittal, but in the next breath is cautioned against believing in them or, at least, of hoping to gain access to them: 'Don't give way to that temptation . . . I don't believe they can be got at.'[72] As such they are simply another source of torment—inaccessible saviours, redeemers who might as well not exist. Belief in acquittal, hope in salvation, *le sale espoir*: this, as the man from the country learns too late, is the greatest anguish of all. Yet, once mentioned, how can the great advocates be dismissed from mind? 'Unfortunately one can never quite forget about them, especially during the night'—that is, when we are most weak and vulnerable.[73]

Yet Block continues himself to dream of salvation and sleeps every night in the advocate's house lest he should miss it, for at any moment he may be summoned and he must be ready. Ready for what? To be rebuffed and humiliated, for, despite all his efforts, he never comes at the right time even when he responds instantaneously to the summons. He does all he can and it is worthless. Given the religious context, it seems to be a comment on the futility of works in the economy of salvation. Grace is what he needs, but *The Trial* is a text without grace: for Block, for the man from the country, for Joseph himself. Joseph's education is furthered as Block becomes a visual aid in a lesson pitilessly staged for Joseph's instruction. When the advocate learns that Joseph intends to dismiss him, he responds that he has treated Joseph too well ('I'd like to show you how other accused men are treated'[74]) and he summons Block to show Joseph what might so easily have been done to him. Here, above all, *The Trial* anticipates Orwell's Room 101, but Kafka's is a subtler depiction of humiliation and abasement, dispensing with the *grand guignol* elements of Orwell's presentation. Winston is felled by a blow from a truncheon; Block staggers at a simple question. This Ministry of Love has no need for rats. 'You were called for . . . and yet you've come at the wrong time . . . You always come at the wrong time.'[75] The sadistic cat-and-mouse treatment cannot be missed: this is a master impossible to please. Block is as ready as Winston to un-man himself, to crawl and lick the tormentor's hand, to offer up his new-found friend Joseph as a victim in his place. Outraged at what he judges to be an insult, not just to Block, but to mankind (all men fall in Block as they did in Adam), Joseph tries to persuade him to act with decency, but is thwarted by the desperate man's determination to degrade himself—Block refuses to see that the advocate is abusing *him* simply to bring Joseph to heel.

What most depresses Joseph is the realization that this is all part of 'a well-rehearsed dialogue,' a long-established ritual, that it has happened many times before and will happen many times in the future.[76] It is the equivalent of Orwell's boot in the face forever but, again, the greater subtlety of the earlier text is what catches attention. As in *Nineteen Eighty-Four*, the religious dimension is impossible to ignore. Leni's role in the ritual provides an opportunity to criticize the cult of the Virgin (although Leni is far from virginal), especially the Catholic doctrine of Mary as mediatrix of all grace. The spectacle of the greybeard businessman shamelessly begging a girl to intercede for him scandalizes Joseph, is 'humiliating even to an onlooker.'[77] The shame is not simply Block's but spills over to pollute us all: there is a solidarity, after all, but it is one of debasement. 'The client ceased to be a client and became the Advocate's dog.' Grovelling before the advocate, Block is treated like a cur when Leni warns him to behave by jerking on his collar. This exhibition of abasement links Kafka with Orwell's Ministry of Love. 'We shall squeeze you empty.'[78] O'Brien's promise to Winston could so easily apply to the abject commercial traveller.

So revolted is Joseph that he cannot bear to look at Block; it is the fear of becoming what nauseates him that makes him turn away. Indeed, if the aim was to bring Joseph back into line, then the lesson seems to have misfired. He is more opposed to the court than ever; the treatment of Block angers as well as sickens him. Hence the importance of the following chapter. No one can say if Kafka would have approved of the way in which his literary executor, Max Brod, arranged the chapter sequence of *The Trial*. What is indisputable is that the chapter following the humiliation of Block is exactly where it should be, depicting as it does the different but equally devastating humiliation of Joseph himself. 'In the Cathedral' makes transparent the links between Joseph, Block and the man from the country. If Block seems guilty of Mariolatry, Joseph is rebuked by the priest for relying too much on women. Block spends a whole day trying to understand the difficult scriptures (echoes of 'In the Penal Settlement') without getting past the first page; Joseph is ensnared by the priest in a labyrinthine exegesis, with as much hope as Sisyphus of reaching a conclusion. Block lives like a dog, Joseph dies like one. All three—Block, Joseph, the man from the country—consume their lives waiting for a judgment that never comes. Could there be a greater humiliation?

Joseph is humiliated in the mind, made to confess how little he knows, even about his own affairs. He goes—more accurately, is brought—to the cathedral to be shown how ignorant he is about himself and the world he lives in. Why is he in the cathedral at all? He believes, mistakenly as it turns out, that he is there to give a guided tour to an Italian, an important customer of Joseph's bank—a task assigned him at the last minute when the Manager, the original guide, capriciously changes his mind. Pressed for time, the Italian suggests to Joseph that they restrict the tour to the cathedral rather than the city and fixes a time for their meeting. The whole affair is haphazard from start to finish—Joseph would have been in the bank but for the Manager's sudden unexplained change of mind or in another part of the city but for the Italian's casually fortuitous proposal of the cathedral. So, at least, it seems to Joseph; his presence in the cathedral is simply the contingent conclusion of a series of accidents—he could so easily have been somewhere else.

It is not the view taken by Leni when he tells her by phone of his cathedral appointment. Surprised to begin with, she interrupts his attempted explanation with a magisterial summation of what's really going on: 'They're driving you hard.' It's a contagious insight, for he finds himself agreeing: 'Yes, they're driving me hard.'[79] What first appeared mere accident is now seen as careful design. 'They'—it is the same unspecified pronoun that Hemingway's stricken hero in *A Farewell to Arms* employs to convey his sense of the forces conspiring our destruction—have arranged the meeting in the cathedral, *not* with the expected Italian (he is simply the ruse to get Joseph there), but with the prison chaplain. Beneath what Joseph thinks is true is what really is true, beneath what he thinks he is doing is what is really being done: there is a destiny that shapes our ends, rough-hew them as we will—but it is a far more baffling business for Joseph than it is for Hamlet.

The priest tells Joseph that he has had him summoned, and, when Joseph understandably replies that he has come to meet an Italian, the priest brusquely dismisses this as irrelevant: what do Joseph's intentions have to do with it? 'They' want him in the cathedral and here he is. And where, for that matter, is the Italian if the visit really is for his sake? Joseph is made to recognize that he has no more dignity than a pawn on a board, but the pawn is at least spared the delusion of believing itself a free-choosing agent. Without this power to imagine and enact the future, to choose to act or abstain, human beings, says Spinoza, would simply be falling stones. Joseph has been battling to maintain a minimum degree of control over his life; shown that even this is a hoax, he capitulates and the chapter ends with him dully resigned to the execution that awaits him.

Nor is this the full measure of his humiliation; it is not simply that he does not manage his own life, neither does he understand it. This is the purpose of the priest's story of the man from the country: to replace certainty with doubt, knowledge with confusion, light with darkness. If Joseph (and the reader) can go astray in misunderstanding so apparently simple and straightforward a story, how can we ever be sure of being right? At first hearing, Joseph has no doubt as to what it means—it is, after all, his own story. The man from the country is another blameless victim of a cruel jest, of irrational persecution and moronic injustice. By the time the priest has spun his web of intricate exegesis (he only finishes because he has run out of time), Joseph wearily concedes that he is no longer sure of anything and will debate no more: how can you stand on ground that won't stay still? It is impossible to know for sure, yet just as impossible to live unperturbed in that state of suspense that Swift condemned as the life of a spider.[80] To need, yet be unable, to know: it's the nadir of cognitive degradation.

The lesson that miscarried in the episode with Block is successfully concluded in the meeting with the priest. Joseph is demoralized: his seeming choices are not really his at all, his reading of events is merely one among many, each as unstable as the next. Descartes found in the *cogito* the unchallengeable fact of personal identity; Kafka finds there the irrefutable conviction of personal insignificance, of nonentity: I think, but to what purpose? Better to be the pawn or the falling stone, for, if they are impotent, it is without knowing and being embarrassed by it.

Kafka is at once the most powerful of Vanni Fucci's heirs, yet scarcely an heir at all. There could be no more devastating account of human life than the one presented in his pages: here, if anywhere, is cause to grieve. But there is no sense of malice in Kafka's work, of an author out to get us as there is in Hardy, Conrad or Wharton. In the humiliations of Tess, Winnie, Ethan, one senses an authorial hostility toward character and reader alike: some enemy hath done this, as the lord of the field says. There is contrivance in the disposals of Tess, Winnie and Ethan—not so much the way things are as the way they are crafted to be. We sense nothing of this in Kafka.

It is not—the mistake of his early readers—that he lines up with his harassed protagonists or tries to enlist our sympathies for them: whatever compassion we find in these texts we have imported. This work occupies a space between tragedy and satire—man as victim or as fool—closer to the second, but lacking the punitive impulse native to satire. There is, rather, a disconcerting neutrality, a detachment, almost an indifference to the harrowing fates presented, whether it be George Bendemann, Gregor Samsa, the Officer in the penal settlement or Joseph K in *The Trial*. These texts reveal, on the surface, all the unemotional factuality of a police notebook: there is no heartache, sorrow, no relish or satisfaction at the events recorded. Below the surface it is another story. Precisely because it is not overt propaganda for any particular world-view, it is the more powerful in its impact. There is no manipulation or rigging of events to resent or react against. If we grieve, it is not because of the palpable intentions of the author.

Every reader of Kafka remarks on the fact that, however bizarre, considered in isolation, the discrete events may be, they assume a strangely compelling force when they come together as an integral whole: the individual details may tax belief, but the overall design commands our acceptance. We move from an initial remonstrative incredulity ('this is impossible') to a sense of unshakeable conviction ('this is true'). It is a tribute to Kafka's uncanny narrative power that at the close of these perplexing texts one should be reminded of Bishop Butler's words: 'Things and actions are what they are, and the consequences of them will be what they will be; why then should we desire to be deceived?'[81] Disagreeing with Kafka seems almost like quarrelling with nature.

NOTES

1. Erich Heller, *Kafka* (Fontana, Collins: London; 1974), 28, 35.

2. Franz Kafka, 'In the Penal Settlement,' *Metamorphosis and Other Stories*, trans. Willa and Edwin Muir (Penguin: Harmondsworth, 1961), 194.

3. Ibid., 198.

4. Ibid., 181, 185.

5. Ibid., 188.

6. Kierkegaard, quoted in Albert Camus, *The Myth of Sisyphus*, trans. Justin O'Brien (Penguin: Harmondsworth, 1975), 120.

7. Ronald Gray, *Franz Kafka* (Cambridge University Press: London and New York, 1973), 134–5.

8. Quoted in Heller, *Kafka*, 88.

9. *The World of Franz Kafka*, ed. J.P. Stern (Weidenfeld & Nicolson: London, 1980), 20–1.

10. Arthur Schopenhauer, *Essays and Aphorisms*, ed. R.J. Hollingdale (Penguin: Harmondsworth, 1970), 49.

11. *Metamorphosis and Other Stories*, 175.

12. Ibid., 174.

13. Emil Henry, quoted in Benjamin R. Barber, *Superman and Common Men: Freedom, Anarchy and the Revolution* (Penguin: Harmondsworth, 1972), 29. See also *The Anarchist Reader*, ed. George Woodcock (Fontana, Collins: Glasgow, 1977), 193.

14. *Metamorphosis and Other Stories*, 186.

15. Quoted in Heller, *Kafka*, 62.

16. Ibid., 64.

17. Ibid., 64.

18. 'Letter to His Father,' in *Wedding Preparations in the Country and Other Stories* (Penguin: Harmondsworth, 1978), 75.

19. Quoted in Heller, *Kafka*, 13.

20. *Metamorphosis and Other Stories*, 184.

21. Ibid., 180.

22. Ibid., 187.

23. Ibid., 191.

24. Ibid., 197.

25. Ibid., 192–3.

26. Ibid., 178.

27. Ibid., 178.

28. Franz Kafka, *The Trial* (Penguin: Harmondsworth and London, 1953), 215.

29. Albert Camus, *The Myth of Sisyphus*, 109.

30. Peter Heller, 'On Not Understanding Kafka,' in *The Kafka Debate: New Perspectives for our Time*, ed. Angel Flores (Gordian Press: New York, 1977), 24–41.

31. *The Trial*, 225, 233.

32. Ludwig Wittgenstein, *Tractatus Logico-Philosophicus* (Routledge: London and New York, 1981), 26, 188.

33. *The Trial*, 240.

34. Franz Kafka, *The Castle*, trans. Willa and Edwin Muir (Penguin: Harmondsworth, 1957), 216.

35. *The Myth of Sisyphus*, 112.

36. T.W. Adorno, quoted in Malcolm Bradbury, *The Modern World: Ten Great Writers* (Penguin: Harmondsworth, 1989), 259.

37. Quoted by George Steiner, *Real Presences: Is There Anything in What We Say?* (Faber & Faber: London and Boston, 1989), 224.

38. *Kafka: A Collection of Critical Essays*, ed. Ronald Gray (Prentice Hall: Englewood Cliffs, NJ, 1962), 94.

39. Quoted in Gray (ed.). *Kafka: A Collection of Critical Essays*, 20.

40. Milan Kundera, *The Art of the Novel*, trans. Linda Asher (Faber & Faber: London and Boston, 1988), 106.

41. *The Trial*, 243.

42. *Metamorphosis and Other Stories*, 111.

43. Bradbury, *The Modern World*, 258.

44. Heller, *Kafka*, 26.

45. *The Poems of Alexander Pope*, ed. John Butt (Methuen: London, 1968), 808.

46. *Wedding Preparations in the Country and Other Stories*, 53.

47. Erich Heller, 'The World of Franz Kafka,' in *The Disinherited Mind* (Penguin: Harmondsworth, 1961), 177.

48. Quoted in Gray (ed.), *Kafka*, 157.

49. *Wedding Preparations in the Country and Other Stories*, 136.

50. Heller, *Kafka*, 94.

51. *The Trial*, 243.

52. Ibid., 97.

53. *Wedding Preparations in the Country and Other Stories*, 41.

54. *The Trial*, 171, 233.

55. Ibid., 247.

56. Ibid., 98–9.

57. Ibid., 7.

58. John Bunyan, *Grace Abounding and The Life and Death of Mr Badman*, intro. G.B. Harrison (Everyman's Library, Dent: London, 1956), 298.

59. *The Trial*, 12–13.

60. *Metamorphosis and Other Stories*, 97.

61. Ibid., 102–3.

62. Ibid., 69, 74.

63. Friedrich Nietzsche, *The Gay Science*, trans. Walter Kaufman (Vintage Books: New York, 1974), 328.

64. Philip Rahv, quoted in John Peter, *Vladimir's Carrot: Modern Drama and the Modern Imagination* (Methuen: London, 1988), 160, 159.

65. Kundera, *The Art of the Novel*, 104–5.

66. *The Castle*, 115.

67. *The Trial*, 167.

68. Ibid., 238–9. See Steiner, *Real Presences*, 103–4.

69. *The Trial*, 243.

70. Kundera, *The Art of the Novel*, 104.

71. *The Trial*, 190.

72. Ibid., 197.

73. Ibid., 198.

74. Ibid., 209.

75. Ibid., 210.

76. Ibid., 213.

77. Ibid., 214.

78. George Orwell, *Nineteen Eighty-Four* (Harmondsworth, 1954), 203.

79. *The Trial*, 224.

80. Jonathan Swift, *The Prose Works of Jonathan Swift* (16 vols), ed. Herbert Davis et al. (Basil Blackwell: Oxford, 1939–68), vol. 1, 244.

81. Bishop Joseph Butler, *Fifteen Sermons*, preached at the Rolls Chapel and *A dissertation upon the nature of virtue*, ed. W.R. Matthews (George Bell: London, 1953). See also Gray (ed.), *Kafka*, 6.

SIMON RYAN

Franz Kafka's Die Verwandlung: *Transformation, Metaphor, and the Perils of Assimilation*

Kafka's *Die Verwandlung* is the story of a son whose transformation into a repulsive, inhuman, and steadily weakening body marks his banishment from society and from the family he loves. In the course of the narrative Gregor Samsa follows an increasingly inevitable path towards extinction, a death that this unlucky son himself eventually agrees has become necessary. Further, it is the story of a son whose language has become incomprehensible. As this article will argue, Gregor's voice, now an unintelligible squeak, is like Kafka's Jewish voice, both heard and overheard in critical readings and finally ignored because the new code in which it is embedded ultimately falls on deaf ears. Since 1912 Kafka's story has wandered a long way from its original home in a Czech-Jewish minority culture. It appeared at a time when the younger generation, many of whose parents had migrated to the city from the country, was widely subordinated to their parents' desire to assimilate into a new cultural environment. The long and tortuous history of the critical reception of *Die Verwandlung* demonstrates over and over again the highly elusive nature of the cultural and aesthetic encoding of the key signifier, the vile body around which the constellation of this family drama endlessly gyrates.

A reexamination of *Die Verwandlung* in relation to issues of ethnicity and gender in the context of recent Kafka scholarship opens a number of

From *Seminar: A Journal of Germanic Studies* 43, no. 1 (February 2007): 1–18. © 2007 by the Canadian Association of University Teachers of German.

interpretative possibilities, including the tantalizing prospect that it may now be possible to uncover with a greater measure of certainty than before the social, linguistic, and ethnopsychological origins of the grotesquely alienated body of the insect man, Gregor Samsa. New evidence supports the hypothesis that the metaphoric body in the text simultaneously expresses and conceals deep-seated anxieties about the writer's ethnic identity during a period of intense cultural transformation. From this perspective, Kafka's narrative may have much to tell us about the fictional representation of a severely alienated body—the writer's body that Deleuze conceptualizes as "an extension of the imagined body of the father." The narrative is also about the destructive power of abusive metaphors and their relationship to cultural and ethnic identity at risk. Although much scholarly enterprise in the past six decades has been devoted to the interpretation of *Die Verwandlung*, it is still unclear what we might learn from this example of "minor literature" about why invoking terms of racial abuse and engendering suspicion of minority groups are not only the linguistic symptoms of a deep social ill, but also to be viewed as modes of behaviour that produce, out of the lives of humiliated fathers and mothers, sons and daughters whose culturally transmitted negative self-perception, in turn, leads to acts of violence and self-destruction.

As prototypical Deleuzean "experimental machines" Kafka's narratives seem to have become the perfect postmodern playthings. Amidst an array of poststructuralist, post-Freudian, and feminist readings, the abject body at the centre of *Die Verwandlung*, Kafka's "ungeheueres Ungeziefer"—or "monstrous vermin"—and the no longer fully human voice that emanates from it threatened to remain abstractions, culturally and temporally disembodied signifiers, divorced, as they are in the original narrative, from their cultural and historical roots. The widespread critical reluctance to engage with issues pertaining to differences of race and gender in relation to the progression of the narrative's central metaphor is puzzling given that Réda Bensmaïa for one considers that as far back as 1975 Deleuze and Guattari revealed Kafka to be a "writer who for the first time throws open the question of 'literature' to the forces and the differences (of class, race, language, or gender) that run through it" (214). Later, in *A Thousand Plateaus* (1980), Deleuze and Guattari laid the theoretical groundwork for a future reading of the text's commercial-traveller insect body as the enunciation of a machinic and collective assemblage. This concept enables an enquiry into the way the fictional transformation of the body in *Die Verwandlung* refracts both the social transmission of order-words (*mots d'ordre*) pertaining to the male Jewish body in Prague at the time of the novella's composition and the incorporeal transformations that produced a shift in the semiotic variables operating within the discourse of race (75–80). If, as Deleuze and Guattari also claimed, the essence of the novella as a literary form "is organised around the question, 'What happened? Whatever could have happened?'" (193) and if, in the critical reception of *Die Verwandlung*, this question still remains open, then compelling grounds remain for not abandoning the quest for the contributing causes of this abrupt bodily transformation. This article argues that, despite the leads suggested by Deleuze and Guattari and the more recent positive reception of some of them by Sander L. Gilman, a reading of the metaphoric body in *Die Verwandlung* that provides an adequate account of the issues of cultural transformation encoded in the text has not taken place.

Since the early 1990s, Kafka scholarship by Mark M. Anderson, Gilman, Walter Sokel, Scott Spector, and John Zilcosky has contributed much to our understanding of the cultural-historical context of Kafka's work. Their approaches underscore the importance of understanding Kafka's Jewishness while simultaneously pursuing deconstructive approaches to his fiction. Anderson's analysis of Kafka's aestheticism argues convincingly that Kafka conceives of the self and the writer's quest for understanding, expression, and spiritual redemption in terms that relate to the assumption and removal of layers of clothing from a body that is defined within its ethnocultural setting (6). Sokel advances the notion that, in *Das Urteil*, *Die Verwandlung*, and *Der Prozess*, there is "a striking resemblance of structure between Kafka's representation of fictional characters with his presentation of the relationship between use of the German language and Jewish being" (852). Spector's research points to the everyday consciousness of an acute territorial crisis registered by Kafka and his contemporaries among the Prague-Jewish intelligentsia. At the heart of this crisis of territoriality he posits a profound anxiety about Central European Jewishness and the question of assimilation in relation to the ways in which culture, language, and the concept of nation were being constructed in the first two decades of the twentieth century. Zilcosky approaches Kafka's narratives of alienation through an exploration of Kafka's intensive reading of travel writing and his own travels, especially the records of his personal experiences while travelling and his reception of travel writing that conveyed the visceral impact on the traveller's subjectivity of journeys to exotic, utopian, or dystopian places. In the case of *Die Verwandlung*, Zilcosky argues that a hidden master trope, that of the *Reisender*, operates in the narrative *ex negativo* in the form of Gregor's radical internalization of the exotic vermin Kafka encountered in the course of his reading (77). The studies cited above all include useful commentary on *Die Verwandlung* that endeavours to locate the narrative in its original cultural and social setting. The argument pursued here is, however, particularly indebted to clues to the enigma of this narrative provided by Gilman in his study of the ethnopsychology of Kafka's cultural milieu, to Stanley Corngold for his early and later revised reflections on Kafka's deconstruction of metaphors (*The Commentator's Despair*; "Kafka's Other Metamorphosis" 41–57), and to Nina Pelikan Straus for her insights into the transfer of gender roles between brother and sister in the course of the tale (651–67). Sokel's reflections on *Die Verwandlung* in the wake of Gilman's book are also drawn on in the course of the argument.

In his 1995 monograph *Franz Kafka, the Jewish Patient*, Gilman reached a new and significant understanding concerning the "desirable but inherently impossible" transformation of the male Jewish body in Europe around the turn of the century (13). This sociocultural analysis elucidates decisive elements in the construction of Kafka's discourse through historical and biographical documents and an analysis of the fiction, but, surprisingly perhaps, does not offer more than brief comments on *Die Verwandlung* itself. The critical reception of Gilman's book among North American scholars has been marked by division over the issue of its historicism. Sokel's review praised Gilman's research for its success in connecting "Kafka's discourse, in life documents and fiction, to specific, fatefully influential discourses of his age" (526), but noted what he considered to be Gilman's apparent lack of attention to what he termed the "uniqueness" in Kafka's art. What Sokel accepted as an understandable effect of the thematic preoccupation and historical focus of Gilman's work, Corngold took to be a glaring and unforgivable omission. Corngold's review presents an oversimplified view of Gilman's evidence and methodology and accuses him, in "this original, obsessive and wrong-headed book," of deliberately ignoring the distinctive literariness of Kafka's work, reducing it to the same, aesthetically banal level as the other historical documents he produces in order to substantiate the claim that Kafka internalized and reproduced stereotypical features of the anti-Semitism of his times. However, Gilman's approach proves on a closer reading to be considerably more differentiated with regard to the literary works than Corngold's review suggests. As its application to the case of *Die Verwandlung* will demonstrate, the resulting sociocultural analysis of Kafka's discourse cannot so easily be dismissed. Concluding his more positive review, Sokel observed that "Gilman's volume is a boon not only to readers of Kafka, but to all who seek to understand our recent past. For future Kafka scholars his book will be indispensable" (526–27). Although Spector does not refer, except in his bibliography, to *Franz Kafka, The Jewish Patient* and cites only Gilman's earlier research on the genealogy of the term *Mauscheln* (90), his exhaustive analysis of the impact of an acute territorial crisis on Kafka and his contemporaries confirms Gilman's conclusions regarding the strategies Kafka adopted as a Prague Jew in an ethnically hostile environment. When combined with important clues provided by other commentators, Gilman's ethnopsychological evidence can indeed be seen to point the way to a new reading of this remarkable fictional account of an ill-fated process of cultural adaptation and transformation.

At the beginning of this enquiry stand the two photographic markers of difference that Kafka has subtly positioned in the narrative. In the first section of the narrative, two photographs are on display in the Samsa apartment. They demand closer examination. The first is above the table in Gregor's bedroom. Gregor has cut it out of an illustrated magazine: "Es stellte eine Dame dar, die, mit einem Pelzhut und einer Pelzboa versehen, aufrecht dasaß und einen schweren Pelzmuff, in dem ihr ganzer Unterarm verschwunden war, dem Beschauer entgegenhob" (*Erzählungen* 57). The erotic qualities of the image are not lost on Gregor, nor have they been overlooked by Kafka's commentators. Some of these commentators, including Anderson—the only recent scholar to take up the issue of the photographs in detail—have found in this episode a playful reference to Leopold von Sacher-Masoch's *Venus im Pelz* (1880). Later, as his mother and sister try to strip his room of his last bachelor possessions, Gregor, in splendid mock-epic fashion, defends it by covering it with his insect body: "[er] kroch eilends hinauf und preßte sich an das Glas, das ihn festhielt und seinem heißen Bauch wohltat" (86). This passage suggests that the photograph is an image of the feminine that in some way Gregor wishes to defend and embrace. Yet apart from the reference to its source in popular reading material and the obvious inference of its relation to Gregor's isolated bachelor state, Kafka provides us with no further explanations as to the photograph's meaning for Gregor. Its wider cultural significance becomes apparent only in the context of Pelikan Straus's and Gilman's research into Kafka's relationship to the feminine and its implications for his portrayal of Gregor.

When he first succeeds in unlocking his door, partly revealing himself in the doorway, the livingroom table has been set for breakfast. As he leans in the doorway, the second photographic portrait of the story hangs opposite him, "eine Photographie Gregors aus seiner Militärzeit, die ihn als Leutnant darstellte, wie er, die Hand am Degen, sorglos lächelnd, Respekt für seine Haltung und Uniform verlangte" (69). The appearance of such an image in a middle-class family narrative written during the late phase of the Austro-Hungarian Empire, when military service was still the norm, is perhaps nothing out of the ordinary. Indeed, the topic of Gregor's military service has not been neglected in critical discussions of the story, but its particular significance in relation to his bodily transformation has not yet been fully explored. The description of the portrait, anchored as it is in Gregor's subjective perception, raises questions about Gregor's suddenly altered relationship to this positive photographic image of himself as a young man fit for military service and therefore to his masculine self-image. Anderson reads the uniform as an expression of the effacement of Gregor's singularity through uniformity (133), a further sign in the text of the oppressive *Verkehr* of work and the social order to which the family is enslaved and from which Gregor in his new animal covering has now supposedly found a means to escape. While this is a most perceptive interpretation, it nonetheless overlooks the double-coding in the text of the photographic image both as the marker of a former state that has been somehow overcome in the process of transformation and as an image of an experience associated with being free of care ("sorglos") and the desire to command social respect ("Respekt [. . .] verlangte"). This passage emphasizes Gregor's military bearing—in other words, the outward appearance of the young lieutenant's body—and conveys a sense of what has been lost that remains unaccounted for. As Gilman's evidence for the cultural significance of Jewishness in relation to fitness for military service will suggest, a direct link may be made between the suggestion of loss when Gregor catches sight of his portrait and his experience, only a few moments before struggling to open the door to the living room, of the loss of his normal human voice. In order for this link between the body clothed in the military uniform and the loss of voice to become explicit, the cultural double-coding of the military uniform and the body it enfolds must first be unlocked. In view of the importance of the paradoxes surrounding locked and unlocked doors in the novella and in Kafka's fiction generally, it is significant that a locksmith ("Schlosser"; 66–67) is sent for but never in fact arrives—a sign perhaps that Kafka was anxious that the ethnocultural source code of the photograph should remain forever well concealed.

Few writers have agonized as much about the body as Kafka. Few writers have entered so self-consciously into the act of writing as a means of constructing the image of the writer's body: "Als es in meinem Organismus klargeworden war, daß das Schreiben die ergiebigste Richtung meines Wesens sei, drängte sich alles hin und ließ alle Fähigkeiten leer stehn, die sich auf die Freuden des Geschlechtes, des Essens, des Trinkens, des philosophischen Nachdenkens, der Musik zu allererst, richteten. Ich magerte nach allen diesen Richtungen ab" (*Tagebücher* 3.1.1912, 167). The complex origins of Kafka's sense of his own body are hinted at on many occasions in his work. Of particular interest in the present context is the following diary entry:

> Ich heiße hebräisch Amschel wie der Großvater meiner Mutter
> von der Mutterseite, der als ein sehr frommer und gelehrter
> Mann mit langem weißen Bart meiner Mutter erinnerlich ist, die
> sechs Jahre alt war als er starb. [. . .] Ein noch gelehrterer Mann
> als der Großvater war der Urgroßvater der Mutter, bei Christen
> und Juden stand er in gleichem Ansehen, bei einer Feuersbrunst

geschah infolge seiner Frömmigkeit das Wunder, daß das Feuer sein Haus übersprang und verschonte, während die Häuser in der Runde verbrannten. [...] Alle außer dem Großvater der Mutter starben bald. Dieser hatte einen Sohn, die Mutter kannte ihn als verrückten Onkel Nathan [...]. Gegen das Fenster laufen und durch die zersplitterten Hölzer und Scheiben, schwach nach Anwendung aller Kraft, die Fensterbrüstung überschreiten. (*Tagebücher* 25.12.1911, 156)

Here Kafka recites his genealogy, naming in Hebrew the inherited body: he thinks fondly and finally somewhat apprehensively of his maternal Jewish forebears. Then, with the next stroke of the pen, he traces in imagination the trajectory of an intensely self-destructive urge. The recollection of the body's ethnic origins in this diary passage is thus spatially and temporally contingent with a violent wish to destroy his own body or at least somehow be free of it.

It is not possible to examine the fate of the protagonist's body in the fictional world of *Die Verwandlung* without reference to the construction of narrative's central metaphor or without taking into account Kafka's unease about the use of metaphors. Corngold's great service has been to remind us of what is often overlooked in critical readings of the story, namely Kafka's intense dislike of metaphor and the despair about writing this negative perception engendered in him:

Die Metaphern sind eines in dem Vielen, was mich am Schreiben verzweifeln läßt. Die Unselbständigkeit des Schreibens, die Abhängigkeit von dem Dienst-mädchen, das einheizt, von der Katze, die sich am Ofen wärmt, selbst vom armen alten Menschen, der sich wärmt. Alles dies sind selbstständige, eigengesetzliche Verrichtungen, nur das Schreiben ist hilflos, wohnt nicht in sich selbst, ist Spaß und Verzweiflung. (*Tagebücher* 6.12.1921, 403)

In particular, Kafka bemoans the difficulty of constructing metaphors for true feelings that would allow him "meinen ganz bangen Zustand ganz aus mir herauszuschreiben und ebenso wie er aus der Tiefe kommt, in die Tiefe des Papiers hinein, oder es so niederzuschreiben, daß ich das Geschriebene vollständig in mich einbeziehen könnte" (*Tagebücher* 8.12.1911, 136; Corngold, *The Commentator's Despair* 7). What Kafka brings to attention in this diary entry is the cultural conditioning of the signifiers on which all writing inevitably depends, the condition that the later Austrian experimental writer, Oswald Wiener, characterized in 1969 as the unbearable nature of the way language organizes reality: "Die Organisation der Wirklichkeit durch die Sprache ist unerträglich" (LII).

The recollection of Corngold's observation concerning Kafka's unease about metaphors suggests the importance of assessing the cultural origins and the expressive function of the metaphoric body in Kafka's "writing out" of anxiety. The original Prague-German phrase for the transformed body is "ungeheueres Ungeziefer." Students of German literature usually learn that English and other translations of the central metaphor vary. "Ungeziefer" is a generic term referring to "vermin," but because the new body in the story resembles an insect or beetle of sorts, it is often translated as such, thus obscuring Kafka's careful choice of the word "Ungeziefer." This choice will be shown to be significant in another context. Collocated with the adjective "ungeheuer" is the noun "Ungeheuer," a word with a wide range of connotations in German and various possible translations into English and other languages generally denoting a monster or ogre of the folk-tale variety. The effect of the two negative prefixes is to intensify the impression of something indeterminate, neither human nor animal: an *Un-Tier*. *Die Verwandlung* relates the consequences of Gregor's transformation into a new and quite "impossible" bodily form: impossible in every sense but especially impossible as a survival capsule for the ill-fated son because it is an ill-adapted creature, a "Mischling," a hybrid or half-breed of some kind (a favourite Kafka theme, as Gilman notes), still partly human on the inside, with a limited life span and no female mate in sight.

Corngold proposes in his reading of *Die Verwandlung* that Kafka has effectively carried out an act of countermetamorphosis or deconstruction by transforming the body metaphor—a strategy inspired by his fundamental objection to the metaphor. Corngold's notion of a playful and uncanny destabilization of the literal and figurative poles of the metaphor is certainly relevant to an understanding of its central role in the text. His reading of the literal pole of the metaphor, which he formulates as "this man is a vermin" (*The Commentator's Despair* 19) or is "said to be a louse" ("Kafka's Other Metamorphosis" 50), nevertheless tends to divert critical attention from its cultural context. He finally adopts the view that "the attempt to interpret *Die Verwandlung* through Kafka's empirical personality suffers by implication from the difficulty of interpreting the vermin through the residual empirical sense of the metaphor of the vermin" (*The Commentator's Despair* 19).

If we accept Corngold's conclusion, we miss the very real sociocultural context of the term "monstrous vermin" at the time and place of the tale's composition. Corngold instead argues that Gregor's alienation is essentially an expression of the estrangement from the family, which Kafka himself endured because he desired to live for literature alone. Kafka so exhausts himself seeking a state of autonomous aesthetic activity that he becomes "a being that cannot be accommodated in a family" (*The Commentator's Despair* 11). Corngold thus assumes that Kafka is driven not by any concern over the empirical referent of "the familiar metaphor"—that is, with the man who is designated as a vermin—but by "a radical aesthetic intention" that deliberately sets out to distort and therefore deconstruct the initially monstrous metaphor (10). Gilman's findings, however, suggest quite the opposite. He suggests that it makes greater sense to assume that in *Die Verwandlung* Kafka is in fact vitally interested in the empirical referent and thus writes against the very idea of metaphor being used at all to establish a relation between a human being and a species of vermin.

Gilman in *Franz Kafka, the Jewish Patient* and Sokel, writing somewhat later on *Die Verwandlung* in "Kafka as a Jew," both argue that, for Kafka, the business of assimilation into the non-Jewish world invokes a sense of shame (Gilman 18–19; Sokel 842–43). Sokel demonstrates perhaps most appositely the double-edged nature of this shame. On the one hand, it is the shame of repressing Jewishness in order to be assimilated and, on the other, it is the shame that the writer-son experiences in failing to fulfil the role of the dutiful Jewish son by helping to further the commercial interests that both drive and support the assimilation project of the Kafka family. Sokel finds this shame metaphorically embodied in "the verminous hulk of the commercial travelling salesman" (851). From the point of view of the family, Gregor is the "parasite no better than vermin," who can no longer work to support them. From Gregor's perspective—which Sokel, referring to Kafka's friendship with the Yiddish actor, Yitzhak Löwy, characterizes as "an internalised Yitzhak Levi's perspective," namely that of an authentic, Yiddish-speaking Eastern European Jew—Gregor is a figure of shame because he has failed to pursue the promise of his own liberation from the economic and cultural servitude in which the family is still enmeshed. Therefore he can only wither away. Without wishing to limit the narrative to an allegory of the dilemmas of assimilation, Sokel establishes a clear link between the appearance of the metaphoric body in the narrative and Kafka's experience of a radical cultural split.

Gilman's research, however, provides the vital key to the apparently seamless encoding of the metaphoric body. He draws on Kafka's notion that the literature written in German by Prague (and Warsaw) Jews is a "minor literature" and on the well-known development of this idea by Deleuze and Guattari in their 1975 study *Kafka: Toward a Minor Literature*. Gilman argues that Kafka tried to "transmute" his "irreducibly Jewish voice" (12) into the discourse of German literary "high modernism." He explains how Kafka smuggles his compelling need to secure his eminently insecure male

Prague-Jewish identity across the linguistic border into the culturally dominant German-speaking world. Prague German, as the language of a ruling
minority, was itself the language of a deterritorialized group—an artificially
cultivated, formal, and lexically somewhat restricted form of German, which
Kafka found he had simultaneously to employ and transcend (22). Gilman
emphasizes the importance of understanding Kafka's self-image when reading his work: "central to the existence of a minor literature is a clear association with the discourse about the body of the writer—bodies and biographies
are never peripheral to the construction of a 'minor literature'" (23).

With the exception of Deleuze and Guattari, Kafka scholars writing
before the 1990s tended to view Kafka's anxiety about his body as a feature
of his individual psychology rather than as a manifestation of wider ethnopsychological issues faced by Western European Jews who were dealing every
day with the very real difficulties of acculturation. Following Deleuze, Gilman contends that the writer's body is "an extension of the imagined body of
the father [. . .] it is not that the father is the (positive) Oedipal aggressor
dominating the son; rather the father is"—and here Gilman cites Deleuze's
1967 essay "Coldness and Cruelty" (60–61)—"not so much the beater as the
beaten. [. . .] Is it not precisely the father-image in him that is miniaturised,
beaten, ridiculed, and humiliated? What the subject atones for is his resemblance to the father and the father's likeness in him: the formula of masochism is the humiliated father'" (23). Building on this causal formulation of the
socially inflicted suffering of the father in the process of assimilation and its
atonement in the son, we can begin to discern the way the writer's body is
projected into the fiction of *Die Verwandlung*.

What Gilman demonstrates through his precise and detailed historical
study of the ethnopsychology of Kafka's time in relation to the prevailing discourses of race, gender, and illness is that Kafka's intense desire to write—to
establish over a textual world the control that the surrounding culture denied
him (158)—was motivated to a considerable degree by an overwhelming
anxiety that the fatally marked Jewish body inherited from his father would
inevitably betray him and, through that betrayal, abort the whole project of
assimilation for which the father intended his son's body should also serve as a
vehicle. As Gilman argues, the form that betrayal would take Kafka glimpsed
all too clearly in the outwardly strong but inwardly weakened, potentially ill,
and socially humiliated body of his own father, who, even as he hastened to
flee his fate by trying to become that impossible creature, a fully assimilated
Western Jew, worked relentlessly to fulfil in his own body the turn-of-the-
century, anti-Semitic stereotype of the male Jew.

Gilman's analysis of the transformation of the anti-Semitic stereotype
also bears implications for a reading of *Die Verwandlung*. He produces a

considerable body of documentary evidence to support the view that towards the end of the nineteenth century the older theological difference of the Jew from his Christian neighbours was in the process of being translated into a new, biologically founded discourse. As Kafka grew to manhood in Prague, the result of this process was a new set of stereotypical traits that overlaid earlier anti-Semitic prejudice and characterized the everyday thinking of many non-Jews about their Jewish neighbours. Fitness for military service was the overarching measure of masculinity in Europe at the time. In spite of the innumerable examples of highly competent Jewish soldiers serving in European armies, male Jews were popularly believed to be physically weak (especially in the lungs and feet), to be cowards, shirkers, and potential traitors. The practice of ritual male circumcision and the traditional restriction of male Jews to certain professions had served in the eyes of non-Jewish men to "feminize" the body of the male Jew. Circumcision was widely equated either with castration or with an unmasculine inclination towards lewdness and depravity. In the popular mind, together with the traditional anti-Semitic images of Jews as ritual murderers of Christian women and children, Jews were believed to be carriers of disease, especially diseases of the blood, syphilis (associated with the practice followed by Eastern Jews of *metsitsah* during circumcision), tuberculosis (which, when associated with speculation about higher levels of immunity amongst Jews, led to deep suspicions about their ritual complicity in spreading the disease), and infectious skin diseases (compare the itching white spots on the belly of Gregor Samsa's insect carapace).

Jewish sexuality was also suspect: they were believed to be either promiscuous or very likely to be homosexual or both. The body of the male Jew becomes "an analog of the body of the homosexual" (160), a site for a conflation of images—a fact that also suggests the importance of reconsidering critical readings of Kafka's homoerotic fantasies. Female Jews were often portrayed as prostitutes or otherwise libeled as seducers of Aryan men. Gilman concludes that the marked body of the Jew as a social construction of European anti-Semitism entered into both the self-perception and self-actualization of the Jew to such an extent that the word "Jew" had clearly become for Kafka's contemporaries a precisely gendered concept that linked the idea of Jewish masculinity with pathological traits (21). As the archetypal "Jewish patient," Kafka, Gilman argues, always lived as if predestined for the illness to which he finally fell victim. When the evidence for the internalization of anti-Semitic views in such celebrated instances of Jewish self-hatred as the case of Otto Weininger and the occasional outbursts of Karl Kraus is also taken into account, Gilman's thesis appears much less extreme and obsessive than Corngold's response to it would suggest.

To this general profile of the anti-Semitic stereotype Gilman adds com-pelling evidence that Kafka's particular belief that assimilation is an impossible bodily transition was nowhere more palpably instilled in him than through the long-running Dreyfus Affair—the trial, incarceration on Devil's Island, and torture of Captain Alfred Dreyfus, a Jewish officer in the French army maliciously accused by conspiring fellow-officers of betraying military secrets to the Germans (Gilman 72–78; 116–18). This infamous abuse and acid-test of the French justice system gripped the whole of Europe and especially its Jews from 1894 to 1906, the year Kafka turned twenty-six. The fate of Drey-fus represented to Kafka and his whole generation the ultimate betrayal of the Jewish body. The letters and diaries of Dreyfus were avidly consumed. Gilman argues that the sketch of the torture machine Kafka included in a letter to Milena Jesenská in March 1920 closely reflects Kafka's reading of the 1901 German edition of Dreyfus's memoirs and letters (87). If the thoroughly acculturated, physically robust, wealthy, cultured, highly educated, confidant, even occasionally arrogant Jew, the impeccable career-officer Alfred Dreyfus, could be falsely accused, roughly seized, exposed to the worst forms of anti-Semitic slander, and physically reduced by torture to manifest the "concealed body" of the stereotypical sick, physically decaying male Jew, what might hap-pen to less secure, less socially prominent male Jews like Kafka who, even while exercising and dieting furiously, believed his body was already primed for some fatal disease or for insanity like his mother's "crazy Uncle Nathan"?

In the context of Gilman's reading of the Dreyfus Affair, the alleged unfitness of male Jews for military service and Kafka's manifest interest in reports of Dreyfus's trial and incarceration, we cannot now overlook the way in which Gregor's early glimpse of the photograph of himself in military uni-form takes on a precise and painful ethnopsychological significance that has not been registered in other accounts of the narrative. The military uniform that had previously held out to this middle-class son the utopian promise of cultural uniformity and ethnic anonymity in a state of full assimilation has turned out like the world of secularized industrial labour for which Gregor has only just now also proved unfit, namely to represent a false hope.

To consider the question of whether the body in which Gregor now finds himself is a body already marked for extinction, it is necessary to return to the cultural history of the term "Ungeziefer." Early in the critical reception of the novella Corngold reminded us that the noun "Ungeziefer" in Mid-dle High German signifies an "unclean animal not suited for sacrifice" (*The Commentator's Despair* 10). Kafka, Corngold argues, was quite likely to have been aware of this. From other sources (Gray; Sokel) we learn that "German usage applies the term 'Ungeziefer' to persons considered low and contempt-ible," equivalent to calling someone in English a "louse" or a "cockroach."

However, it is not until Gilman's 1995 study that we are made incontrovertibly aware of the anti-Semitic connotations that the word "Ungeziefer" carried for Kafka in Prague around the turn of the century. In German and Austrian anti-Semitic political publications, Jews were frequently referred to as "rats," "mice," "insects," and "vermin"—"Ungeziefer der Menschheit" (31; 80, the last descriptor cited from Hiemer 34–40). In the intense anti-Semitic language that the French anti-Dreyfusards employed in their newspaper, *La Libre Parole*, the Jew was described as "a stinking and dangerous animal, a plague, a centipede, a microbe, a mite, a cancer, an ugly spider and synagogue lice. […] 'Long live the sabre that will rid us of the vermin.' […] 'God's goodness ends where the Jew begins'" (Denis-Bredin 351).

The conclusion reached on the basis of Gilman's research—namely, that the empirical referent of the central metaphor cannot be overlooked as securely as Corngold insists—gains further support from Sokel. He clarifies a number of issues concerning Kafka's realization of the false consciousness arising out of the unresolved tension between Prague German as the language of his "official, assimilated, Germanised surface consciousness" and Yiddish as the language of "the submerged Jewish self" (848). The result is a Germanized surface consciousness that is out of step with the inner emotional life: "[s]ince emotional reality can no longer find expression in speech, it is stifled and condemned to wither" (848). In evidence, Sokel cites Kafka's own statements expressing his awareness among his parents' generation and that of his contemporaries of an agonizing social and cultural rift between assimilated Central European Jews and Eastern European Jews. Such "Ostjuden" were frequently viewed with a mixture of disdain and disgust as the culturally backward inhabitants of a narrow, dark, and poverty-stricken world that their parents had been anxious to leave behind. In addition to Kafka's well-known speech of February 1912 on the significance of Yiddish for his contemporaries in Prague, Sokel refers to the appearance of what he takes to be the striking insect metaphor in the often cited letter to Max Brod of June 1921: "so they wanted to write in German; but with their little hind legs they remained stuck in the Jewishness of their fathers and with their little front legs they were finding no new ground. The despair over that was their inspiration" (844–45).[1] Gilman interprets the same image in the immediate context of Kafka's letter to Brod, where he likens the tendency of Kraus's wit to mimic Yiddish-German *Mauscheln*, as depicting "a mouse caught in a glue trap" (31–32). Insect or mouse, in either reading of the image the association between Jewish writers and a species of vermin remains unmistakable. Sokel also cites Kafka's letter to Milena Jesenská, which the writer penned after several afternoons of "bathing in *Judenhaß*" (850; *Briefe an Milena* 240). In the context of a comment on Jews' insistence on living where they are not welcome, Kafka compares them directly with cockroaches ("Schaben") that cannot be eradicated from the bathroom (*Briefe an Milena* 240).

By concentrating exclusively on the aesthetic dimension of the metaphor and its reflection of a self trying to exist in an impossible field of tension between the demands of everyday life and the allure of a pure aesthetic realm, Corngold overlooks the copresence of another code that reflects Kafka's enormous anxiety over an equally unresolvable tension between the social and familial pressure to assimilate and his manifest desire to enter into a state of authentic Jewishness. Kafka clearly recognized that such a desire was popularly associated with living like vermin that are difficult to eradicate from the European social terrain. His father's contemptuous comparison of his son's association with Yitzhak Löwy to the condition of a man who beds down with dogs and gets up with fleas was undoubtedly still ringing in his ears when he wrote *Die Verwandlung*. The entry in the diary for 2 November 1911 recording this event reads: "Mein Vater über ihn: 'Wer sich mit Hunden zu Bett legt, steht mit Wanzen auf'" (*Tagebücher* 103). Like the word "Ungeziefer," "Wanzen" is also a generic rather than a specific term that presents a problem to the translator. "Fleas" is the natural English rendering, but the word obscures Kafka's preference for the more indeterminate sense of "Wanzen." Now, in the face of the vilification of Jewishness that was inseparable feature of the process of the cultural transformation in which he was enmeshed in Prague, the prospect of an authentic Jewish existence perhaps appeared forever out of reach.

Without repressing other forms of alienation to be encountered in *Die Verwandlung*, Gilman's study provides firm evidence in support of the hypothesis that the "monstrous vermin" in this family drama is, at perhaps the deepest level of Kafka's writerly imagination, a manifestation of the "impossible body" of what for him at least had become the "impossible transformation" into that shameful being, the fully assimilated westernized male Jew. The anxieties that Kafka both reveals and conceals in the narrative are then, in this reading, the cruel results of the struggle to repress the truth of one's origins in the process of trying to acculturate. Exhausted by an unequal struggle with the harshly competitive and commercial values of what is portrayed in the sketch of labour relations early in the narrative as a replica of the invasive, industrialized, secular or gentile world of modern capitalism, Gregor betrays the father's wish to integrate the family into an inhospitable social environment. His betrayal takes the form of an involuntary reversion to what the dominant culture, in which the family is embedded, soon believes him to be: the physically weak, lazy, "feminine" (in as far as he is a male no longer fit for military service and now dependent on the labour of others, including his mother and sister), and contagiously infected monster that, as Gilman shows, was socially constructed in Western and Central Europe as the anti-Semitic stereotype of the male Jew. And the implication of the opening descriptor, "ungeheueres Ungeziefer," is that it is the abusive, "ordinary language" metaphors of European anti-Semitism that have signalled so clearly to Gregor what he must inevitably become.

The body in the text is revealed as a creature akin to "the savage one" that Evelyn Torton Beck finds invoked in a speech in Yakov Gordin's Yiddish play *Der Vilder Mentsch* (1907). When viewed in the context of Gilman's analysis, this figure must be seen to represent the grotesque body of the male Jew condemned to self-extinction as a nasty half-breed because he has, in contravention of Kafka's scrupulous ethic, bowed down before "the graven idol" of gross materialism and attempted complete assimilation:

> What—where is this savage one? A savage who observes our behaviour and our ways is buried deep within each of us [...]. When we improve ourselves, when the spirit in us wakens, when our souls reign over our bodies, then the savage one within us sleeps. But when we strive only for material goals, when we have no ideals, when our spirit sleeps, then the savage one awakens and forces us to go against civilisation, against the laws of humanity. (145)

In an essay that investigates the narrative's presentation of relationship of the son to the *Schuld der Eltern* and the *Schuld des Vaters*, Sokel examined the literalization of self-alienation in the sudden transformation of Gregor into a bestial form. He made use of a number of theoretical models ranging from the writings of early Marx on alienation to the primitive myth of the scapegoat. Beck's discovery of the tale's incorporation of structural and thematic links to Gordin's play and Sokel's analysis of the father's double betrayal of the family—first through the father's surrender of the family to the entrepreneurial individualism of capitalism and then through his duplicitous enslavement of the son to the ensuing debt—underscore Walter Benjamin's prescient remark in 1934 that "[n]o other writer has obeyed the commandment 'Thou shalt not make unto thee a graven image' so faithfully" (808). From Kafka's perspective at the time of writing *Die Verwandlung*, it must have indeed appeared that the struggle to assimilate into a culture of pure commercialism and material striving represented an abhorrent abandonment of his Jewish cultural heritage. For many young male Jews of Kafka's generation in Europe it appeared that there might well be no psychological or culturally coherent way forward.

In an almost symbiotic relationship to the transformation experienced by Gregor are the changes affecting his sister, Grete, who grows in determination and purpose even as her brother declines. This parallel series of events also warrants closer investigation. Gilman's study provides convincing evidence for the notion that the male Jew was subjected to a process of feminization. The process of an exchange of signifiers whereby this particular transformation enters into the text had already been elucidated by Nina Pelikan Straus in 1991. From a feminist position she views Kafka as "a prophet of the complexities engendered by the woman question." She demonstrates clearly Kafka's "discomfort with the male role" (667) and advances the significant notion that Grete's experience is crucial to the understanding of the story. While Gregor exchanges responsibility for regressive dependency, "Grete exchanges dependency for the burdensome efficiency and independence that Gregor formerly displayed" (655).

Here we find a cogent explanation of Grete's newfound "determination" and "confidence." In addition we see Gregor (and Kafka himself) "caught between the shameful desire to identify himself with women and the consciousness that he cannot identify himself with man" (657). The hidden purpose in Gregor's metamorphosis, this time in the zoological sense, is seen in the butterfly-like blossoming of the sister Grete out of the pupa or chrysalis of Gregor, who in the narrative is left "mager" and "vollständig flach und trocken" (104). The hard, armoured shell of Gregor's doomed masculinity is finally crushed. Grete's anima at the end the narrative is exchanged for the collapsed "Ich" of the protagonist.

Biographical evidence for this fantasized exchange with a female double is provided by Kafka's close relationship with and enormous regard for his youngest sister, Ottla. "Im übrigen ist meine jüngste Schwester (schon über 20 Jahre alt) meine beste Prager Freundin," says Kafka in a letter to Felice Bauer that is exactly coeval with *Die Verwandlung* (*Briefe an Felice* 11.11.1912, 87). In his biography of Kafka, Ernst Pawel makes the projection of the brother's wishes onto the sister explicit: "Throughout her rebellion and search for self—defying the father, working the land, breaking away from home, marrying a non-Jew—she in fact acted out her brother's wildest and most impossible dreams" (87). What Sokel implies but does not explicitly state in his article, "Kafka as a Jew," is the repressed cultural subtext of Gregor's desire to send his sister to the conservatory and his craving for that seemingly impossible other "food." It must not be forgotten that for many educated Central and Western European Jews during Kafka's lifetime a career in the arts, especially literature, music, and the theatre, was seen as a way to overcome the dilemmas imposed on them by their Jewishness. Moved as he is by his sister Grete's violin recital, Gregor feels he might now be able to find the way to the "ersehnten unbekannten Nahrung" (98), the unknown nourishment that he craved. The projection of this wish for a form of cultural attainment acceptable to the gentile world onto the figure of the sister in *Die Verwandlung* can be seen to reflect Kafka's shame over his own stifled Jewish voice and his conviction that, for him at least, any genuine cultural reconnection with it was impossible. Sokel and Spector both argue that this was Kafka's actual position on the matter. While it is certainly possible, as Erich Heller suggested in the 1970s, to link Gregor's desire for this unknown nourishment to Kafka's interest in Schopenhauer's view of music as the only art form that promises to overcome the suffering caused by individuation (38), it also makes sense to link it to a last fleeting wish to recover for the young male European Jews of Kafka's generation the lost ground of a positive Jewish acculturation. The rejection of this projected wish through the philistine behaviour towards Grete of the three bearded boarders, who, as Sokel reminds us, are present only by dint of a commercial and contractual arrangement in the Samsa apartment, adds a further twist of the knife to Gregor's dying hope for some small, albeit vicarious or, in the context of his apparently incestuous desire to kiss her on the neck, even vampiristic, share in this longed-for social acceptance and cultural nourishment.

In the context of the disrupted trajectory of male Jewish assimilation into Western and Central European society, the transformation of Gregor's human voice into an inhuman twittering squeak demands a reading that links it to the critically well-established discussion of Kafka's awareness of the absence of an authentic literary language for Western Jews like himself. As established or aspiring *Kulturjuden*, they were always in danger of slipping back into the Yiddish-derived habits of articulation represented in the popular discourse of the period as *Mauscheln*, or at least of being unfairly accused of doing so. In *Jewish Self-Hatred: Anti-Semitism and the Hidden Language of the Jews* (1990) Gilman exposed the origins of the term in anti-Semitic discourse. Spector draws on Gilman's analysis of the term to show how two of Kafka's contemporaries, Heinrich Teweles, a Prague German liberal, and the Bohemian Jewish German nationalist and philosopher of language, Fritz Mauthner, interpreted the persistence of *das Mauscheln* in Jewish speech and writing as a considerable barrier to the attainment of authentic German nationality (90–91). Mauthner maintained that any German text by a Jewish author inevitably remains "Jew talk" and that the German Jew "will become a full German only when *Mauschel* expressions become a foreign language or when he no longer understands them" (91). In *Franz Kafka, The Jewish Patient*, Gilman makes explicit Kafka's awareness of the association in popular German usage between *Mauscheln* and things "mouse-like" (23). The application of this association to *Josefine, die Sängerin oder das Volk der Mäuse* needs no further commentary here. The link between Kafka's suppressed, unattainable, or perhaps forever "lost" authentic Jewish

voice and what is perceived by the family and the irascible chief clerk as
Gregor Samsa's incomprehensible language must be drawn over the concealed bridge that joins the figurative and literal poles of the central metaphor. Kafka's strict injunction, sent in October 1915 to his publisher Kurt
Wolff, against any attempt to offer a visual representation of the "monstrous
vermin" clearly signalled that Kafka meant it to be an indeterminate creature,
not any particular insect or bug but a generic species of vermin, a hybrid
thing, a true *Mischling*. Part human, part animal, part insect, the "ungeheueres Ungeziefer" suffers from intense anxieties about employment, has a form
of skin disease, exhibits dietary peculiarities, finds itself in intense conflict
with the father, agonizes about cultural matters, is progressively stripped of
its masculinity, is forced to retreat into increasingly filthy quarters as soon
as it advances into the "living room," and, instead of communicating in the
human voice it imagines it possesses, is perceived as emitting only what the
enthnocultural context of Kafka's writing invites us to hear as a "mouselike"
squeak. Faced with intolerable stress, Gregor's human voice recedes and,
with it, both his command of the language of the dominant order in which
the family is located and everything else he holds dear. He thus regresses to
an increasingly primitive and abject state. His potential for communication
with an alluring feminine other has been reduced to the silent contempla-
tion of a mere image clipped from a magazine. The young lieutenant in the
photographic portrait has been exposed for the hybrid creature that he really
is: he can no more pronounce words of command than Gregor can make his
case understood in a language that the chief clerk from his employer's office
can understand. *Mauscheln* will out.

The coda to the narrative sketches the liberation of the family and
the blossoming of Grete. In order to relate Kafka's ending to the argument
above, it remains only to apply to the encoded body the ethnopsychological
conversion factor suggested by Gilman's research and the significance of the
"hourglass-shaped" exchange between brother and sister depicted in Pelikan
Straus's account of Gregor's "feminization" becomes alarmingly clear (655).
For the male Jew there is indeed no possible way forward. The repressed
bachelor Gregor is literally replaced by the marriageable Grete with her
lovely "young body":

> Stiller werdend und fast unbewußt durch Blicke sich verständigend,
> dachten sie daran, daß es nun Zeit sein werde, auch einen braven
> Mann für sie zu suchen. Und es war ihnen wie eine Bestätigung
> ihrer neuen Träume und guten Absichten, als am Ziele ihrer
> Fahrt die Tochter als erste sich erhob und ihren jungen Körper
> dehnte. (107)

"[M]eine kleine Geschichte ist beendet, nur macht mich der heutige Schluß gar nicht froh, er hätte schon besser sein dürfen, das ist kein Zweifel," wrote Kafka in a letter to Felice Bauer (*Briefe an Felice* 6–7.12.1912, 163). The melancholy tone of this remark is hardly surprising, nor, given the nature of the story's ending, is Kafka's dislike of metaphors: metaphorically at least, he had just written himself out of existence.

NOTE

1. Sokel's translation from Franz Kafka, *Briefe 1902–1924*, ed. Max Brod, New York: Schocken, 1958.

WORKS CITED

Anderson, Mark. *Kafka's Clothes: Ornament and Aestheticism in the Habsburg Fin de Siècle.* New York: Oxford UP, 1992.

Beck, Evelyn Torton. *Kafka and the Yiddish Theater. Its Impact on his Work.* Madison: U of Wisconsin P, 1971.

Benjamin, Walter. "Franz Kafka: On the Tenth Anniversary of His Death." *Walter Benjamin. Selected Writings. Vol. 2: 1927–1934.* Trans. Robert Livingston et al. Ed. Michael W. Jennings et al. Cambridge: Belknap Press, 1999. 794–818.

Bensmaïa, Réda. "On the Concept of Minor Literature from Kafka to Kateb Yacine." *Gilles Deleuze and the Theater of Philosophy.* Ed. Constantin V. Boundas and Dorothea Olkowski. New York: Routledge, 1994. 213–28.

Corngold, Stanley. *The Commentator's Despair: The Interpretation of Kafka's 'Metamorphosis.'* Washington: National University Publications, 1973.

———. "Kafka's Other Metamorphosis." *Kafka and the Contemporary Critical Performance: Centenary Reading.* Ed. Alan Udoff. Bloomington: Indiana UP, 1987. 41–57.

———. "Franz Kafka, The Jewish Patient, by Sander Gilman." Book Review. *Shofar* 15 (1997): 110–12.

Deleuze, Gilles. "Coldness and Cruelty." *Masochism: Coldness and Cruelty.* Trans. Jean McNeil. Ed. Gilles Deleuze and Leopold von Sacher-Masoch. New York: Zone Books, 1991. 9–142.

Deleuze, Gilles, and Félix Guattari. *Kafka: Toward a Minor Literature.* Trans. Dana Polan with a foreword by Réda Bensmaïa. Minneapolis: U of Minnesota P, 1986.

———. *A Thousand Plateaus: Capitalism and Schizophrenia.* Trans. Brian Massumi. Minneapolis: U of Minnesota P, 1987.

Denis-Bredin, Jean. *The Affair: The Case of Alfred Dreyfus.* New York: George Braziller, 1986.

Gilman, Sander L. *Franz Kafka, the Jewish Patient.* New York: Routledge, 1995.

———. *Jewish Self-Hatred: Anti-Semitism and the Hidden Language of the Jews.* Baltimore: Johns Hopkins UP, 1986.

Heller, Erich. *Franz Kafka.* London: Fontana, 1974.

Hiemer, Ernst. *Der Jude im Sprichwort der Völker.* Nürnberg: Der Stürmer, 1942.

Kafka, Franz. *Briefe 1902–1924.* Ed. Max Brod. New York: Schocken, 1958.

———. *Briefe an Felice und andere Korrespondenz aus der Verlobungszeit.* Ed. Erich Heller and Jürgen Born. Frankfurt/M.: Fischer, 1976.

———. *Briefe an Milena.* Ed. Willy Haas. Frankfurt/M.: Fischer, 1952.

———. *Erzählungen*. Frankfurt/M.: Fischer, 1983.

———. *Tagebücher 1910–1923*. Frankfurt/M. Fischer, 1983.

Pawel, Ernst. *The Nightmare of Reason: A Life of Franz Kafka*. London: Harvill Press, 1984.

Pelikan Straus, Nina. "Transforming Franz Kafka's Metamorphosis." *Signs: Journal of Women in Culture and Society* 14 (1988–89): 651–67.

Sokel, Walter H. "Franz Kafka, The Jewish Patient." *Modern Fiction Studies* 43.2 (1997): 522–27.

———. "Kafka as a Jew." *New Literary History* 30 (1999): 837–53.

Spector, Scott. *Prague Territories: National Conflict and Cultural Innovation in Franz Kafka's Fin de Siècle*. Berkeley: U of California P, 2000.

Wiener, Oswald. *Die Verbesserung von Mitteleuropa*. Reinbek: Rowohlt, 1969.

Zilcosky, John. *Kafka's Travels: Exoticism, Colonialism and the Traffic of Writing*. New York: Palgrave Macmillan, 2003.

Chronology

1883	Born in Prague on July 3.
1901–06	Studies law at Ferdinand-Karls University in Prague.
1906	Begins working in a law office. Receives law degree. Embarks on his year of practical training in Prague law courts.
1907	Takes position with insurance company in Prague.
1908	Accepts position with Workers' Accident Insurance Institute.
1910	Starts diary.
1911	Official trip to Bohemia. Trip, with Max Brod, to Switzerland, Italy, and France, writing travelogues. Becomes interested in Yiddish theater and literature.
1913	*Betrachtung* (*Meditations*) published.
1914	Engagement to Felice Bauer. Breaks off engagement.
1915	Reconciliation with Felice Bauer. *Die Verwandlung* (later translated as *The Metamorphosis*) published.
1917	Re-engagement to Felice Bauer. Tuberculosis diagnosed. Takes extended sick leave. Engagement to Bauer broken off again.
1918	Continued poor health. Intermittent stays at sanatoria.

1919   Brief engagement to Julie Wohryzek. *In der Strafkolonie* (later
            translated as *The Penal Colony*) and *Ein Landarzt* (later trans-
            lated as *The Country Doctor*) published.

1920   Begins correspondence with Milena Jesenká. Intermittent stays
            at sanatoria.

1921   Returns to work at the Workers' Accident Insurance Institute.

1922   Breaks off relations with Milena Jesenská. Retires from Work-
            ers' Accident Insurance Institute.

1923   Meets Dora Dymant. Lives with Dora Dymant in Berlin.

1924   Moves back to Prague. Moves to sanitorium near Vienna. Dies
            June third in Austria of tuberculosis of the larynx. Collection
            Ein Hungerkunstler (A Hunger Artist) published shortly after his
            death.

1925   Novel *Der Prozess* published (later translated as *The Trial*).

1926   Novel *Das Schloss* published (later translated as *The Castle*).

1927   Novel *Amerika* published (translation published later under the
            same title).

1931   *Beim Bau der Chinesischen Mauer, Ungedruckte Erzaehlungen und
            Prosa aus dem Nachlass* published (later published as *The Great
            Wall of China and Other Pieces*).

Contributors

HAROLD BLOOM is Sterling Professor of the Humanities at Yale University. He is the author of 30 books, including *Shelley's Mythmaking, The Visionary Company, Blake's Apocalypse, Yeats, A Map of Misreading, Kabbalah and Criticism, Agon: Toward a Theory of Revisionism, The American Religion, The Western Canon,* and *Omens of Millennium: The Gnosis of Angels, Dreams, and Resurrection. The Anxiety of Influence* sets forth Professor Bloom's provocative theory of the literary relationships between the great writers and their predecessors. His most recent books include *Shakespeare: The Invention of the Human,* a 1998 National Book Award finalist, *How to Read and Why, Genius: A Mosaic of One Hundred Exemplary Creative Minds, Hamlet: Poem Unlimited, Where Shall Wisdom Be Found?,* and *Jesus and Yahweh: The Names Divine.* In 1999, Professor Bloom received the prestigious American Academy of Arts and Letters Gold Medal for Criticism. He has also received the International Prize of Catalonia, the Alfonso Reyes Prize of Mexico, and the Hans Christian Andersen Bicentennial Prize of Denmark.

ANTHONY THORLBY is an honorary professor at the University of Sussex, where he was for many years professor of comparative literature. He authored *Kafka: A Study* as well as works on Flaubert, the romantic movement, and Tolstoy. He coedited *The Penguin Companion to Literature* and served as editor on other volumes on literature as well.

WALTER H. SOKEL is Commonwealth Professor Emeritus of German and English literature at the University of Virginia. He published *The Myth of Power and the Self: Essays on Franz Kafka, The Writer in Extremis: Expressionism*

219

in Twentieth Century German Literature, and many other books and articles on Kafka. He is honorary president of the Kafka Society of America.

HENRY SUSSMAN is a professor of comparative literature at the State University of New York, Buffalo, and a recurrent visiting professor in the German department at Yale University. He is the author of *The Trial: Kafka's Unholy Trinity*, *Franz Kafka: Geometrician of Metaphor*, and many other titles.

STEPHEN D. DOWDEN is an associate professor of German at Brandeis University, where he also is chairperson of the Germanic and Slavic languages program and head of undergraduate advising. Among the titles he has written is *Sympathy for the Abyss: Study in the Novel of German Modernism—Kafka, Broch, Musil and Thomas Mann*.

ROBERT ALTER is a professor of Hebrew and comparative literature at the University of California, Berkeley. He has published widely on the modern European and American novel, on modern Hebrew literature, and on literary aspects of the Bible. Among his works is *Necessary Angels: Tradition and Modernity in Kafka, Benjamin, and Scholem*.

STANLEY CORNGOLD is a professor of German and comparative literature at Princeton University. He has published widely on modern German writers and thinkers, in addition to translating and writing on the work of Franz Kafka. His recent work involved coediting *Franz Kafka: The Office Writings*.

RUSSELL A. BERMAN is a professor of German studies and comparative literature and Walter A. Haas Professor in the Humanities at Stanford University. He is the author of articles, reviews, and books, including *Enlightenment or Empire: Colonial Discourse in German Culture*. He is also the editor of *TELOS*, a quarterly journal of politics, philosophy, critical theory, culture, and the arts.

CLAYTON KOELB is Guy B. Johnson Professor of German, English and comparative literature and chairperson of the department of Germanic languages and literatures at the University of North Carolina, Chapel Hill. He coedited *A Franz Kafka Encyclopedia* and authored *Kafka's Rhetoric: The Passion of Reading* and many other titles.

MARTIN PUCHNER holds the H. Gordon Garbedian Chair in English and Comparative Literature at Columbia University, where he also serves as the cochair of the doctorate program in theater. He is coeditor of the *Norton Anthology of Drama* and published *Stage Fright: Modernism, Anti-*

Theatricality, and Drama as well as other work. He served as editor of *Theatre Survey* from 2007 to 2009.

PATRICK REILLY has been a professor in the Graduate School of Arts and Humanities at the University of Glasgow, Scotland. He is the author of *The Literature of Guilt: From Gulliver to Golding* and *Jonathan Swift: The Brave Desponder.*

SIMON RYAN teaches courses in German language and literature, European studies, German cinema, and digital culture at the University of Otago, New Zealand. He coauthored an essay that was published in *The Pleasures of Computer Gaming,* and his work has been published in several journals as well.

Bibliography

Alter, Robert. *Imagined Cities: Urban Experience and the Language of the Novel*. New Haven: Yale University Press, 2005.

Armstrong, Raymond. *Kafka and Pinter: Shadow-Boxing: The Struggle between Father and Son*. Basingstoke, England; New York: Macmillan; St. Martin's, 1999.

Beall, Joshua. "The Owl's Perch: Expressions of Subjective Trauma in Kafka." *Exit 9: The Rutgers Journal of Comparative Literature* 6 (2004): 23–41.

Beicken, Peter U. "Kafka's Gays/Gaze." *Journal of the Kafka Society of America* 23, nos. 1–2 (June–December 1999): 3–22.

Bloom, Harold, ed. *Franz Kafka's* The Metamorphosis. New York: Chelsea House, 2007.

Bridgwater, Patrick. *Kafka, Gothic and Fairytale*. Amsterdam, Netherlands: Rodopi, 2003.

———. *Kafka's Novels: An Interpretation*. Amsterdam, Netherlands: Rodopi, 2003.

Corbella, Walter. "Panopticism and the Construction of Power in Franz Kafka's *The Castle*." *Papers on Language and Literature* 43, no. 1 (Winter 2007): 68–88.

Corngold, Stanley. *Lambent Traces: Franz Kafka*. Princeton, N.J.: Princeton University Press, 2004.

Cornwell, Neil. *The Absurd in Literature*. Manchester, England: Manchester University Press, 2006.

Damrosch, David. *What Is World Literature?* Princeton, N.J.: Princeton University Press, 2003.

Danta, Chris. "Sarah's Laughter: Kafka's Abraham." *Modernism/Modernity* 15, no. 2 (April 2008): 343–359.

de la Durantaye, Leland. "Kafka's Reality and Nabokov's Fantasy: On Dwarves, Saints, Beetles, Symbolism, and Genius." *Comparative Literature* 59, no. 4 (Fall 2007): 315–331.

Dern, John A. "'Sin without God': Existentialism and *The Trial*." *Interdisciplinary Literary Studies* 5, no. 2 (Spring 2004): 94–109.

Doctorow, E.L. *Creationists: Selected Essays, 1993–2006*. New York: Random House; 2006.

Duttlinger, Carolin. "Kafka, Der Proceß." In *Landmarks in the German Novel, I*, edited by Peter Hutchinson, pp. 135–150. Oxford, England: Peter Lang, 2007.

Gilman, Sander L. *Franz Kafka*. London, England: Reaktion, 2005.

Goebel, Rolf J. *Constructing China: Kafka's Orientalist Discourse*. Columbia, S.C.: Camden House, 1997.

Gottlieb, Susannah Young-ah, ed. *Reflections on Literature and Culture*. Stanford, Calif.: Stanford University Press, 2007.

Hollington, Michael. "Dickens and Kafka Revisited: The Case of *Great Expectations*." *Dickens Quarterly* 20, no. 1 (March 2003): 14–33.

Isenberg, Noah. *Between Redemption and Doom: The Strains of German-Jewish Modernism*. Lincoln: University of Nebraska Press, 1999.

Kafalenos, Emma. *Narrative Causalities*. Columbus: Ohio State University Press, 2006.

Kalinowski, G.M. "Beckett's 'Reversed Metamorphosis': What Constitutes a Serious Reading of *The Castle*?" *Comparative Literature* 56, no. 4 (Fall 2004): 317–330.

Karl, Frederick R. "In the Struggle between You and Kafka, Back Yourself." *American Imago: Psychoanalysis and the Human Sciences* 55, no. 2 (Summer 1998): 189–204.

Kittler, Wolf. "Burial Without Resurrection: On Kafka's Legend 'Before the Law.'" *Modern Language Notes* 121, no. 3 (April 2006): 647–678.

Kohl, Markus. "Struggle and Victory in Kafka's *Das Schloss*." *Modern Language Review* 101, no. 4 (October 2006): 1,035–1,043.

Kuhlken, Pam Fox. "The Picaresque Landscape in Franz Kafka's *Amerika*." *Journal of the Kafka Society of America* 25, nos. 1–2 (June–December 2001): 35–45.

Levin, David, ed. Kafka Symposium. *Modernism/Modernity* 8, no. 2 (April 2001): 277–334.

Levine, Michael G. "'A Place So Insanely Enchanting': Kafka and the Poetics of Suspension." *Modern Language Notes* 123, no. 5 (December 2008): 1,039–1,067.

Librett, Jeffrey S. "'With These Repulsive Things Indissolubly Bound': Kafka as Primal Scene." *American Imago: Psychoanalysis and the Human Sciences* 64, no. 4 (Winter 2007): 513–533.

Lothe, Jakob. "Aspects of the Fragment in Joyce's *Dubliners* and Kafka's *The Trial*." In *The Art of Brevity: Excursions in Short Fiction Theory and Analysis*, edited by Per Winther, Jakob Lothe, and Hans H. Skei, pp. 96–105. Columbia: University of South Carolina Press, 2004.

Martin, Ruth. "Love at a Distance: Kafka and the Sirens." In *Sexual Politics of Desire and Belonging*, edited by Nick Rumens and Alejandro Cervantes-Carson, pp. 81–99. Amsterdam, Netherlands: Rodopi, 2007.

Melaney, William D. "Kafka's Nietzschean Risk: Writing Against Memory." *Journal of the Kafka Society of America: New International Series* 26, nos. 1–2 (June–December 2002): 24–33.

Nolan, Kevin. "Getting Past Odradek." In *Contemporary Poetics*, edited by Louis Armand, pp. 41–56. Evanston, Ill.: Northwestern University Press, 2007.

Olshan, Matthew. "Franz Kafka: The Unsinging Singer." In *Modern Jewish Mythologies*, edited by Glenda Abramson, pp. 174–190. Cincinnati: Hebrew Union College, 1999.

Parlej, Piotr. *The Romantic Theory of the Novel: Genre and Reflection in Cervantes, Melville, Flaubert, Joyce, and Kafka*. Baton Rouge: Louisiana State University Press, 1997.

Preece, Julian, ed. *The Cambridge Companion to Kafka*. Cambridge, England: Cambridge University Press, 2002.

Reitter, Paul. "Bad Writing in Franz Kafka's 'Das Urteil.'" *Seminar: A Journal of Germanic Studies* 38, no. 2 (May 2002): 134–141.

Ryan, Michael P. "Samsa and Samsara: Suffering, Death, and Rebirth in 'The Metamorphosis.'" *German Quarterly* 72, no. 2 (Spring 1999): 133–152.

Shahar, Galili. "Fragments and Wounded Bodies: Kafka after Kleist." *German Quarterly* 80, no. 4 (Fall 2007): 449–467.

Sharkey, E. Joseph. *Idling the Engine: Linguistic Skepticism in and around Cortazar, Kafka, and Joyce*. Washington, D.C.: Catholic University of America Press, 2006.

Sokel, Walter H. *The Myth of Power and the Self: Essays on Franz Kafka*. Detroit, Mich.: Wayne State University Press, 2002.

———. "Toward the Myth." *Journal of the Kafka Society of America* 22, nos. 1–2 (June–December 1998): 7–15.

Suchoff, David. "Kafka's Canon: Hebrew and Yiddish in *The Trial* and *Amerika*." In *Bilingual Games: Some Literary Investigations*, edited by Doris Sommer, pp. 251–274. New York: Palgrave Macmillan, 2003.

Tambling, Jeremy. *Lost in the American City: Dickens, James and Kafka*. Basingstoke, England: Palgrave, 2001.

Tiedemann, Rolf. "Kafka Studies, the Culture Industry, and the Concept of Shame: Improper Remarks between Moral Philosophy and Philosophy of History." *Cultural Critique* 60 (Spring 2005): 245–258.

Türk, Johannes. "Rituals of Dying, Burrows of Anxiety in Freud, Proust, and Kafka: Prolegomena to a Critical Immunology." *Germanic Review* 82, no. 2 (Spring 2007): 141–156.

Vaughan, Larry. "'The Metamorphosis' and 'The Transformation': Franz Kafka's *Die Verwandlung.*" *Germanisch-Romanische Monatsschrift* 56, no. 2 (2006): 239–242.

Wagner, Benno. "Insuring Nietzsche: Kafka's Files." *New German Critique* 99 (Fall 2006): 83–119.

Webber, Andrew. "Kafka, *Die Verwandlung.*" In *Landmarks in German Short Prose*, edited by Peter Hutchinson, pp. 175–190. Oxford, England: Peter Lang, 2003.

Weinstein, Philip. *Unknowing: The Work of Modernist Fiction.* Ithaca, N.Y.: Cornell University Press, 2005.

Acknowledgments

Anthony Thorlby, "Kafka's Narrative: A Matter of Form." From *Kafka and the Contemporary Critical Performance: Centenary Readings*, edited by Alan Udoff. © 1987 by Indiana University Press.

Walter H. Sokel, "Kafka and Modernism." From *Approaches to Teaching Kafka's Short Fiction*, edited by Richard T. Gray. © 1995 by and reprinted by permission of the Modern Language Association of America.

Henry Sussman, "The Text That Was Never a Story: Symmetry and Disaster in 'A Country Doctor.'" From *Approaches to Teaching Kafka's Short Fiction*, edited by Richard T. Gray. © 1995 by and reprinted by permission of the Modern Language Association of America.

Stephen D. Dowden, "The Impossibility of Crows." From *Kafka's Castle and the Critical Imagination*. © 1995 by Camden House, an imprint of Boydell & Brewer.

Robert Alter, "Franz Kafka: Wrenching Scripture." From *New England Review: Middlebury Series* 21, no. 3 (Summer 2000): 7–19. © 2000 by *New England Review: Middlebury Series*.

Stanley Corngold, "Allotria and Excreta in 'In the Penal Colony.'" From *Modernism/Modernity* 8, no. 2 (April 2001): 281–93. © 2001 by The Johns Hopkins University Press. Reprinted with permission of The Johns Hopkins University Press.

Russell A. Berman, "Tradition and Betrayal in 'Das Urteil.'" From *A Companion to the Works of Franz Kafka*, edited by James Rolleston. Published by Camden House, an imprint of Boydell & Brewer. © 2002 by the editor and contributors.

Clayton Koelb, "Kafka Imagines His Readers: The Rhetoric of 'Josefine die Sängerin' and 'Der Bau.'" From *A Companion to the Works of Franz Kafka*, edited by James Rolleston. Published by Camden House, an imprint of Boydell & Brewer. © 2002 by the editor and contributors.

Martin Puchner, "Kafka's Antitheatrical Gestures." From *Germanic Review* 78, no. 3 (Summer 2003): 177–93. Reprinted with permission of the Helen Dwight Reid Educational Foundation. Published by Heldref Publications, 1319 Eighteenth St., NW, Washington, DC 20036-1802. Copyright © 2003.

Patrick Reilly, "Kafka." From *The Dark Landscape of Modern Fiction*, published by Ashgate. © 2003 by Patrick Reilly.

Simon Ryan, "Franz Kafka's Die Verwandlung: Transformation, Metaphor, and the Perils of Assimilation." From *Seminar: A Journal of Germanic Studies* 43, no. 1 (February 2007): 1–18. © 2007 by the Canadian Association of University Teachers of German.

Every effort has been made to contact the owners of copyrighted material and secure copyright permission. Articles appearing in this volume generally appear much as they did in their original publication with few or no editorial changes. In some cases, foreign language text has been removed from the original essay. Those interested in locating the original source will find the information cited above.

Index